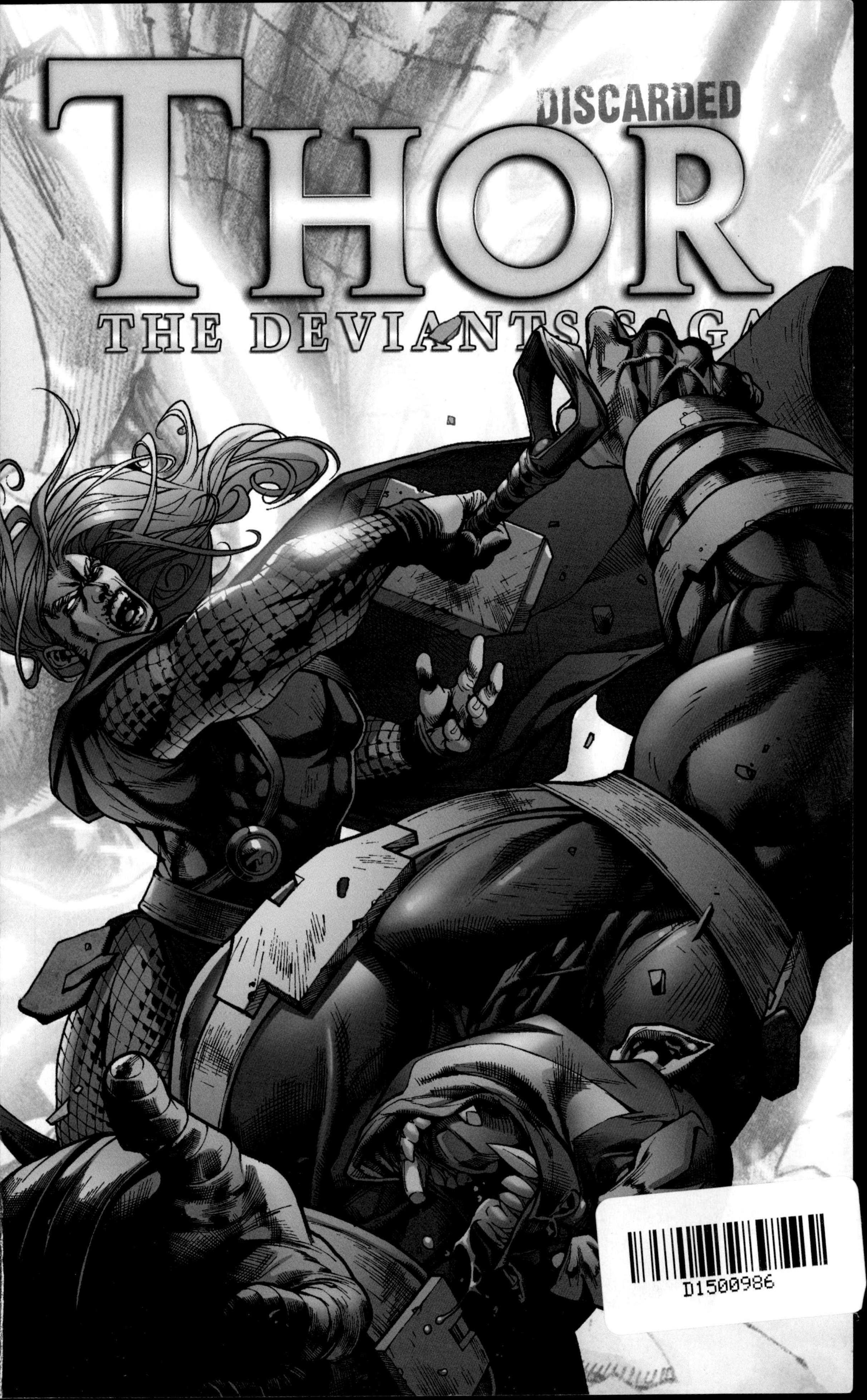
THOR
THE DEVIANTS SAGA

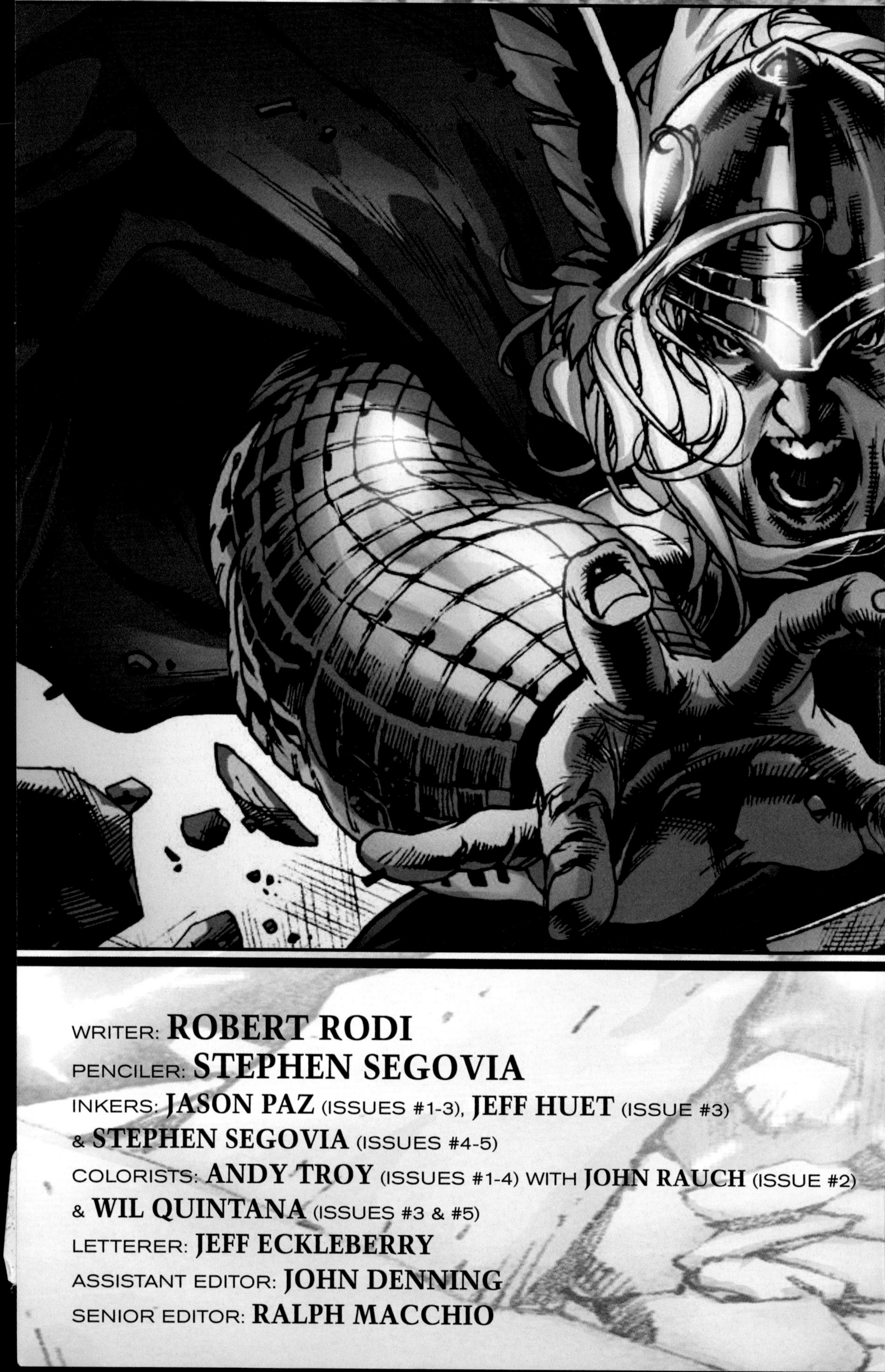

WRITER: **ROBERT RODI**
PENCILER: **STEPHEN SEGOVIA**
INKERS: **JASON PAZ** (ISSUES #1-3), **JEFF HUET** (ISSUE #3)
& **STEPHEN SEGOVIA** (ISSUES #4-5)
COLORISTS: **ANDY TROY** (ISSUES #1-4) WITH **JOHN RAUCH** (ISSUE #2)
& **WIL QUINTANA** (ISSUES #3 & #5)
LETTERER: **JEFF ECKLEBERRY**
ASSISTANT EDITOR: **JOHN DENNING**
SENIOR EDITOR: **RALPH MACCHIO**

COLLECTION EDITOR & DESIGN: **CORY LEVINE**
ASSISTANT EDITORS: **ALEX STARBUCK** & **NELSON RIBEIRO**
EDITORS, SPECIAL PROJECTS: **JENNIFER GRÜNWALD** & **MARK D. BEAZLEY**
SENIOR EDITOR, SPECIAL PROJECTS: **JEFF YOUNGQUIST**
SENIOR VICE PRESIDENT OF SALES: **DAVID GABRIEL**
SVP OF BRAND PLANNING & COMMUNICATIONS: **MICHAEL PASCIULLO**
EDITOR IN CHIEF: **AXEL ALONSO**
CHIEF CREATIVE OFFICER: **JOE QUESADA**
PUBLISHER: **DAN BUCKLEY**
EXECUTIVE PRODUCER: **ALAN FINE**

THOR: THE DEVIANTS SAGA. Contains material originally published in magazine form as THOR: THE DEVIANTS SAGA #1-5. First printing 2012. ISBN# 978-0-7851-6306-0. Published by MARVEL WORLDWIDE, INC., a subsidiary of MARVEL ENTERTAINMENT, LLC. OFFICE OF PUBLICATION: 135 West 50th Street, New York, NY 10020. Copyright © 2011 and 2012 Marvel Characters, Inc. All rights reserved. $16.99 per copy in the U.S. and $18.99 in Canada (GST #R127032852); Canadian Agreement #40668537. All characters featured in this issue and the distinctive names and likenesses thereof, and all related indicia are trademarks of Marvel Characters, Inc. No similarity between any of the names, characters, persons, and/or institutions in this magazine with those of any living or dead person or institution is intended, and any such similarity which may exist is purely coincidental. **Printed in the U.S.A.** ALAN FINE, EVP - Office of the President, Marvel Worldwide, Inc. and EVP & CMO Marvel Characters B.V.; DAN BUCKLEY, Publisher & President - Print, Animation & Digital Divisions; JOE QUESADA, Chief Creative Officer; TOM BREVOORT, SVP of Publishing; DAVID BOGART, SVP of Operations & Procurement, Publishing; RUWAN JAYATILLEKE, SVP & Associate Publisher, Publishing; C.B. CEBULSKI, SVP of Creator & Content Development; DAVID GABRIEL, SVP of Publishing Sales & Circulation; MICHAEL PASCIULLO, SVP of Brand Planning & Communications; JIM O'KEEFE, VP of Operations & Logistics; DAN CARR, Executive Director of Publishing Technology; SUSAN CRESPI, Editorial Operations Manager; ALEX MORALES, Publishing Operations Manager; STAN LEE, Chairman Emeritus. For information regarding advertising in Marvel Comics or on Marvel.com, please contact Niza Disla, Director of Marvel Partnerships, at ndisla@marvel.com. For Marvel subscription inquiries, please call 800-217-9158. **Manufactured between 6/7/2012 and 7/10/2012 by QUAD/GRAPHICS, DUBUQUE, IA, USA.**

10 9 8 7 6 5 4 3 2 1

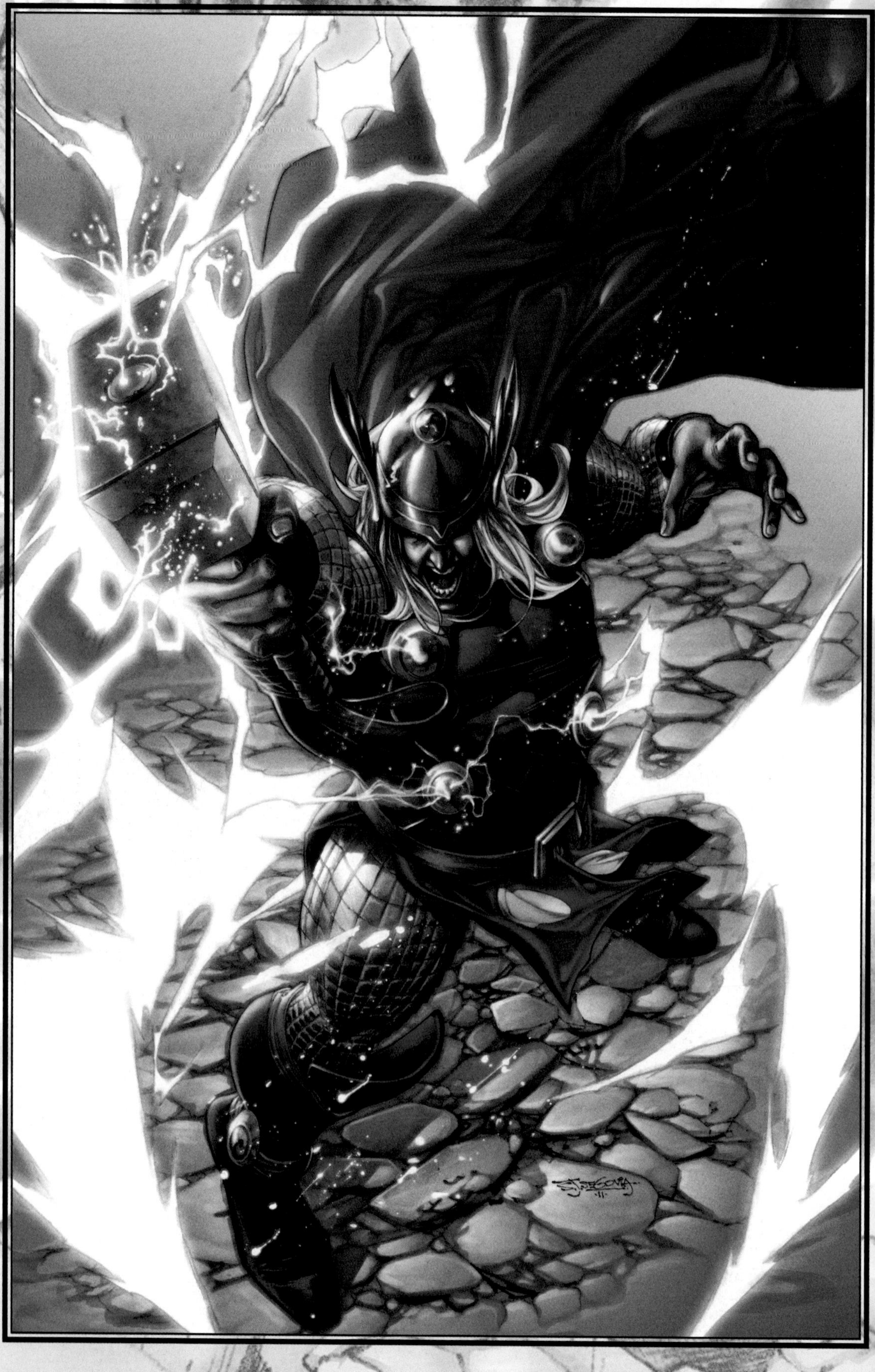

ONE

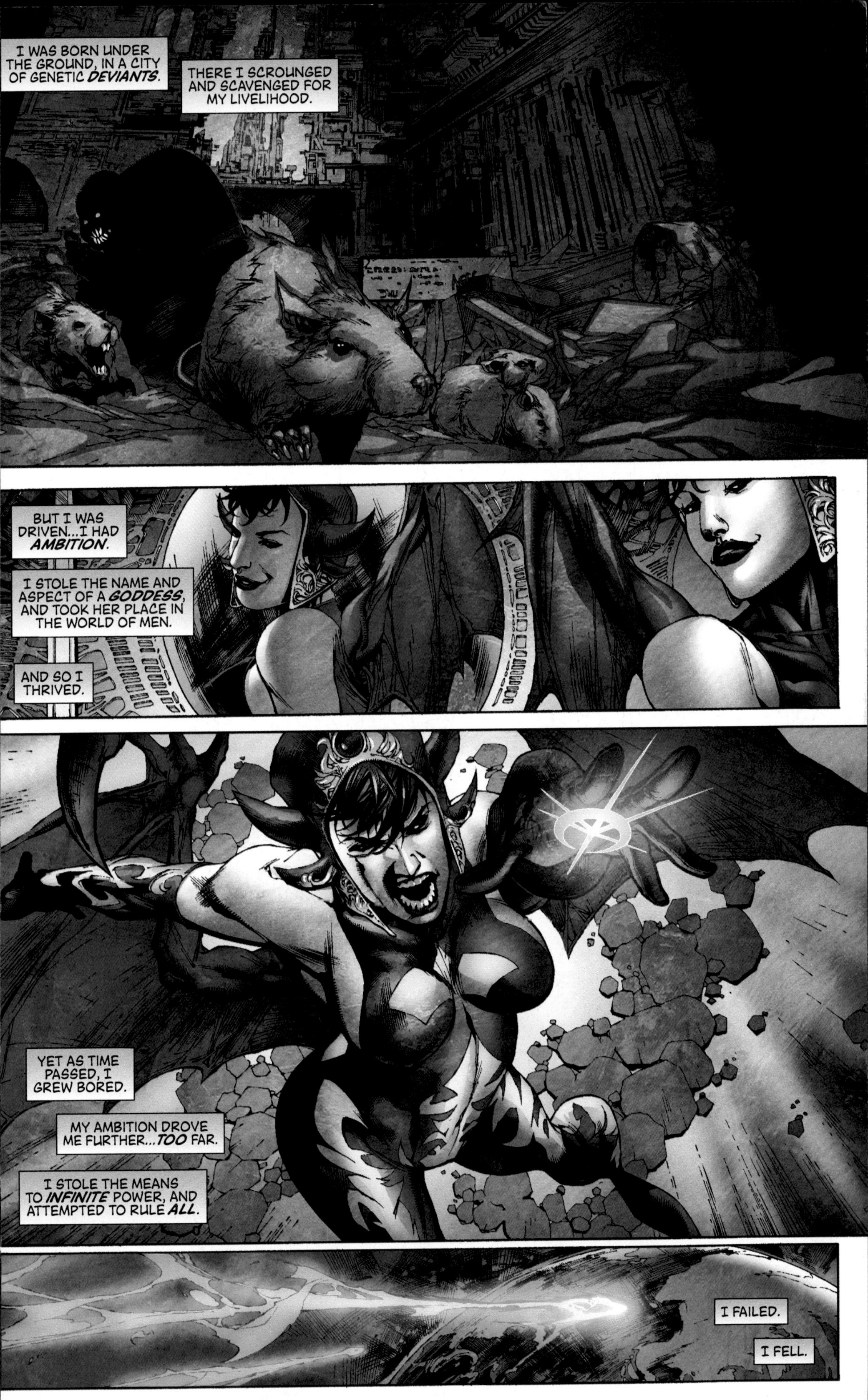

I WAS BORN UNDER THE GROUND, IN A CITY OF GENETIC *DEVIANTS*.
THERE I SCROUNGED AND SCAVENGED FOR MY LIVELIHOOD.
BUT I WAS DRIVEN...I HAD *AMBITION*.
I STOLE THE NAME AND ASPECT OF A *GODDESS*, AND TOOK HER PLACE IN THE WORLD OF MEN.
AND SO I THRIVED.
YET AS TIME PASSED, I GREW BORED.
MY AMBITION DROVE ME FURTHER...*TOO* FAR.
I STOLE THE MEANS TO *INFINITE* POWER, AND ATTEMPTED TO RULE *ALL*.
I FAILED.
I FELL.

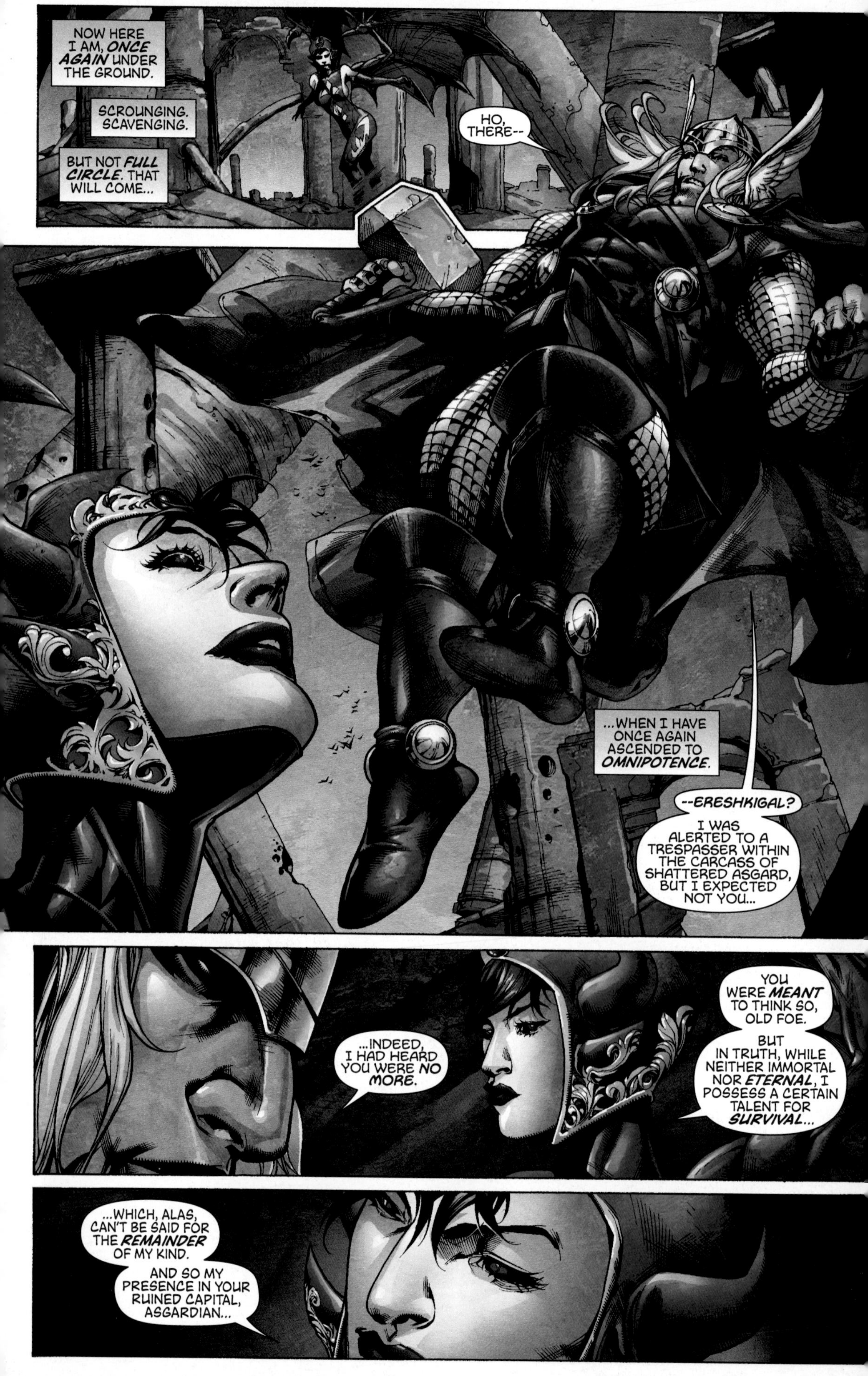

NOW HERE I AM, ONCE AGAIN UNDER THE GROUND.
SCROUNGING. SCAVENGING.
BUT NOT FULL CIRCLE. THAT WILL COME...
HO, THERE--
...WHEN I HAVE ONCE AGAIN ASCENDED TO OMNIPOTENCE.
--ERESHKIGAL?
I WAS ALERTED TO A TRESPASSER WITHIN THE CARCASS OF SHATTERED ASGARD, BUT I EXPECTED NOT YOU...
...INDEED, I HAD HEARD YOU WERE NO MORE.
YOU WERE MEANT TO THINK SO, OLD FOE.
BUT IN TRUTH, WHILE NEITHER IMMORTAL NOR ETERNAL, I POSSESS A CERTAIN TALENT FOR SURVIVAL...
...WHICH, ALAS, CAN'T BE SAID FOR THE REMAINDER OF MY KIND.
AND SO MY PRESENCE IN YOUR RUINED CAPITAL, ASGARDIAN...

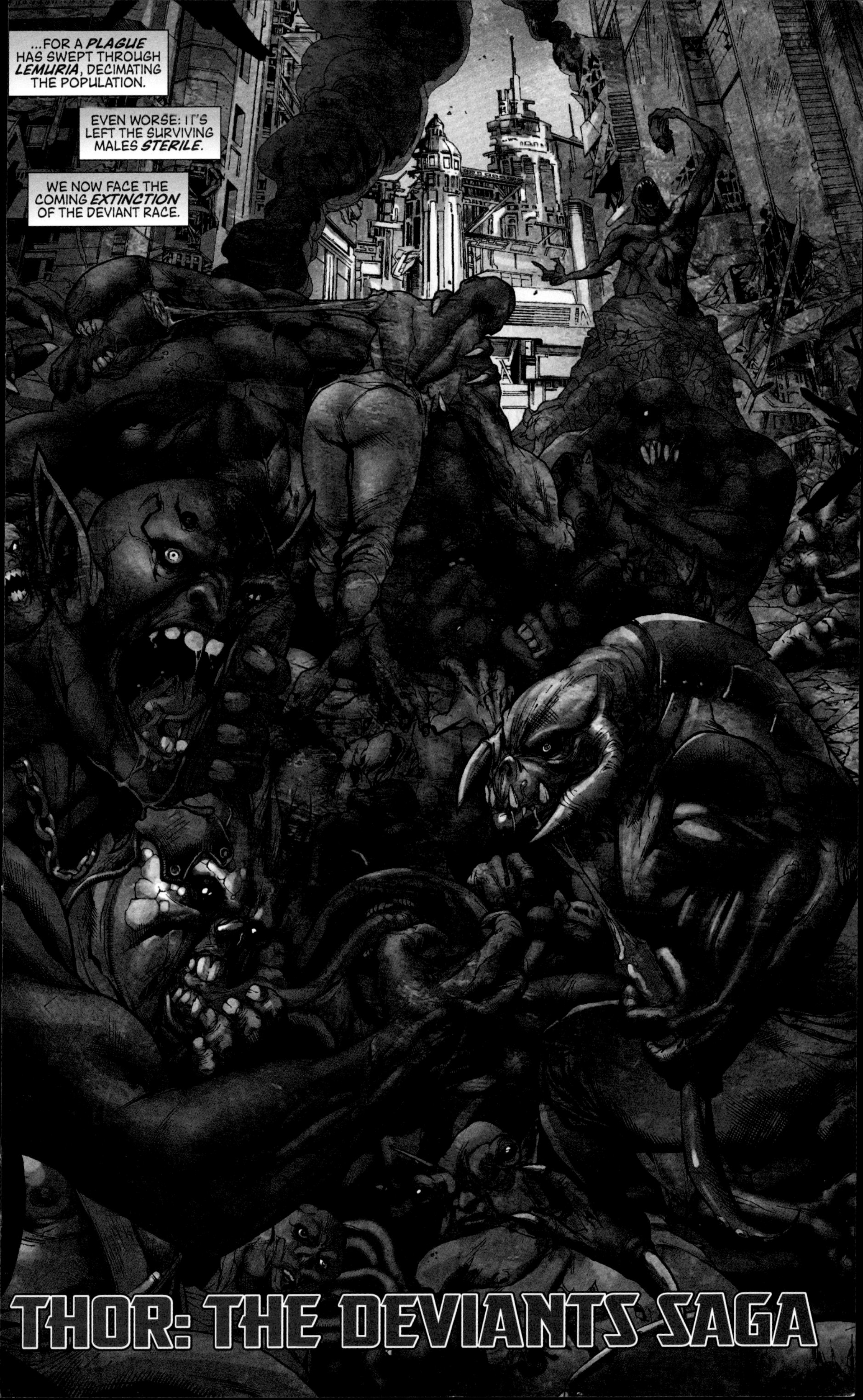
...FOR A PLAGUE HAS SWEPT THROUGH LEMURIA, DECIMATING THE POPULATION.
EVEN WORSE: IT'S LEFT THE SURVIVING MALES STERILE.
WE NOW FACE THE COMING EXTINCTION OF THE DEVIANT RACE.
THOR: THE DEVIANTS SAGA

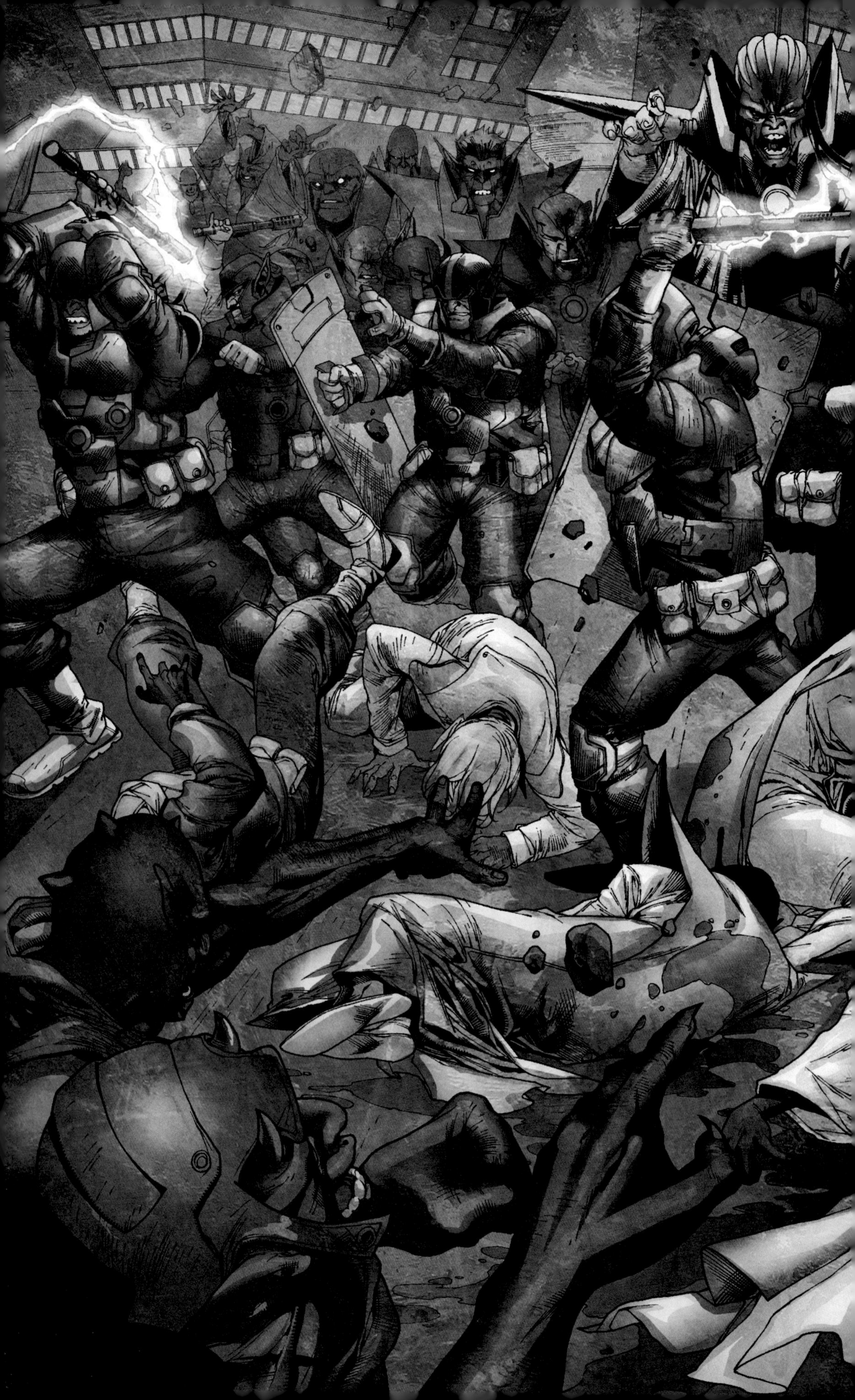

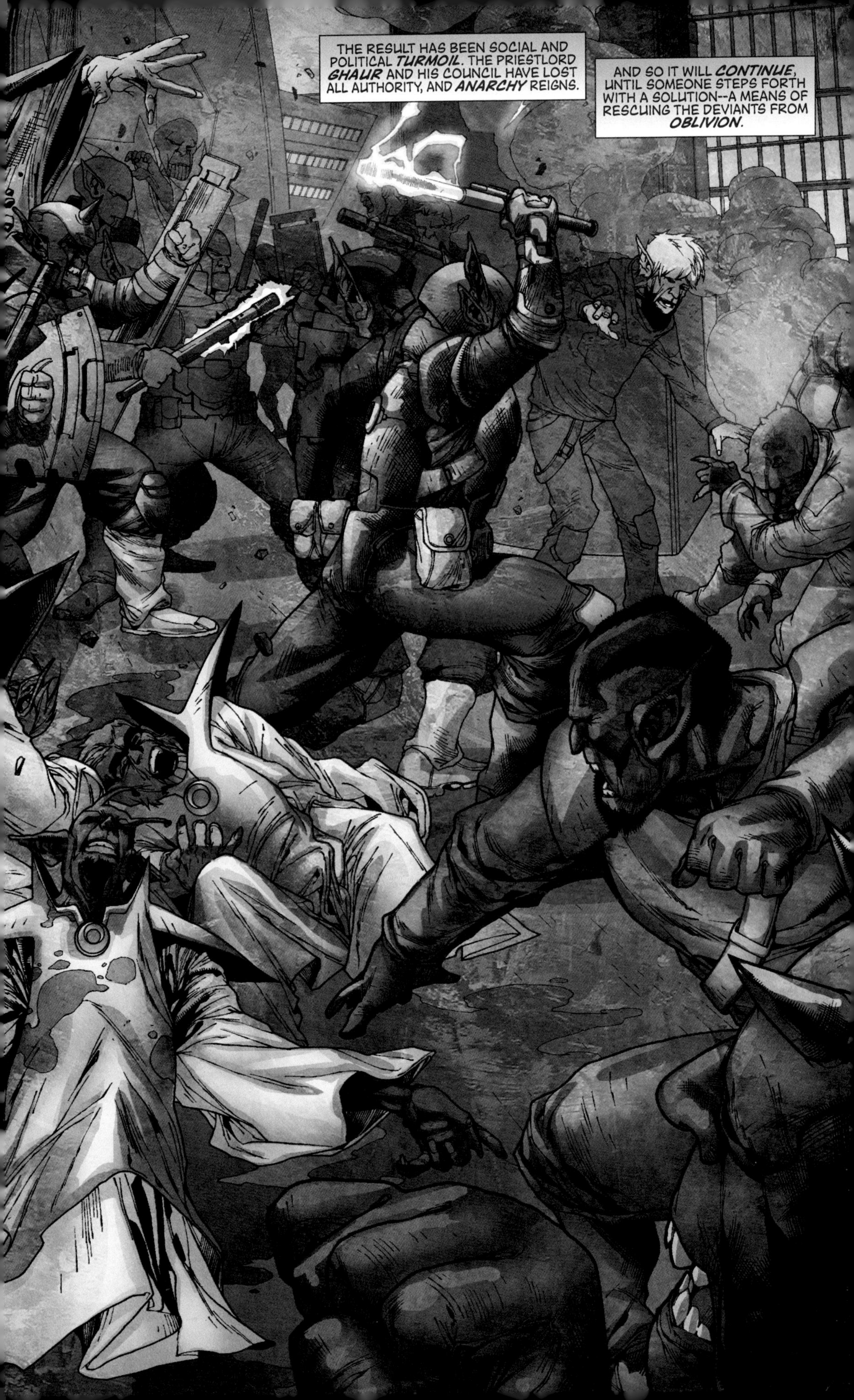
THE RESULT HAS BEEN SOCIAL AND POLITICAL TURMOIL. THE PRIESTLORD GHAUR AND HIS COUNCIL HAVE LOST ALL AUTHORITY, AND ANARCHY REIGNS.
AND SO IT WILL CONTINUE, UNTIL SOMEONE STEPS FORTH WITH A SOLUTION--A MEANS OF RESCUING THE DEVIANTS FROM OBLIVION.

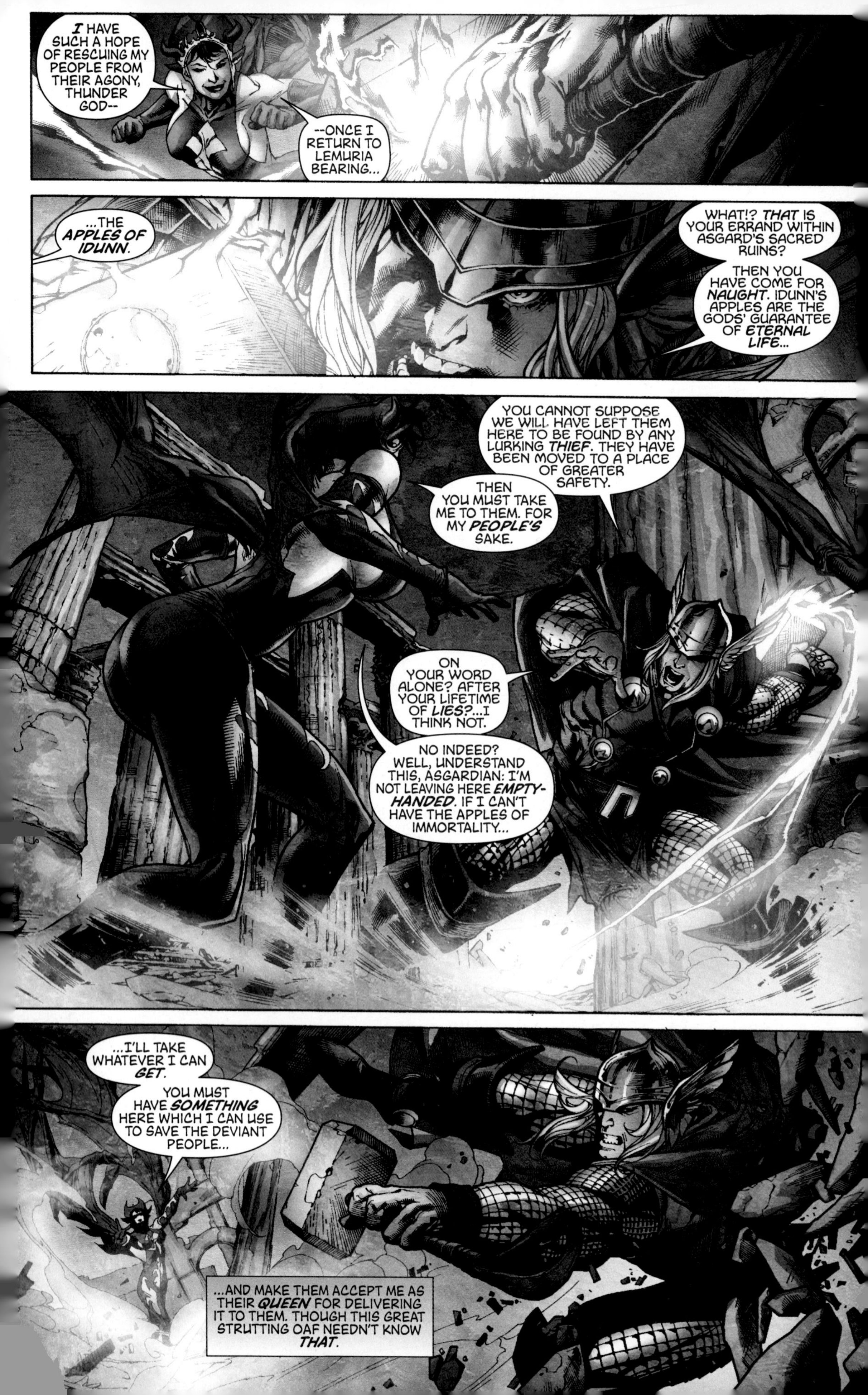
I HAVE SUCH A HOPE OF RESCUING MY PEOPLE FROM THEIR AGONY, THUNDER GOD--
--ONCE I RETURN TO LEMURIA BEARING...
...THE APPLES OF IDUNN.
WHAT!? THAT IS YOUR ERRAND WITHIN ASGARD'S SACRED RUINS?
THEN YOU HAVE COME FOR NAUGHT. IDUNN'S APPLES ARE THE GODS' GUARANTEE OF ETERNAL LIFE...
YOU CANNOT SUPPOSE WE WILL HAVE LEFT THEM HERE TO BE FOUND BY ANY LURKING THIEF. THEY HAVE BEEN MOVED TO A PLACE OF GREATER SAFETY.
THEN YOU MUST TAKE ME TO THEM. FOR MY PEOPLE'S SAKE.
ON YOUR WORD ALONE? AFTER YOUR LIFETIME OF LIES?...I THINK NOT.
NO INDEED? WELL, UNDERSTAND THIS, ASGARDIAN: I'M NOT LEAVING HERE EMPTY-HANDED. IF I CAN'T HAVE THE APPLES OF IMMORTALITY...
...I'LL TAKE WHATEVER I CAN GET.
YOU MUST HAVE SOMETHING HERE WHICH I CAN USE TO SAVE THE DEVIANT PEOPLE...
...AND MAKE THEM ACCEPT ME AS THEIR QUEEN FOR DELIVERING IT TO THEM. THOUGH THIS GREAT STRUTTING OAF NEEDN'T KNOW THAT.

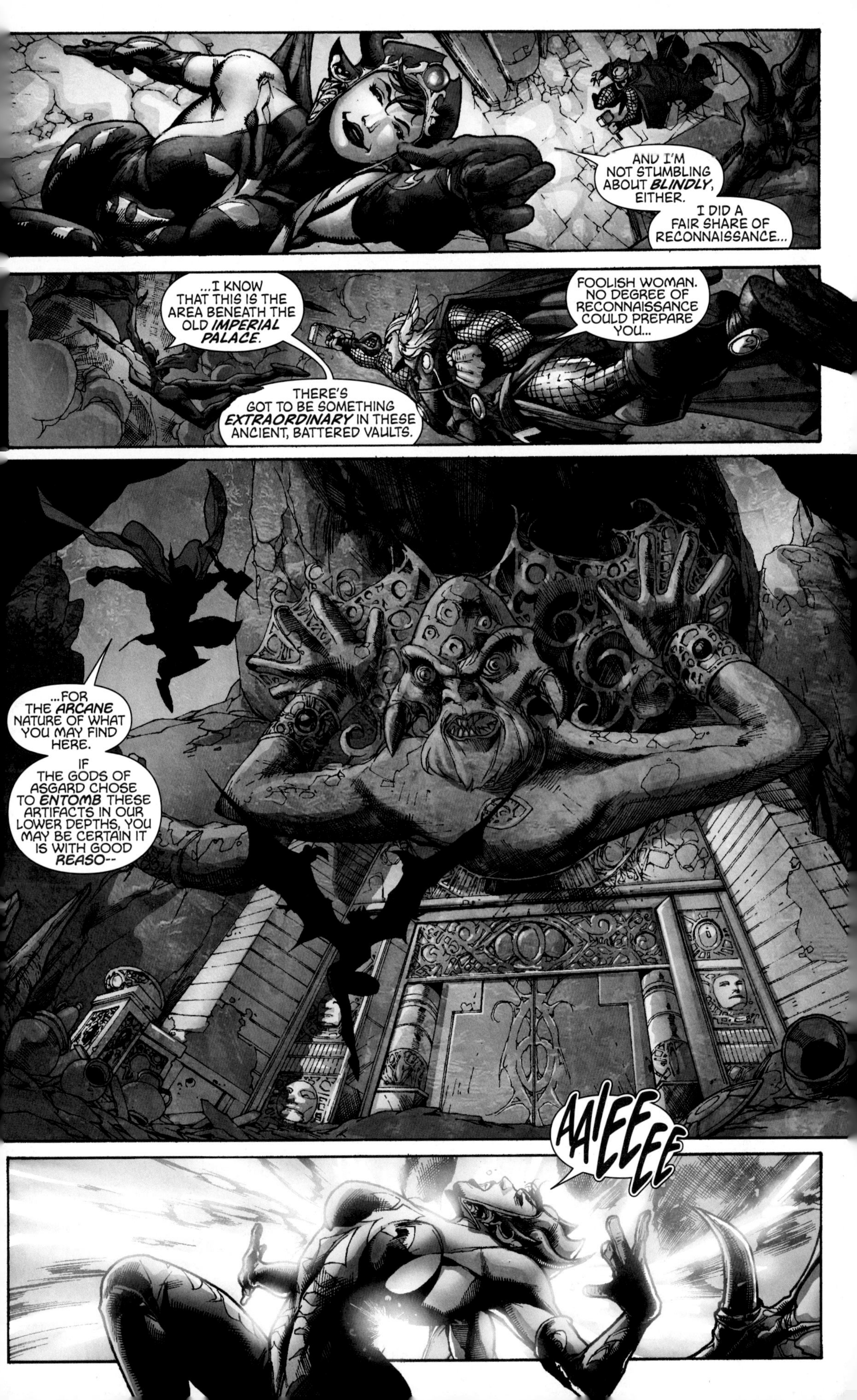
AND I'M NOT STUMBLING ABOUT BLINDLY, EITHER.
I DID A FAIR SHARE OF RECONNAISSANCE...
...I KNOW THAT THIS IS THE AREA BENEATH THE OLD IMPERIAL PALACE.
THERE'S GOT TO BE SOMETHING EXTRAORDINARY IN THESE ANCIENT, BATTERED VAULTS.
FOOLISH WOMAN. NO DEGREE OF RECONNAISSANCE COULD PREPARE YOU...
...FOR THE ARCANE NATURE OF WHAT YOU MAY FIND HERE.
IF THE GODS OF ASGARD CHOSE TO ENTOMB THESE ARTIFACTS IN OUR LOWER DEPTHS, YOU MAY BE CERTAIN IT IS WITH GOOD REASO--
AAIEEEE

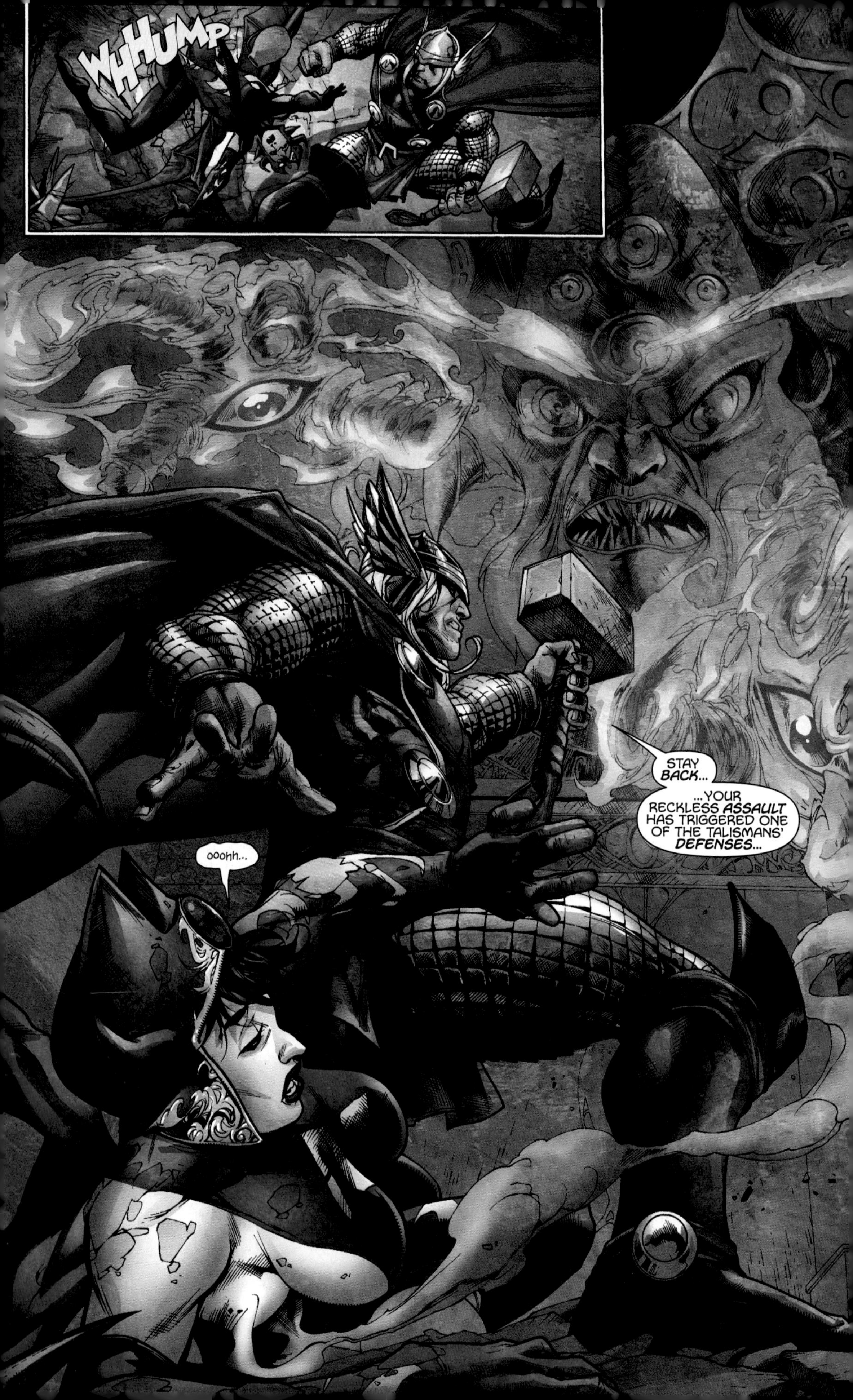
WHHUMP
STAY BACK...
...YOUR RECKLESS ASSAULT HAS TRIGGERED ONE OF THE TALISMANS' DEFENSES...
ooohh...

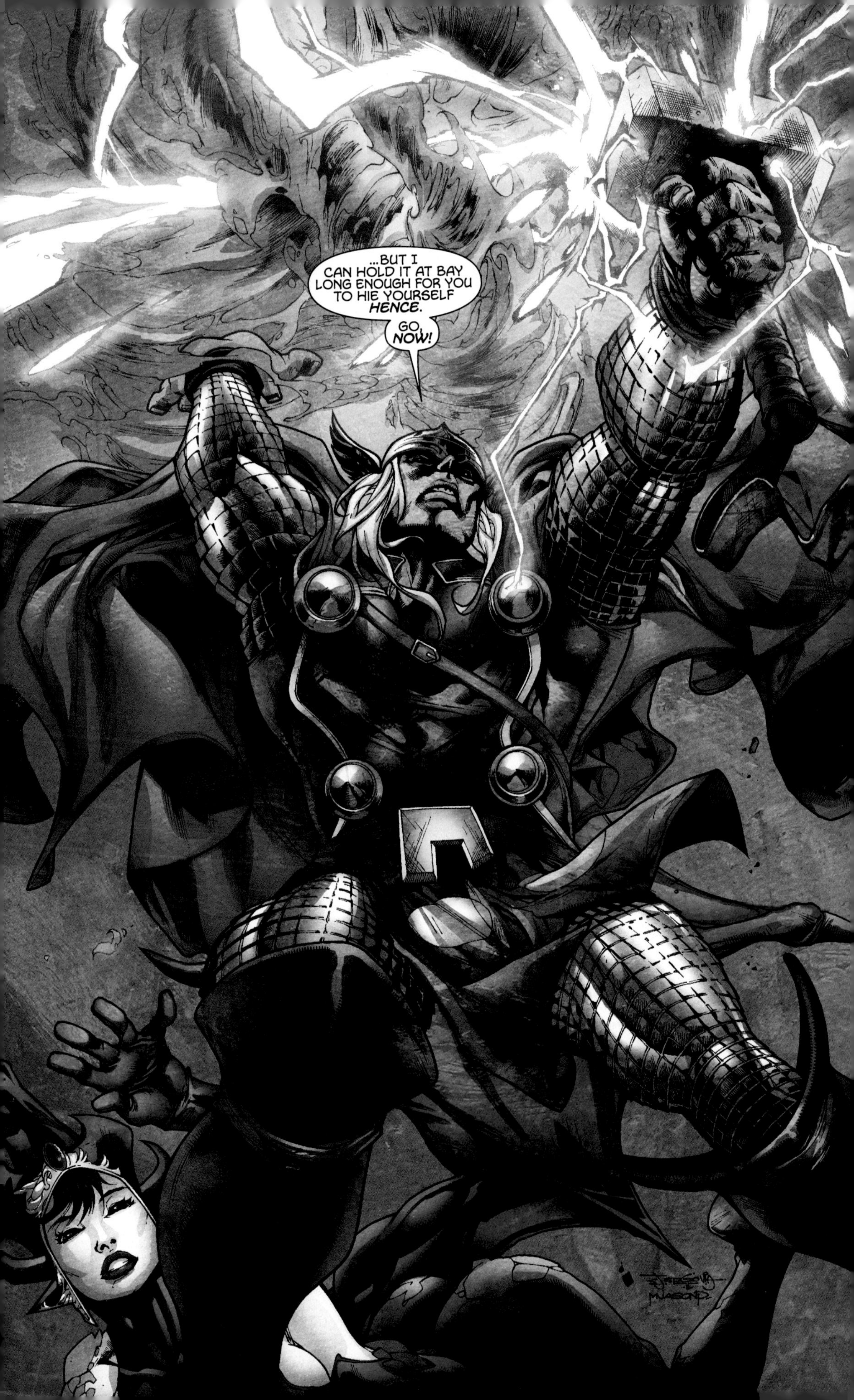
...BUT I CAN HOLD IT AT BAY LONG ENOUGH FOR YOU TO HIE YOURSELF *HENCE*.
GO, *NOW!*

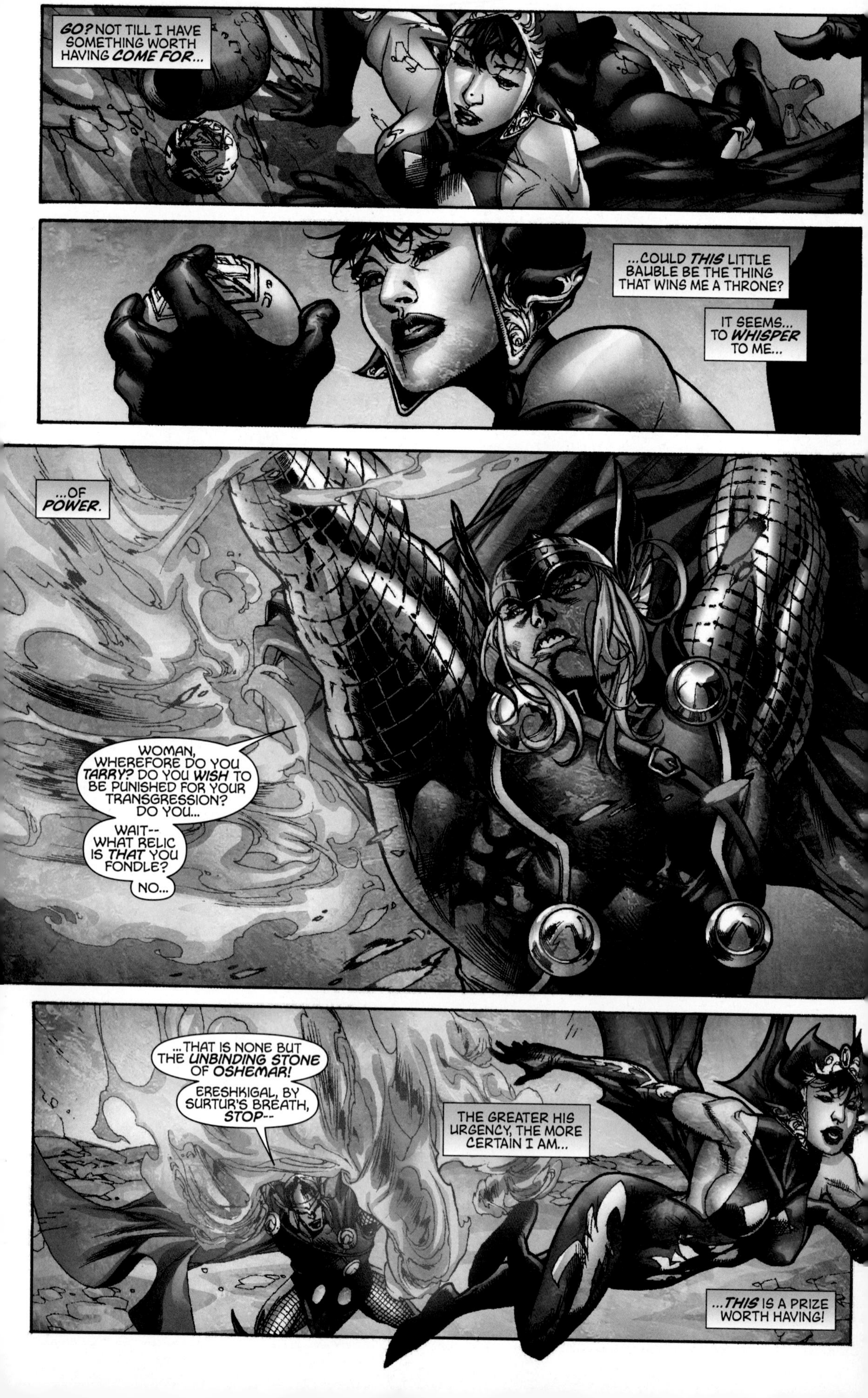
GO? NOT TILL I HAVE SOMETHING WORTH HAVING COME FOR...
...COULD THIS LITTLE BAUBLE BE THE THING THAT WINS ME A THRONE?
IT SEEMS... TO WHISPER TO ME...
...OF POWER.
WOMAN, WHEREFORE DO YOU TARRY? DO YOU WISH TO BE PUNISHED FOR YOUR TRANSGRESSION? DO YOU...
WAIT-- WHAT RELIC IS THAT YOU FONDLE?
NO...
...THAT IS NONE BUT THE UNBINDING STONE OF OSHEMAR!
ERESHKIGAL, BY SURTUR'S BREATH, STOP--
THE GREATER HIS URGENCY, THE MORE CERTAIN I AM...
...THIS IS A PRIZE WORTH HAVING!

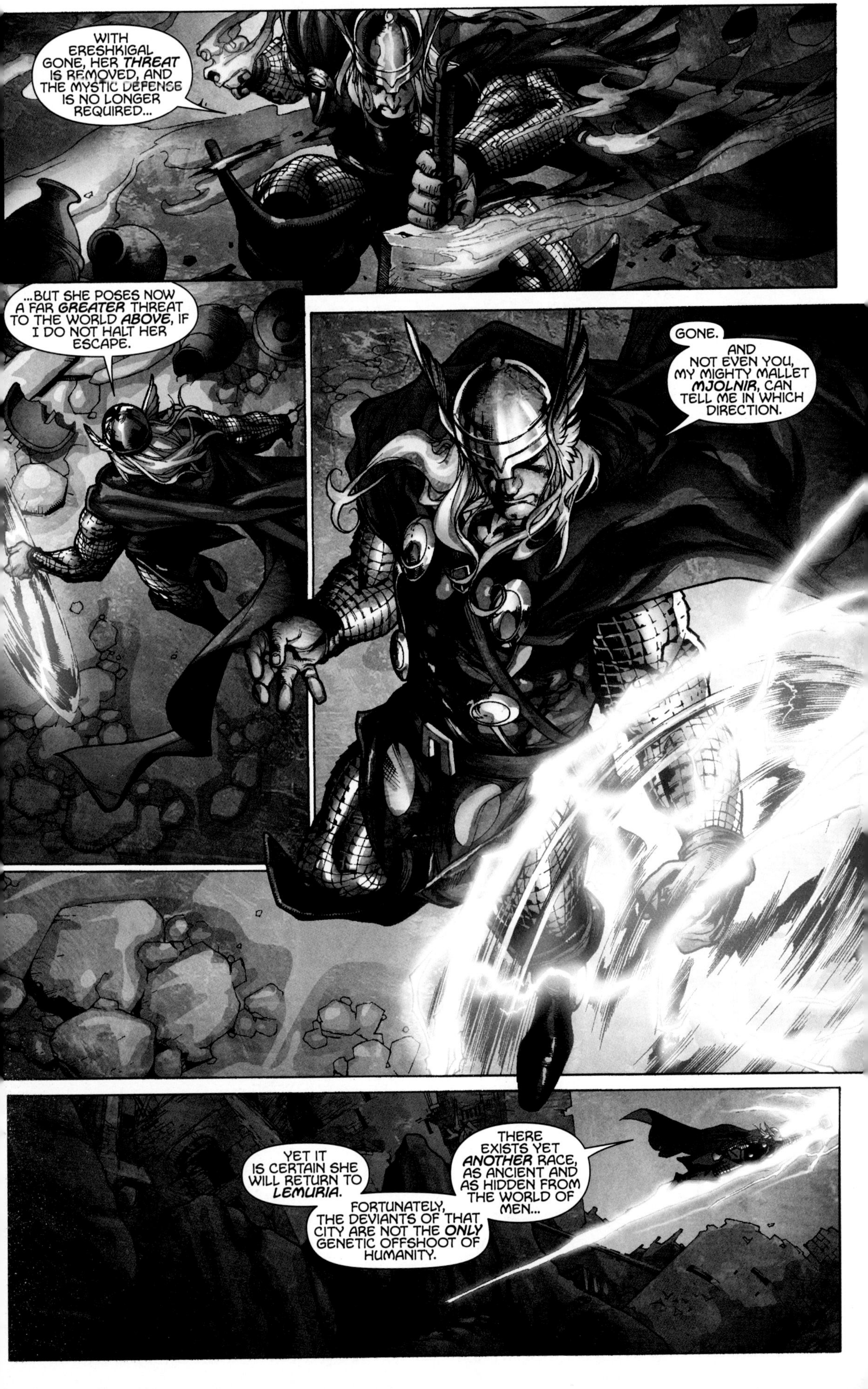
WITH ERESHKIGAL GONE, HER THREAT IS REMOVED, AND THE MYSTIC DEFENSE IS NO LONGER REQUIRED...
...BUT SHE POSES NOW A FAR GREATER THREAT TO THE WORLD ABOVE, IF I DO NOT HALT HER ESCAPE.
GONE.
AND NOT EVEN YOU, MY MIGHTY MALLET MJOLNIR, CAN TELL ME IN WHICH DIRECTION.
YET IT IS CERTAIN SHE WILL RETURN TO LEMURIA.
FORTUNATELY, THE DEVIANTS OF THAT CITY ARE NOT THE ONLY GENETIC OFFSHOOT OF HUMANITY.
THERE EXISTS YET ANOTHER RACE, AS ANCIENT AND AS HIDDEN FROM THE WORLD OF MEN...

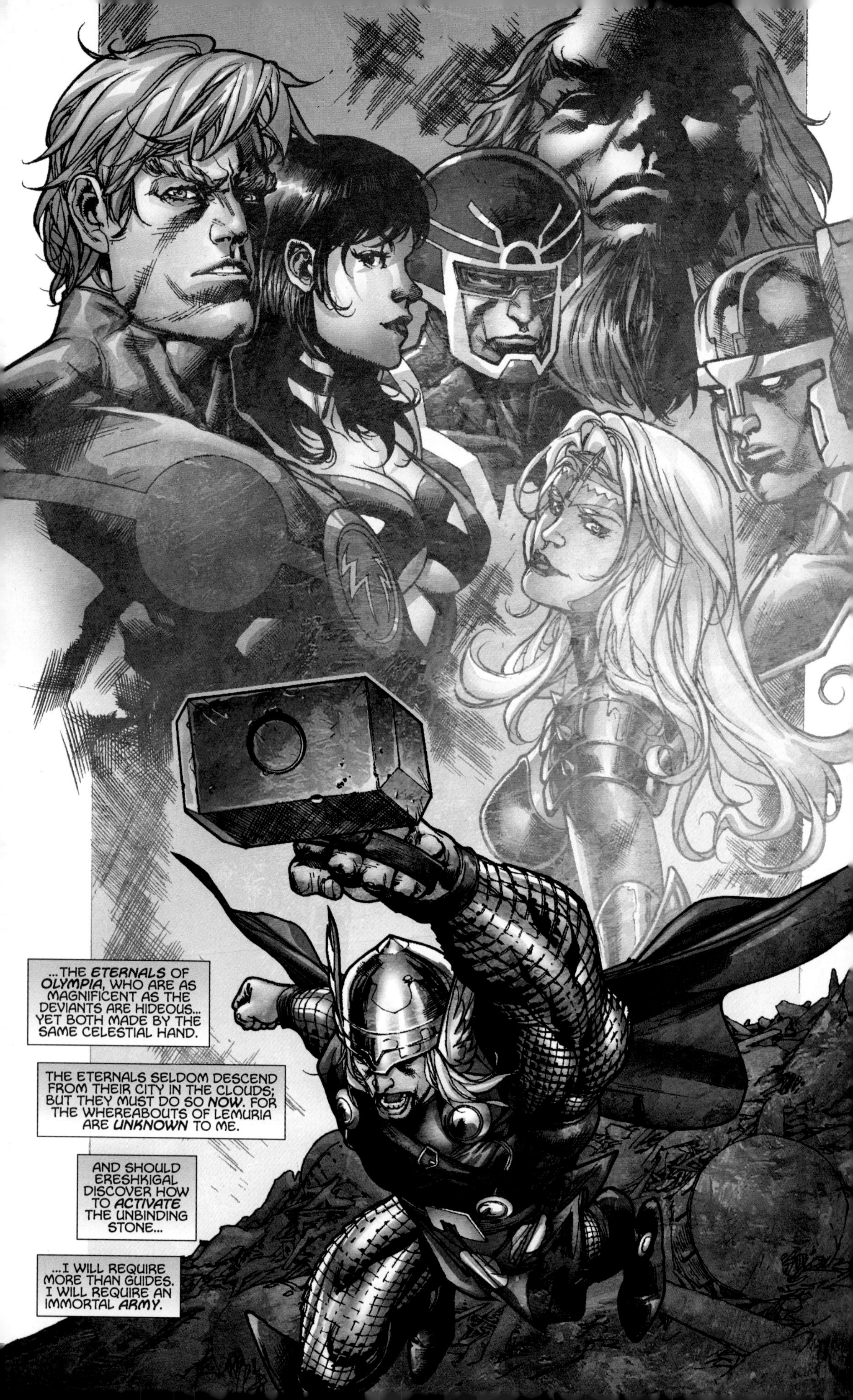
...THE ETERNALS OF OLYMPIA, WHO ARE AS MAGNIFICENT AS THE DEVIANTS ARE HIDEOUS... YET BOTH MADE BY THE SAME CELESTIAL HAND.
THE ETERNALS SELDOM DESCEND FROM THEIR CITY IN THE CLOUDS; BUT THEY MUST DO SO NOW. FOR THE WHEREABOUTS OF LEMURIA ARE UNKNOWN TO ME.
AND SHOULD ERESHKIGAL DISCOVER HOW TO ACTIVATE THE UNBINDING STONE...
...I WILL REQUIRE MORE THAN GUIDES. I WILL REQUIRE AN IMMORTAL ARMY.

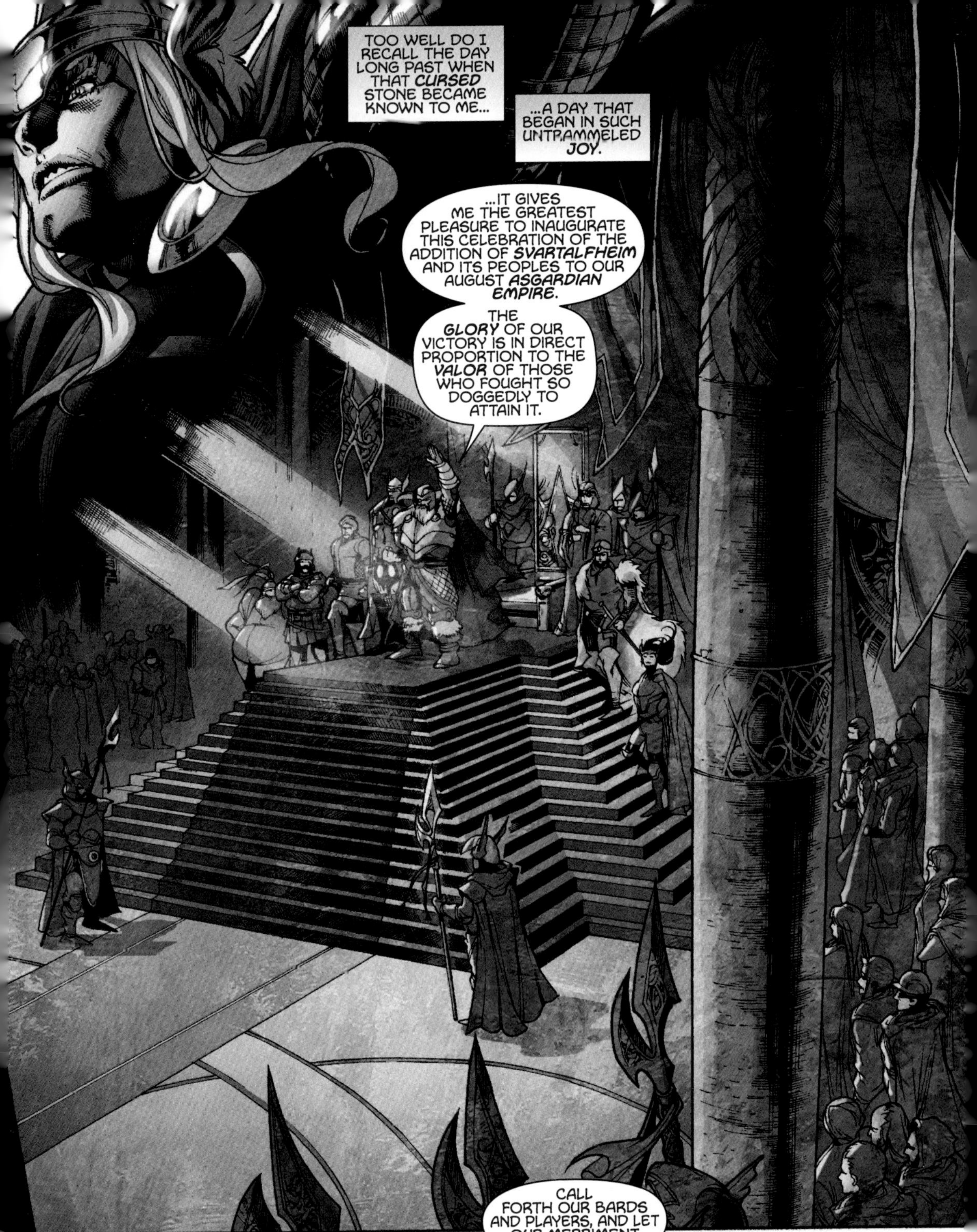
TOO WELL DO I RECALL THE DAY LONG PAST WHEN THAT CURSED STONE BECAME KNOWN TO ME...
...A DAY THAT BEGAN IN SUCH UNTRAMMELED JOY.
...IT GIVES ME THE GREATEST PLEASURE TO INAUGURATE THIS CELEBRATION OF THE ADDITION OF SVARTALFHEIM AND ITS PEOPLES TO OUR AUGUST ASGARDIAN EMPIRE.
THE GLORY OF OUR VICTORY IS IN DIRECT PROPORTION TO THE VALOR OF THOSE WHO FOUGHT SO DOGGEDLY TO ATTAIN IT.
CALL FORTH OUR BARDS AND PLAYERS, AND LET OUR MERRIMENT COMMENC--

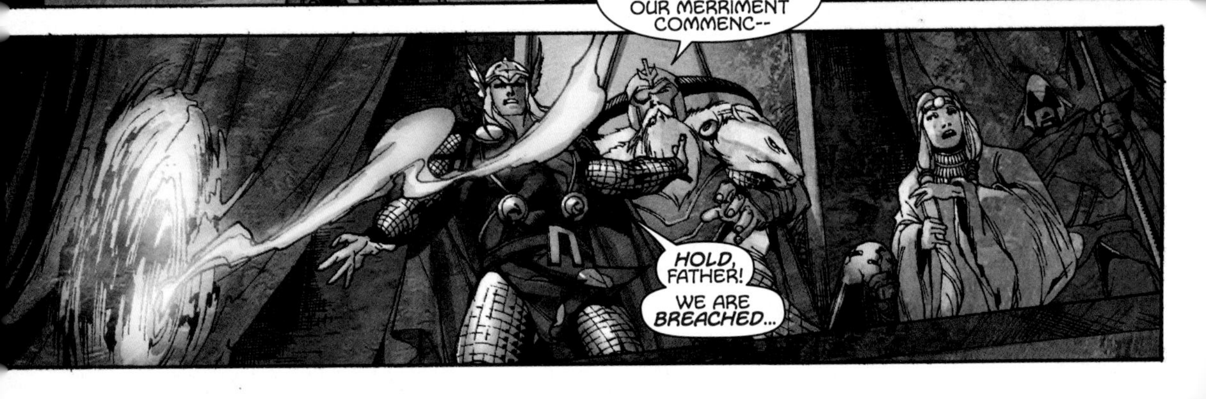
HOLD, FATHER!
WE ARE BREACHED...

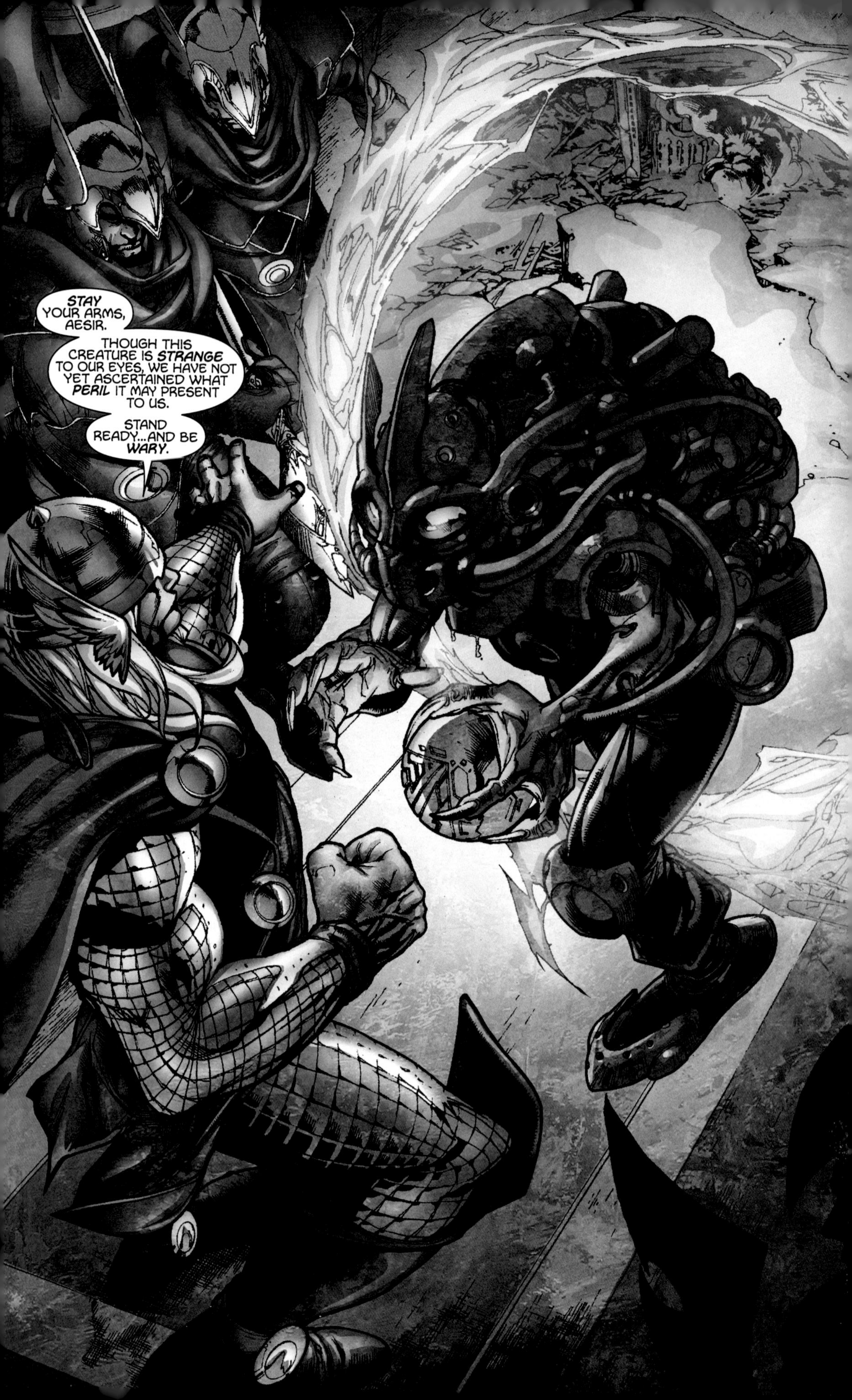
STAY YOUR ARMS, AESIR.
THOUGH THIS CREATURE IS STRANGE TO OUR EYES, WE HAVE NOT YET ASCERTAINED WHAT PERIL IT MAY PRESENT TO US.
STAND READY...AND BE WARY.

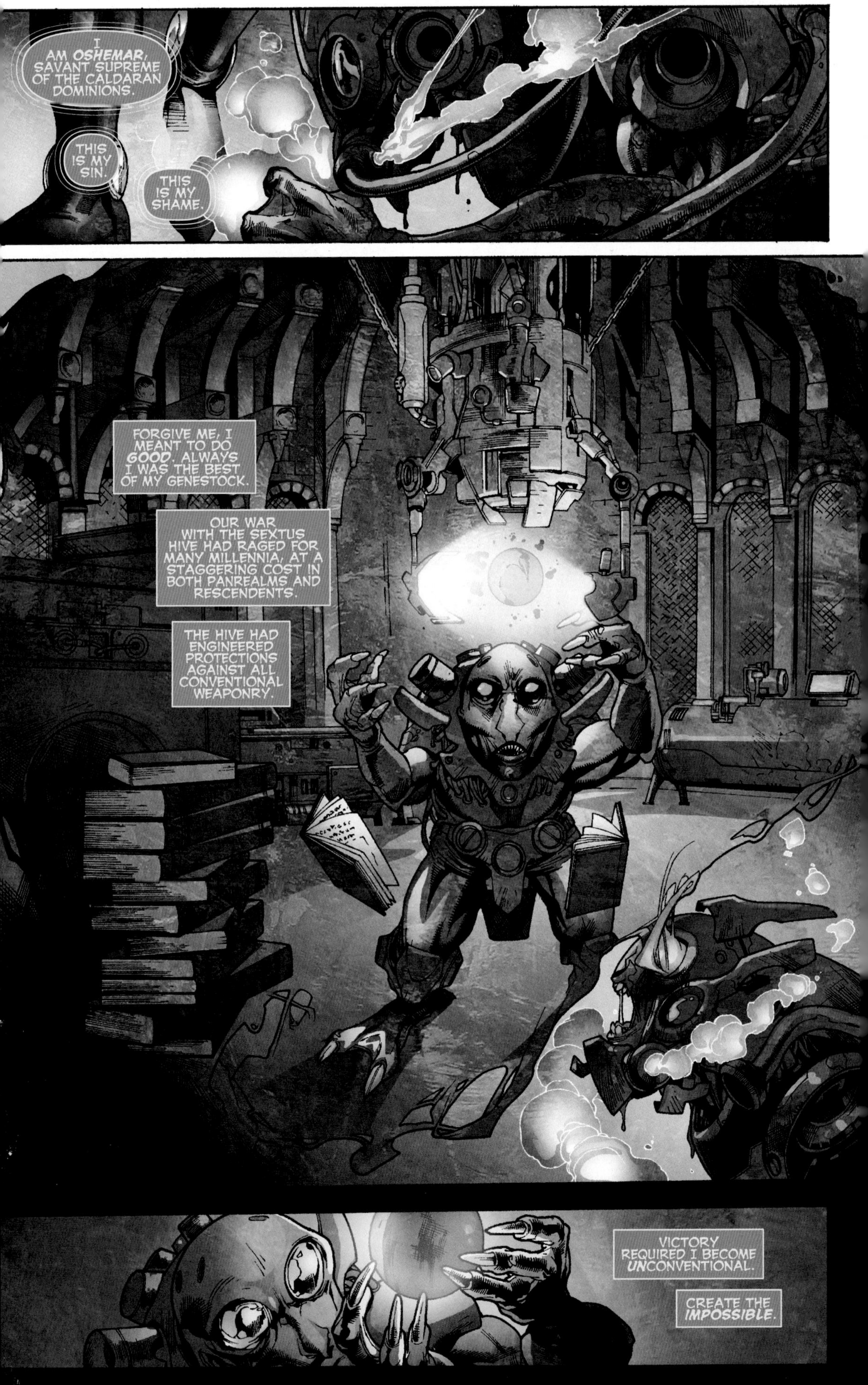
I AM OSHEMAR, SAVANT SUPREME OF THE CALDARAN DOMINIONS.
THIS IS MY SIN.
THIS IS MY SHAME.
FORGIVE ME, I MEANT TO DO GOOD. ALWAYS I WAS THE BEST OF MY GENESTOCK.
OUR WAR WITH THE SEXTUS HIVE HAD RAGED FOR MANY MILLENNIA, AT A STAGGERING COST IN BOTH PANREALMS AND RESCENDENTS.
THE HIVE HAD ENGINEERED PROTECTIONS AGAINST ALL CONVENTIONAL WEAPONRY.
VICTORY REQUIRED I BECOME UNCONVENTIONAL.
CREATE THE IMPOSSIBLE.

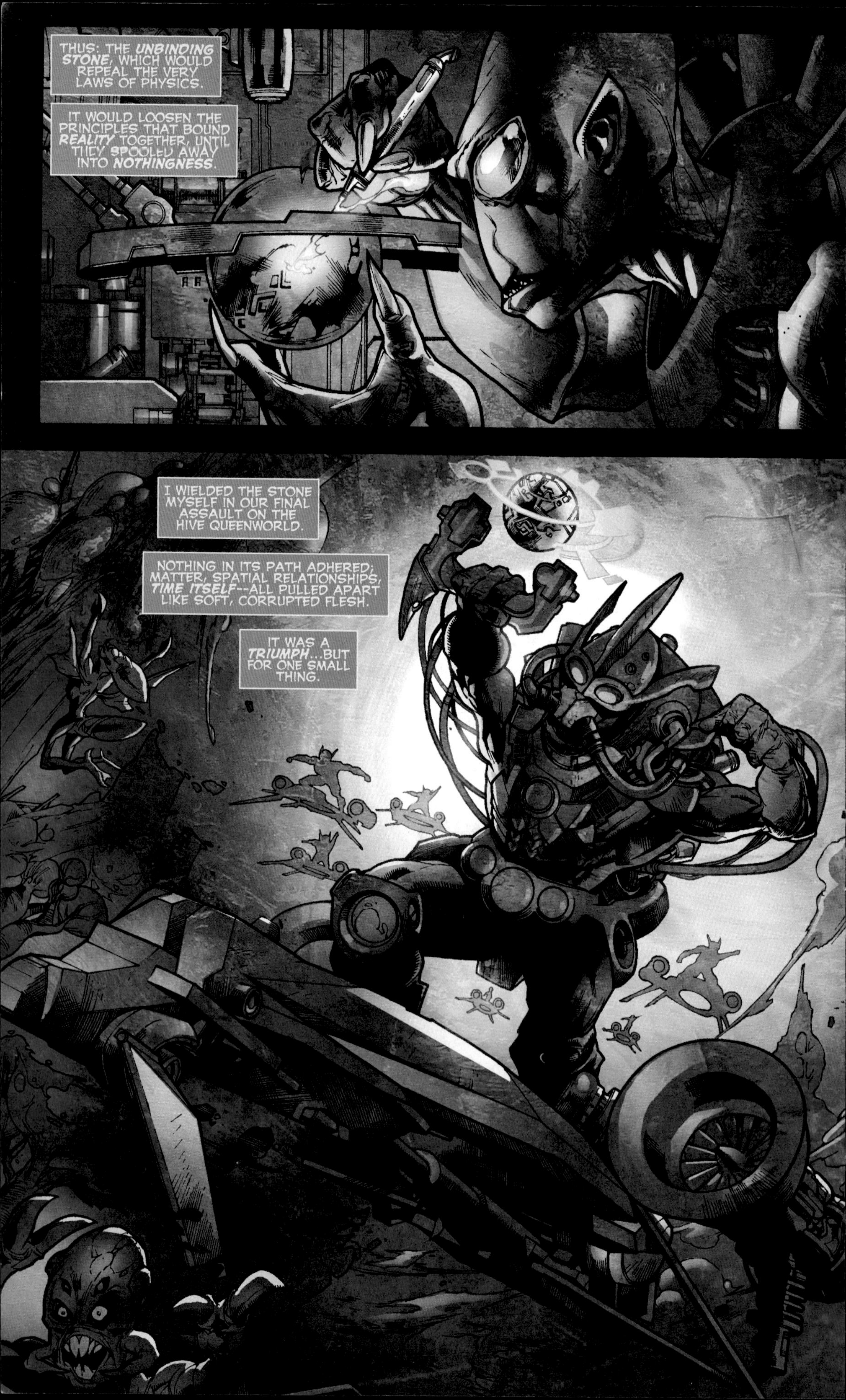
THUS: THE *UNBINDING STONE*, WHICH WOULD REPEAL THE VERY LAWS OF PHYSICS.
IT WOULD LOOSEN THE PRINCIPLES THAT BOUND *REALITY* TOGETHER, UNTIL THEY SPOOLED AWAY INTO *NOTHINGNESS*.
I WIELDED THE STONE MYSELF IN OUR FINAL ASSAULT ON THE HIVE QUEENWORLD.
NOTHING IN ITS PATH ADHERED; MATTER, SPATIAL RELATIONSHIPS, *TIME ITSELF*--ALL PULLED APART LIKE SOFT, CORRUPTED FLESH.
IT WAS A *TRIUMPH*...BUT FOR ONE SMALL THING.

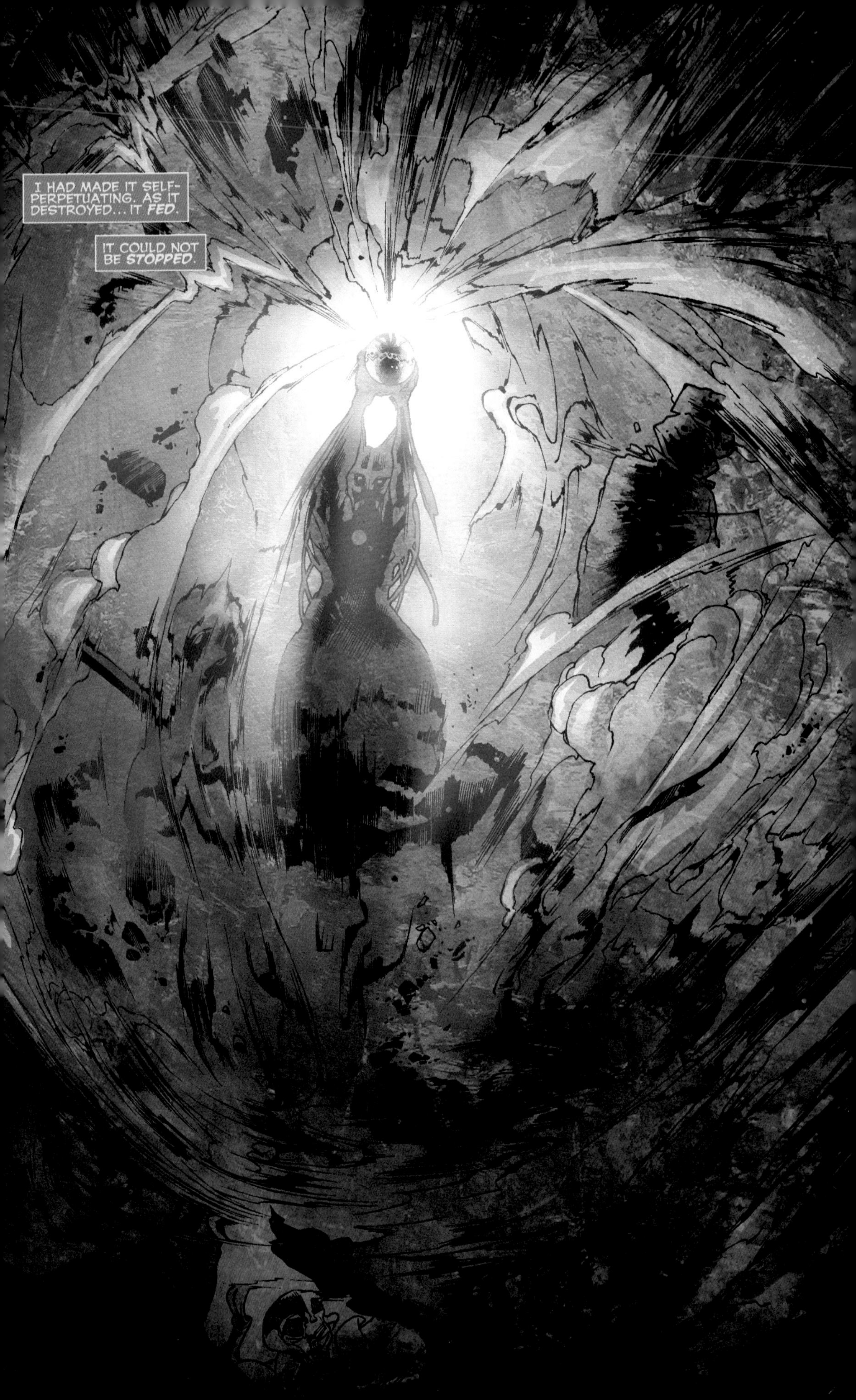
I HAD MADE IT SELF-PERPETUATING. AS IT DESTROYED... IT FED.
IT COULD NOT BE STOPPED.

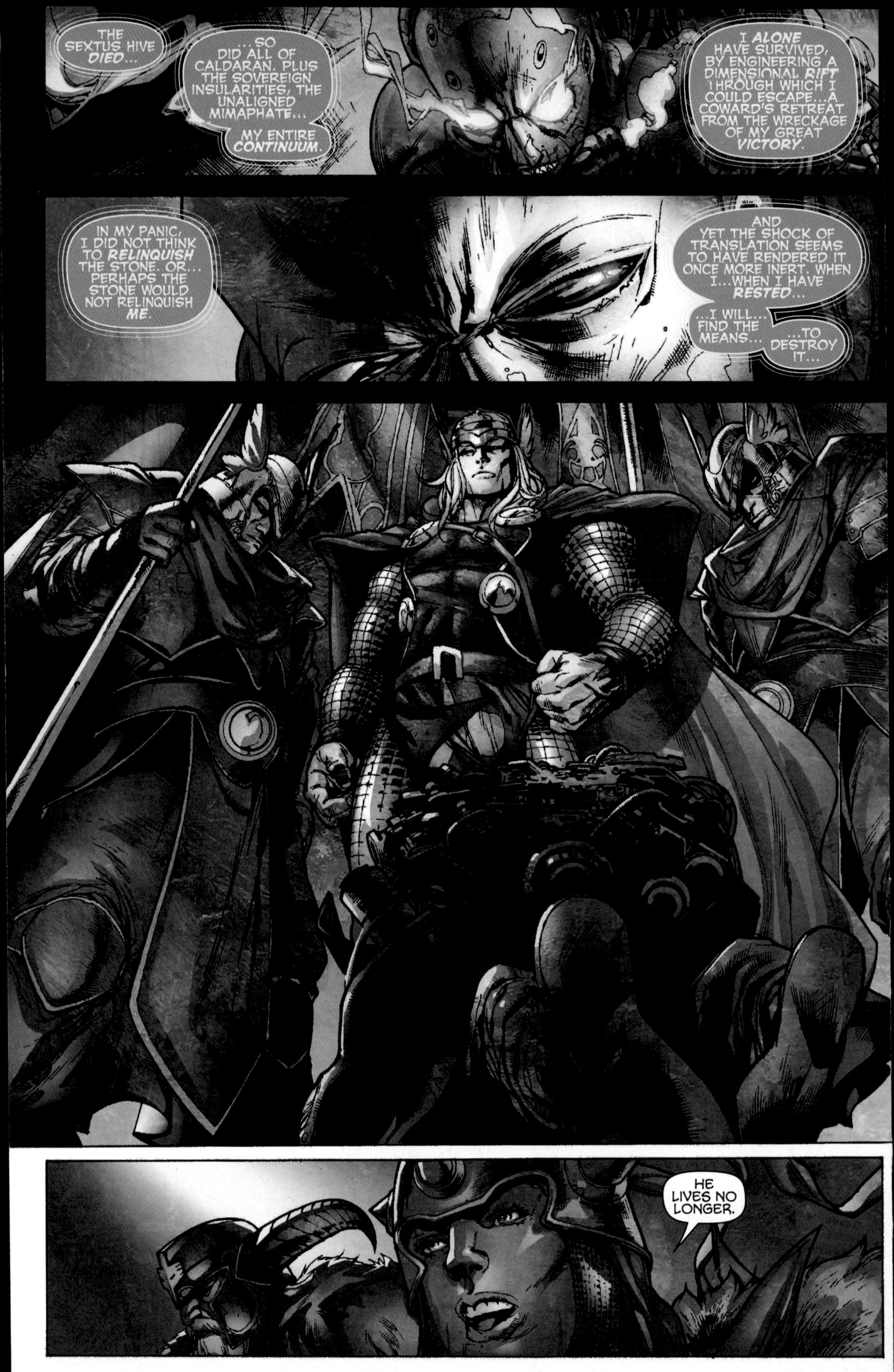
THE SEXTUS HIVE DIED...
...SO DID ALL OF CALDARAN. PLUS THE SOVEREIGN INSULARITIES, THE UNALIGNED MIMAPHATE...
MY ENTIRE CONTINUUM.
I ALONE HAVE SURVIVED, BY ENGINEERING A DIMENSIONAL RIFT THROUGH WHICH I COULD ESCAPE...A COWARD'S RETREAT FROM THE WRECKAGE OF MY GREAT VICTORY.
IN MY PANIC, I DID NOT THINK TO RELINQUISH THE STONE. OR... PERHAPS THE STONE WOULD NOT RELINQUISH ME.
AND YET THE SHOCK OF TRANSLATION SEEMS TO HAVE RENDERED IT ONCE MORE INERT. WHEN I...WHEN I HAVE RESTED...
...I WILL... FIND THE MEANS...
...TO DESTROY IT...
HE LIVES NO LONGER.

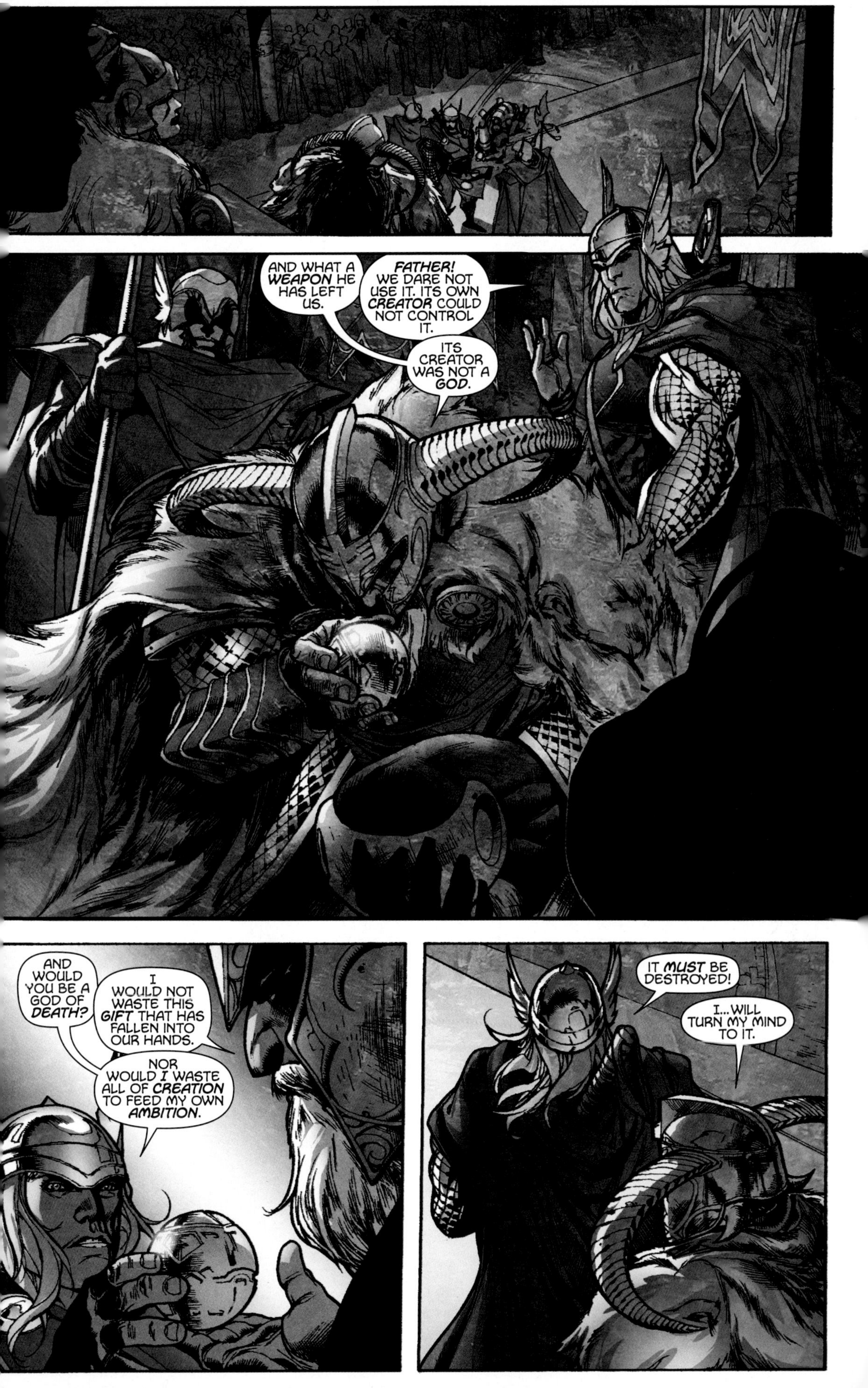
AND WHAT A WEAPON HE HAS LEFT US.
FATHER! WE DARE NOT USE IT. ITS OWN CREATOR COULD NOT CONTROL IT.
ITS CREATOR WAS NOT A GOD.
AND WOULD YOU BE A GOD OF DEATH?
I WOULD NOT WASTE THIS GIFT THAT HAS FALLEN INTO OUR HANDS.
NOR WOULD I WASTE ALL OF CREATION TO FEED MY OWN AMBITION.
IT MUST BE DESTROYED!
I...WILL TURN MY MIND TO IT.

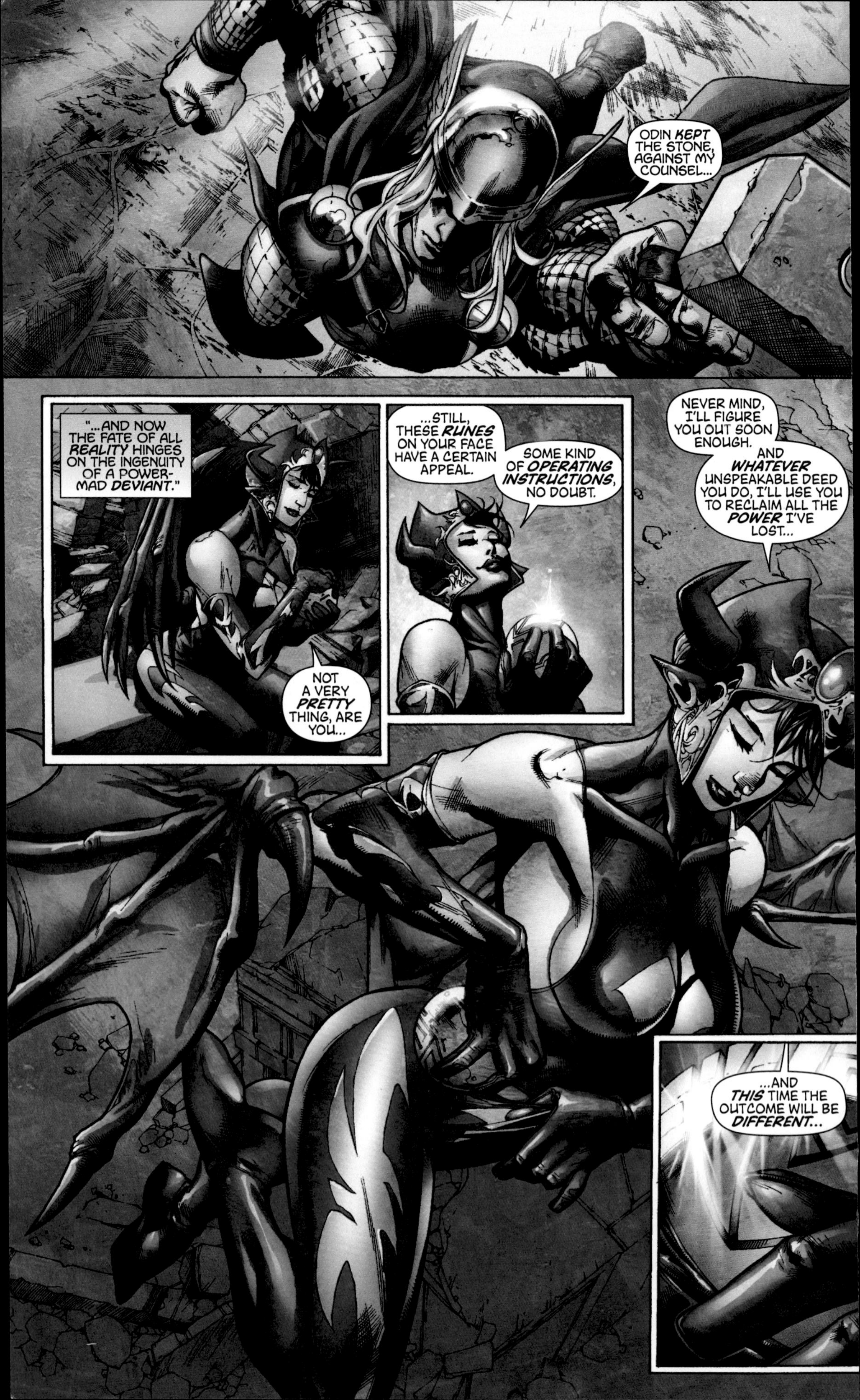

ODIN **KEPT** THE STONE, AGAINST MY COUNSEL...
"...AND NOW THE FATE OF ALL **REALITY** HINGES ON THE INGENUITY OF A POWER-MAD **DEVIANT**."
NOT A VERY **PRETTY** THING, ARE YOU...
...STILL, THESE **RUNES** ON YOUR FACE HAVE A CERTAIN APPEAL.
SOME KIND OF **OPERATING INSTRUCTIONS**, NO DOUBT.
NEVER MIND, I'LL FIGURE YOU OUT SOON ENOUGH.
AND **WHATEVER** UNSPEAKABLE DEED YOU DO, I'LL USE YOU TO RECLAIM ALL THE **POWER** I'VE LOST...
...AND **THIS** TIME THE OUTCOME WILL BE **DIFFERENT**...

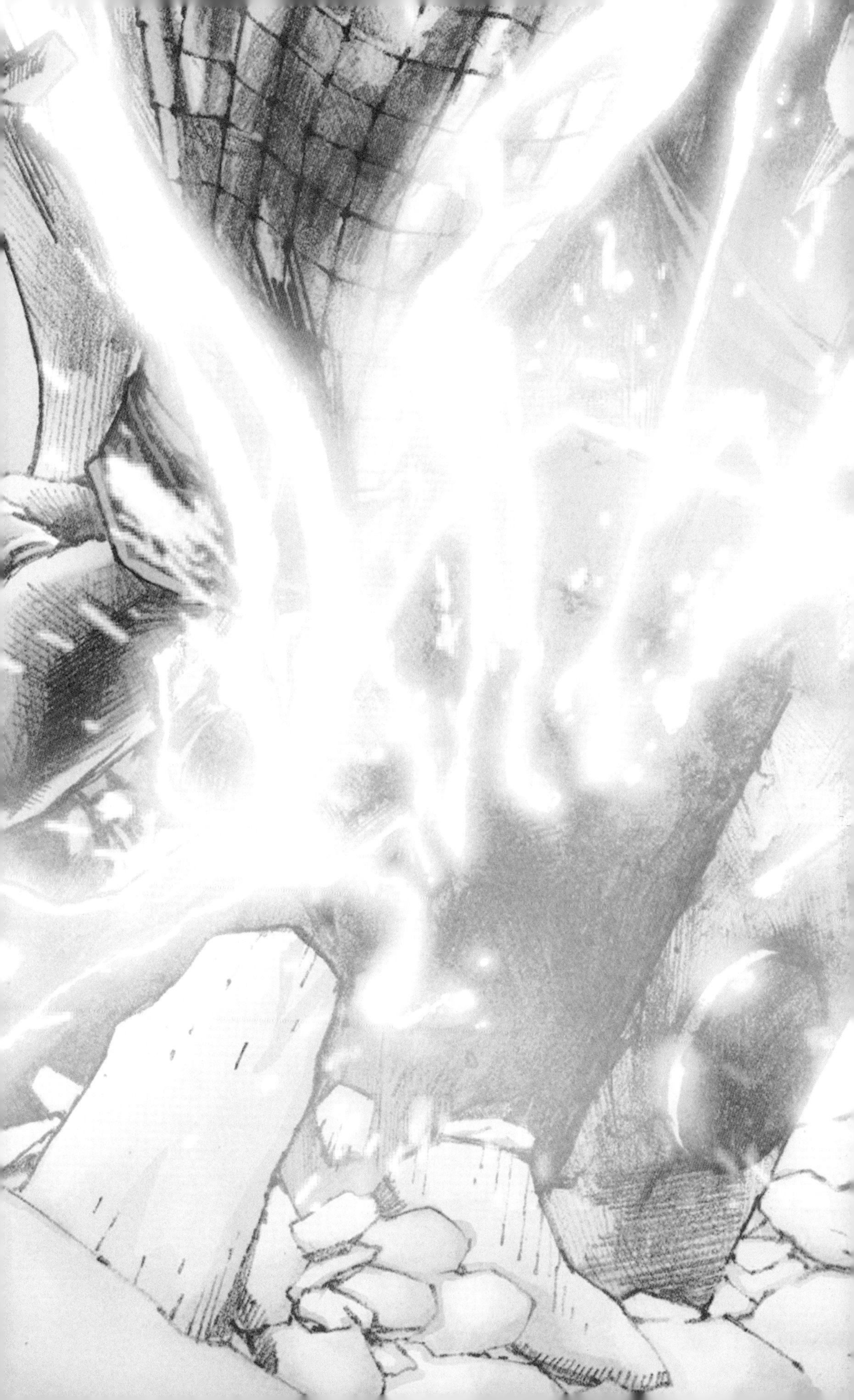

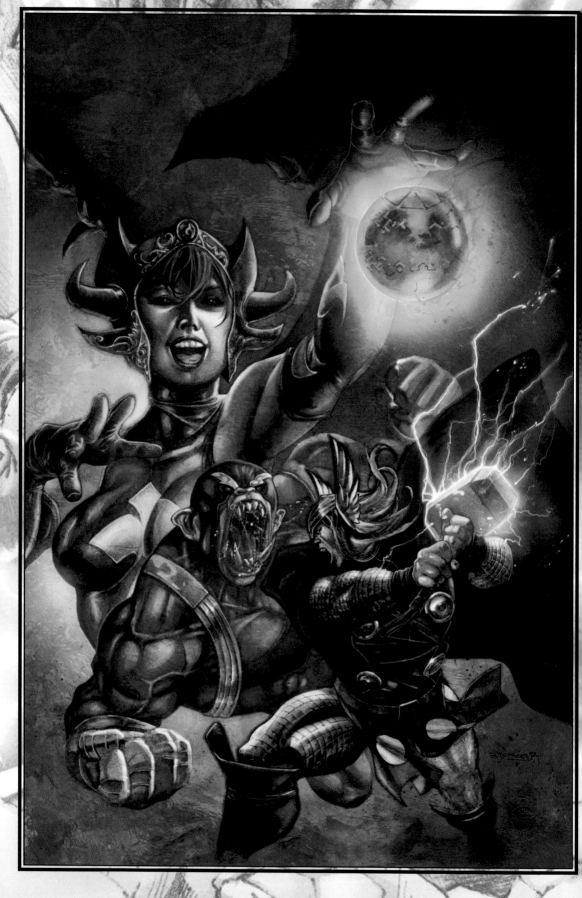

TWO

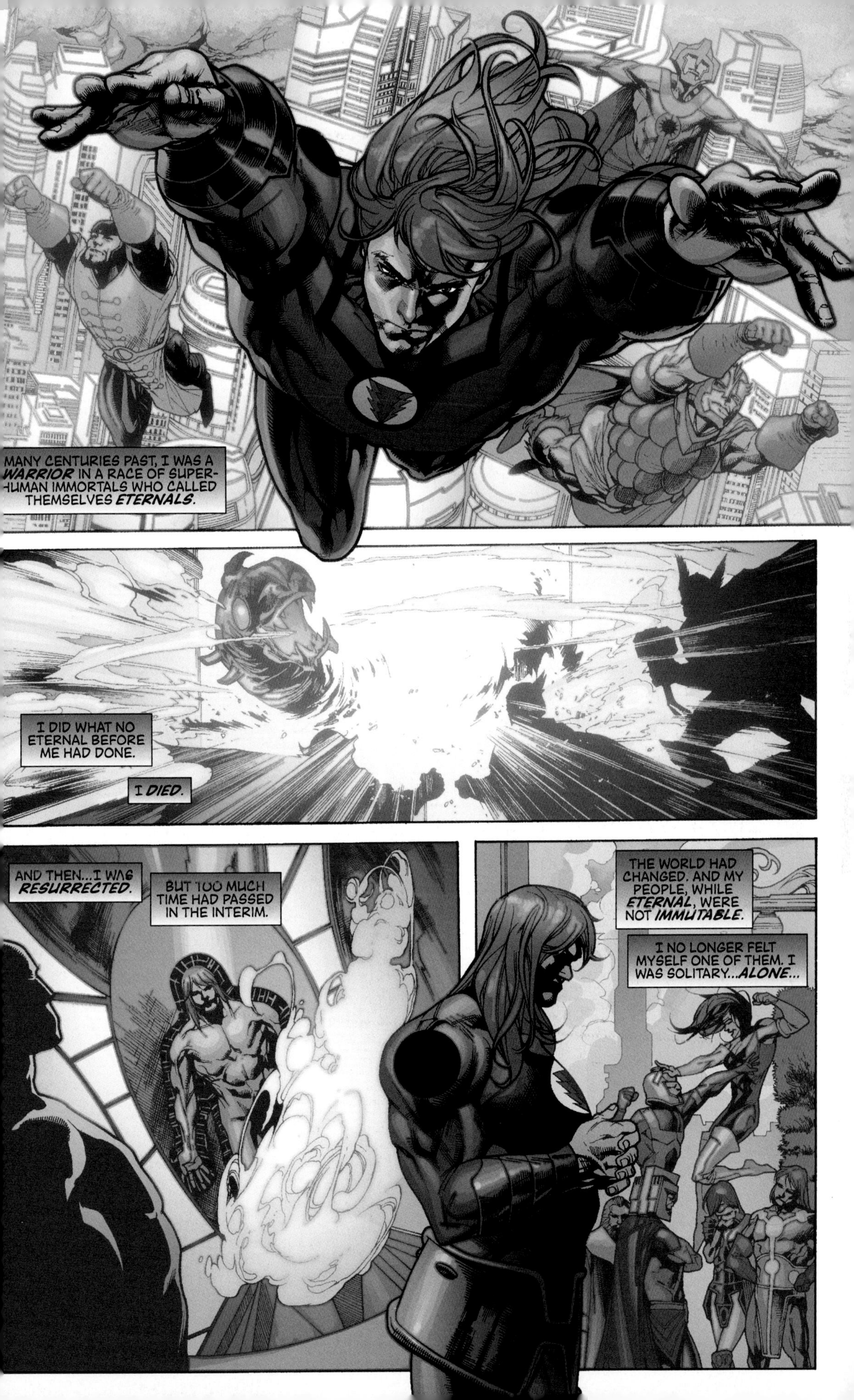
MANY CENTURIES PAST, I WAS A WARRIOR IN A RACE OF SUPER-HUMAN IMMORTALS WHO CALLED THEMSELVES ETERNALS.
I DID WHAT NO ETERNAL BEFORE ME HAD DONE.
I DIED.
AND THEN...I WAS RESURRECTED.
BUT TOO MUCH TIME HAD PASSED IN THE INTERIM.
THE WORLD HAD CHANGED. AND MY PEOPLE, WHILE ETERNAL, WERE NOT IMMUTABLE.
I NO LONGER FELT MYSELF ONE OF THEM. I WAS SOLITARY...ALONE...

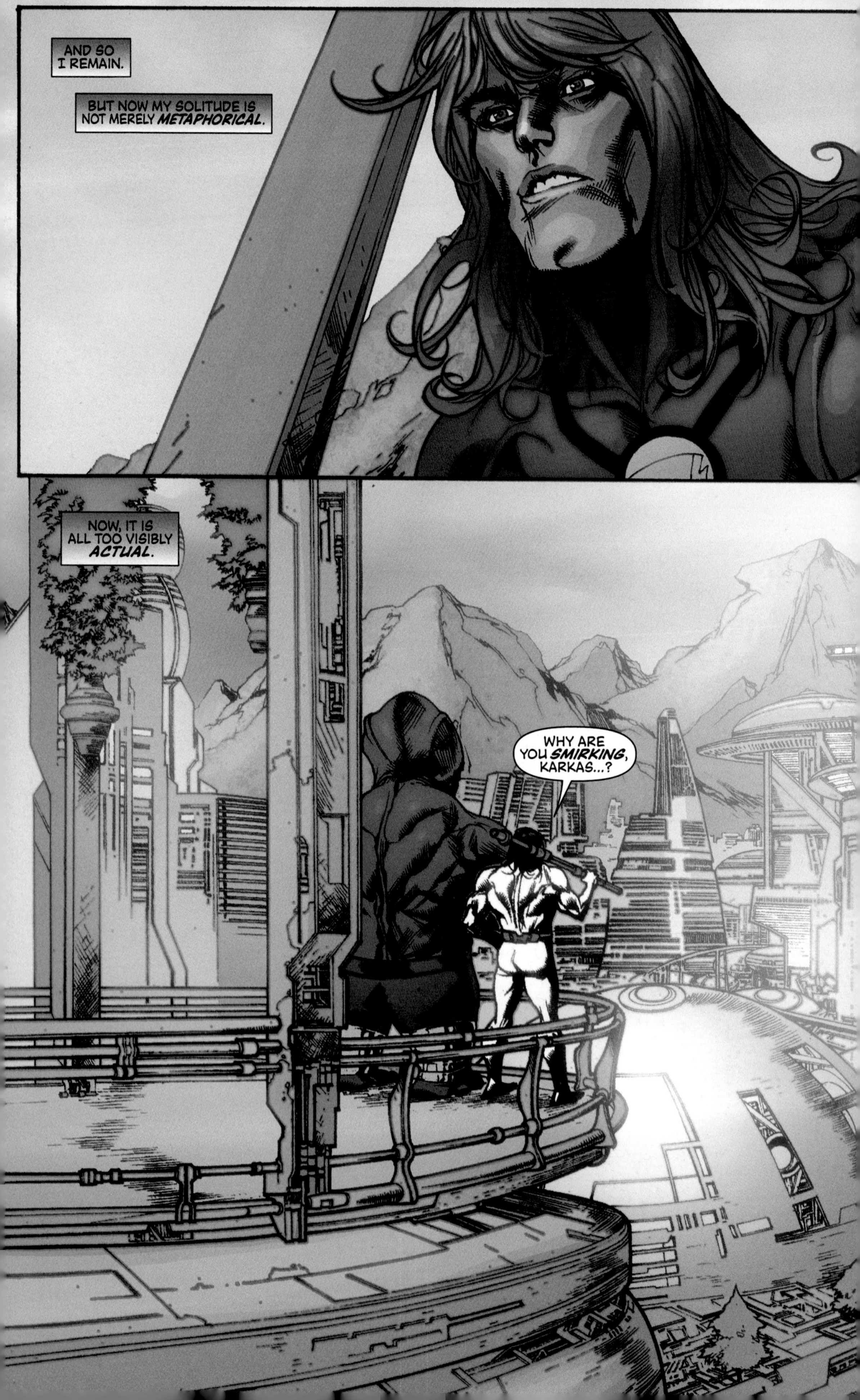
AND SO I REMAIN.
BUT NOW MY SOLITUDE IS NOT MERELY METAPHORICAL.
NOW, IT IS ALL TOO VISIBLY ACTUAL.
WHY ARE YOU SMIRKING, KARKAS...?

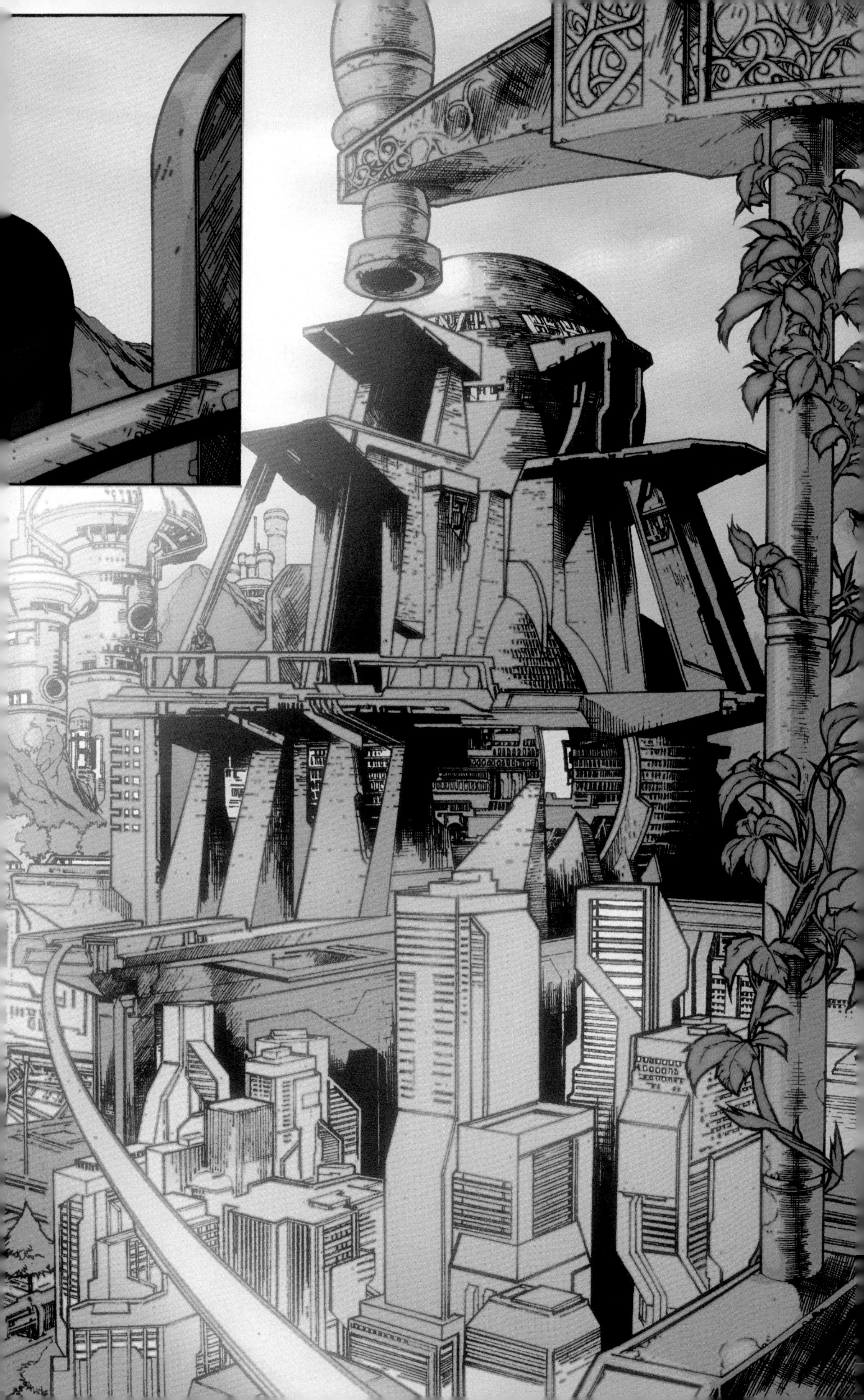

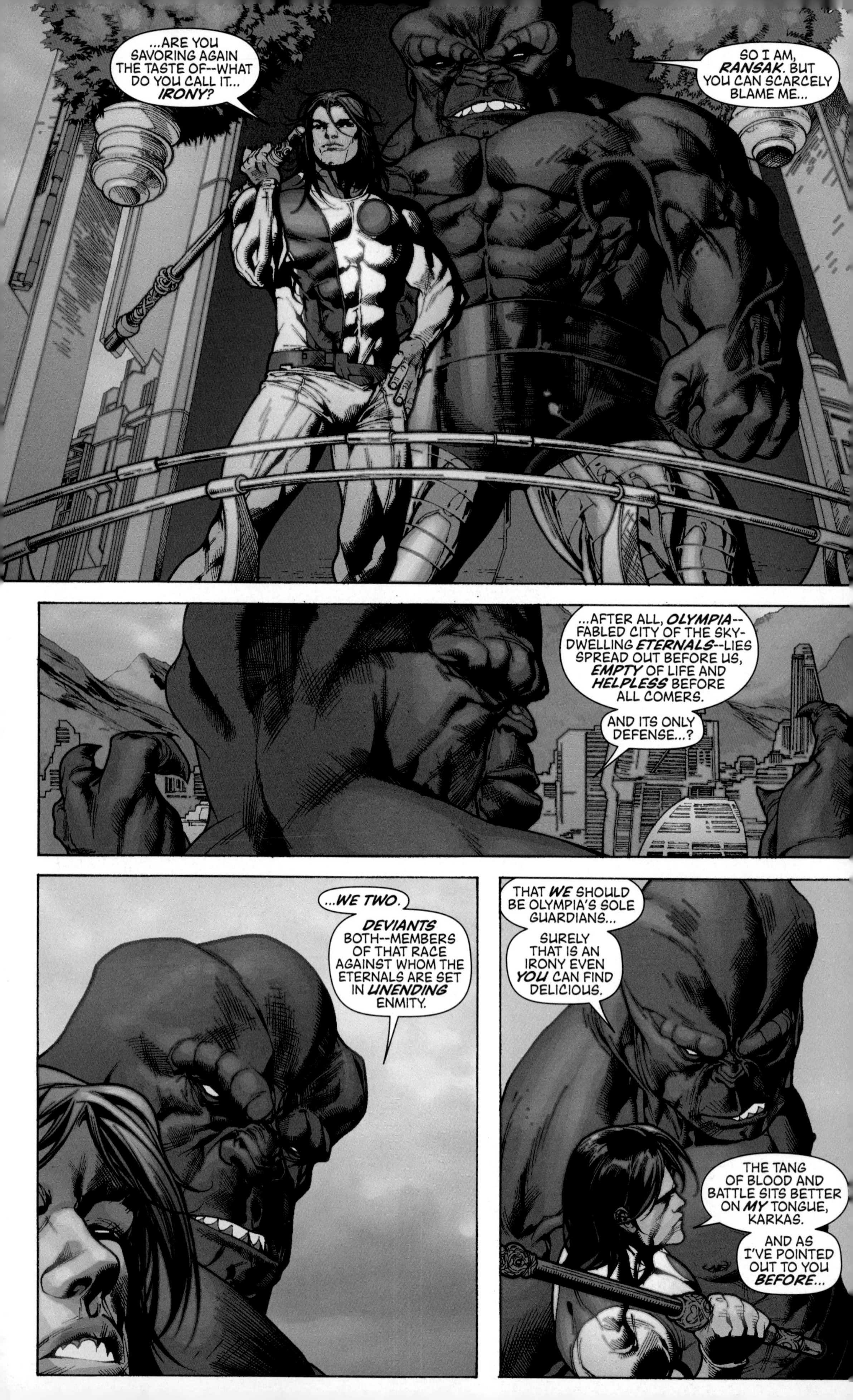
...ARE YOU SAVORING AGAIN THE TASTE OF--WHAT DO YOU CALL IT... IRONY?
SO I AM, RANSAK. BUT YOU CAN SCARCELY BLAME ME...
...AFTER ALL, OLYMPIA--FABLED CITY OF THE SKY-DWELLING ETERNALS--LIES SPREAD OUT BEFORE US, EMPTY OF LIFE AND HELPLESS BEFORE ALL COMERS.
AND ITS ONLY DEFENSE...?
...WE TWO.
DEVIANTS BOTH--MEMBERS OF THAT RACE AGAINST WHOM THE ETERNALS ARE SET IN UNENDING ENMITY.
THAT WE SHOULD BE OLYMPIA'S SOLE GUARDIANS...
SURELY THAT IS AN IRONY EVEN YOU CAN FIND DELICIOUS.
THE TANG OF BLOOD AND BATTLE SITS BETTER ON MY TONGUE, KARKAS.
AND AS I'VE POINTED OUT TO YOU BEFORE...

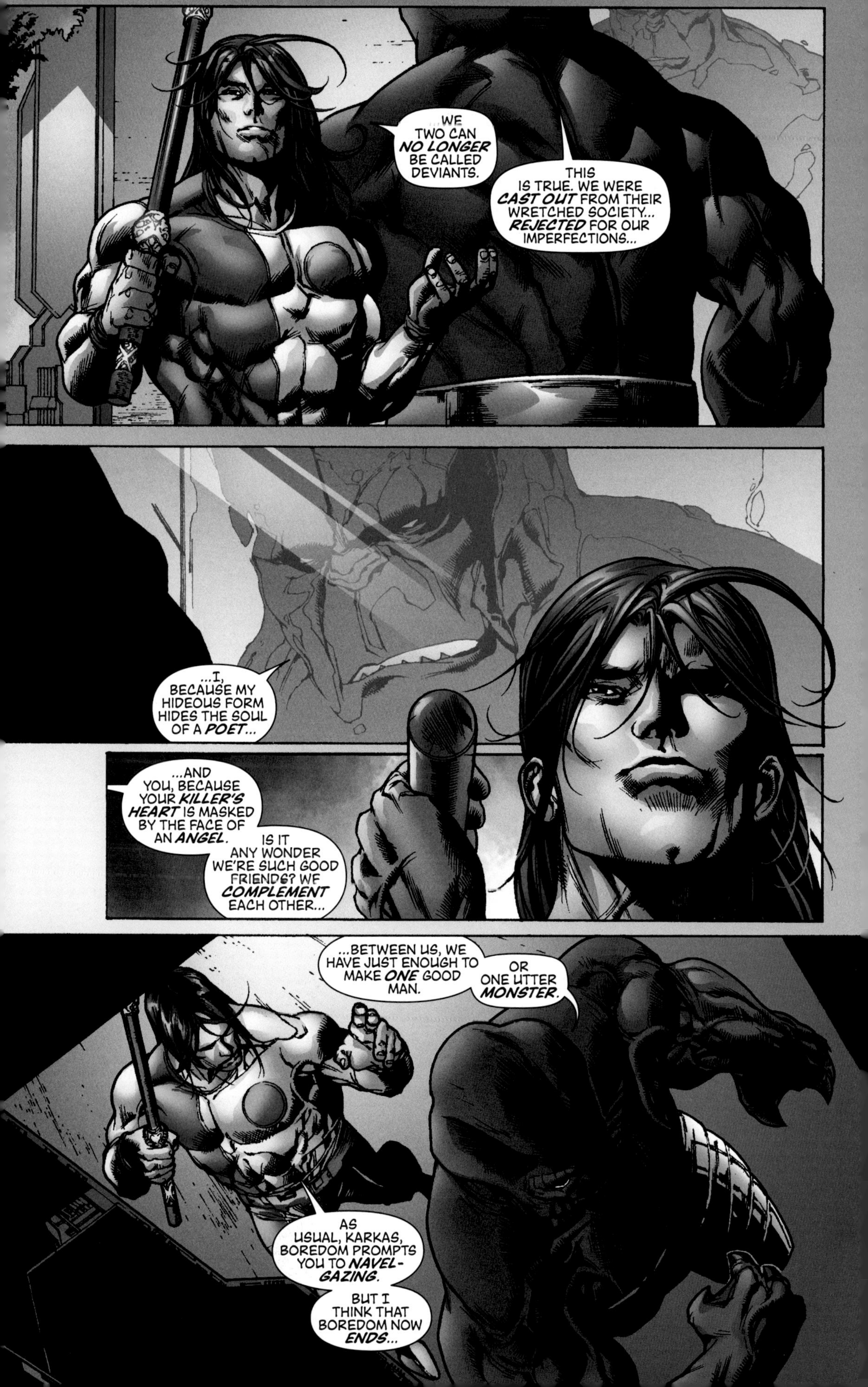
...WE TWO CAN NO LONGER BE CALLED DEVIANTS.
THIS IS TRUE. WE WERE CAST OUT FROM THEIR WRETCHED SOCIETY... REJECTED FOR OUR IMPERFECTIONS...
...I, BECAUSE MY HIDEOUS FORM HIDES THE SOUL OF A POET...
...AND YOU, BECAUSE YOUR KILLER'S HEART IS MASKED BY THE FACE OF AN ANGEL.
IS IT ANY WONDER WE'RE SUCH GOOD FRIENDS? WE COMPLEMENT EACH OTHER...
...BETWEEN US, WE HAVE JUST ENOUGH TO MAKE ONE GOOD MAN.
OR ONE UTTER MONSTER.
AS USUAL, KARKAS, BOREDOM PROMPTS YOU TO NAVEL-GAZING.
BUT I THINK THAT BOREDOM NOW ENDS...

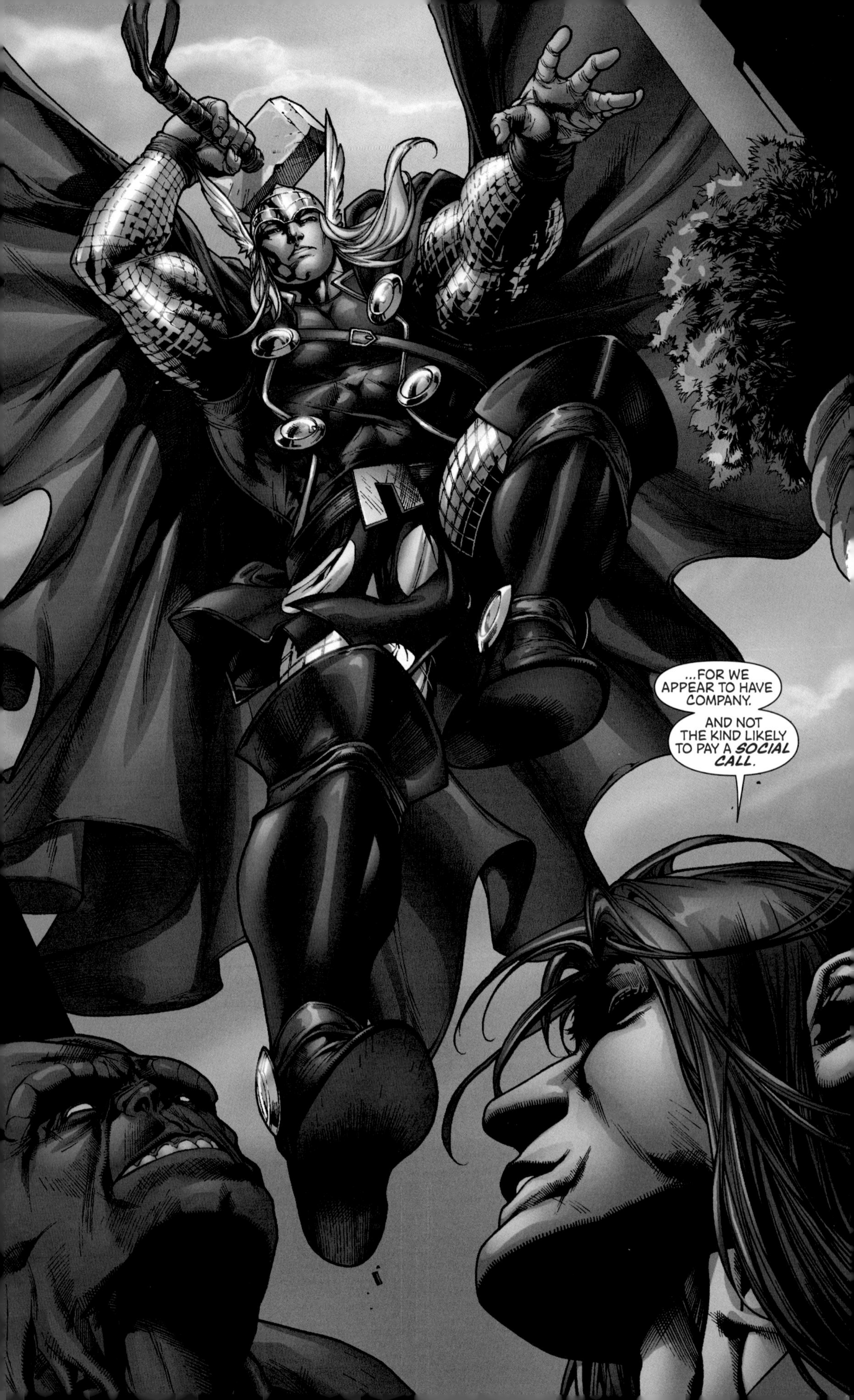
...FOR WE APPEAR TO HAVE COMPANY.
AND NOT THE KIND LIKELY TO PAY A *SOCIAL CALL*.

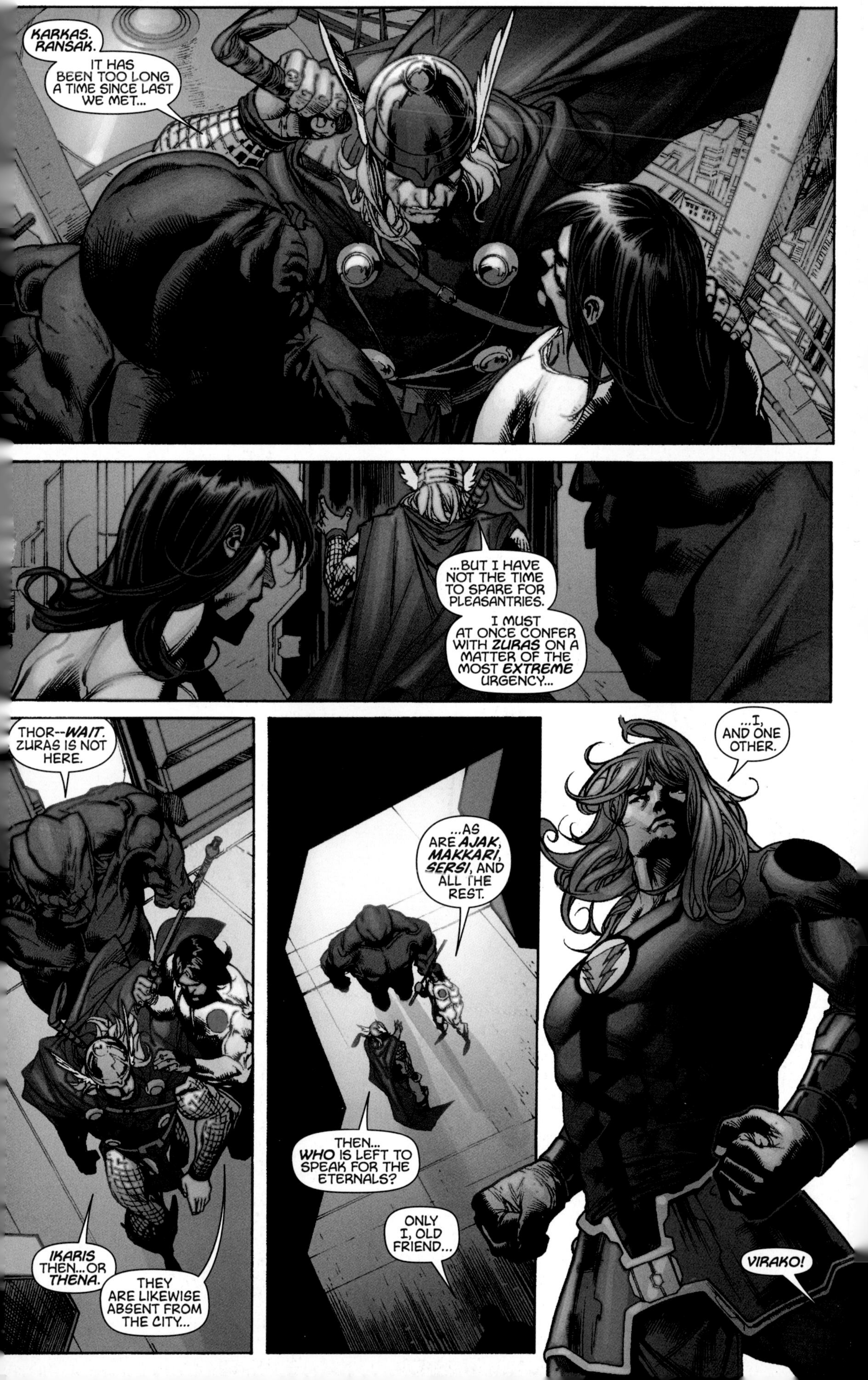
KARKAS. RANSAK.
IT HAS BEEN TOO LONG A TIME SINCE LAST WE MET...
...BUT I HAVE NOT THE TIME TO SPARE FOR PLEASANTRIES.
I MUST AT ONCE CONFER WITH ZURAS ON A MATTER OF THE MOST EXTREME URGENCY...
THOR--WAIT. ZURAS IS NOT HERE.
IKARIS THEN...OR THENA.
THEY ARE LIKEWISE ABSENT FROM THE CITY...
...AS ARE AJAK, MAKKARI, SERSI, AND ALL THE REST.
THEN... WHO IS LEFT TO SPEAK FOR THE ETERNALS?
ONLY I, OLD FRIEND...
...I, AND ONE OTHER.
VIRAKO!

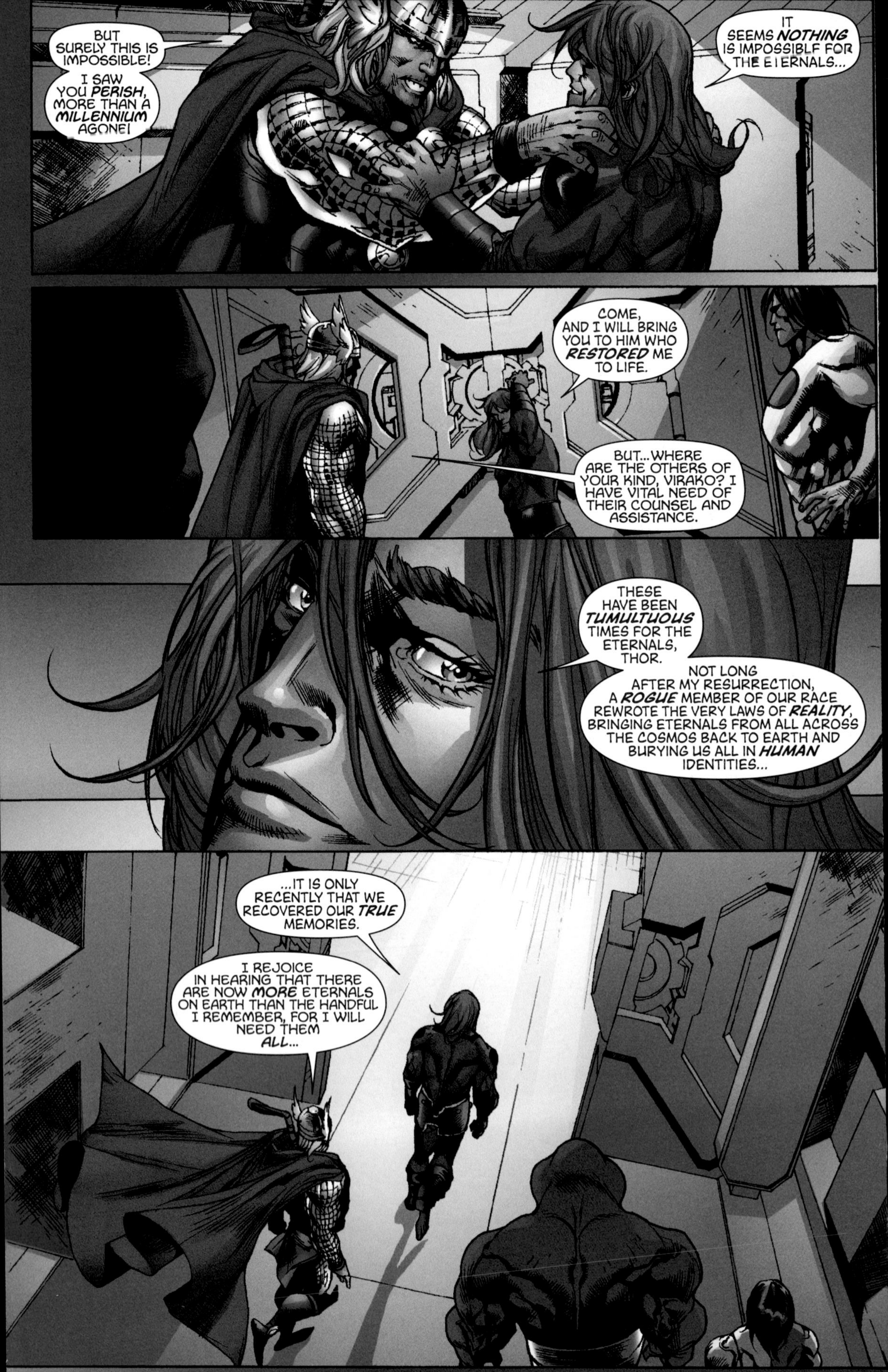
BUT SURELY THIS IS IMPOSSIBLE!
I SAW YOU PERISH, MORE THAN A MILLENNIUM AGONE!
IT SEEMS NOTHING IS IMPOSSIBLE FOR THE ETERNALS...
COME, AND I WILL BRING YOU TO HIM WHO RESTORED ME TO LIFE.
BUT...WHERE ARE THE OTHERS OF YOUR KIND, VIRAKO? I HAVE VITAL NEED OF THEIR COUNSEL AND ASSISTANCE.
THESE HAVE BEEN TUMULTUOUS TIMES FOR THE ETERNALS, THOR.
NOT LONG AFTER MY RESURRECTION, A ROGUE MEMBER OF OUR RACE REWROTE THE VERY LAWS OF REALITY, BRINGING ETERNALS FROM ALL ACROSS THE COSMOS BACK TO EARTH AND BURYING US ALL IN HUMAN IDENTITIES...
...IT IS ONLY RECENTLY THAT WE RECOVERED OUR TRUE MEMORIES.
I REJOICE IN HEARING THAT THERE ARE NOW MORE ETERNALS ON EARTH THAN THE HANDFUL I REMEMBER, FOR I WILL NEED THEM ALL...

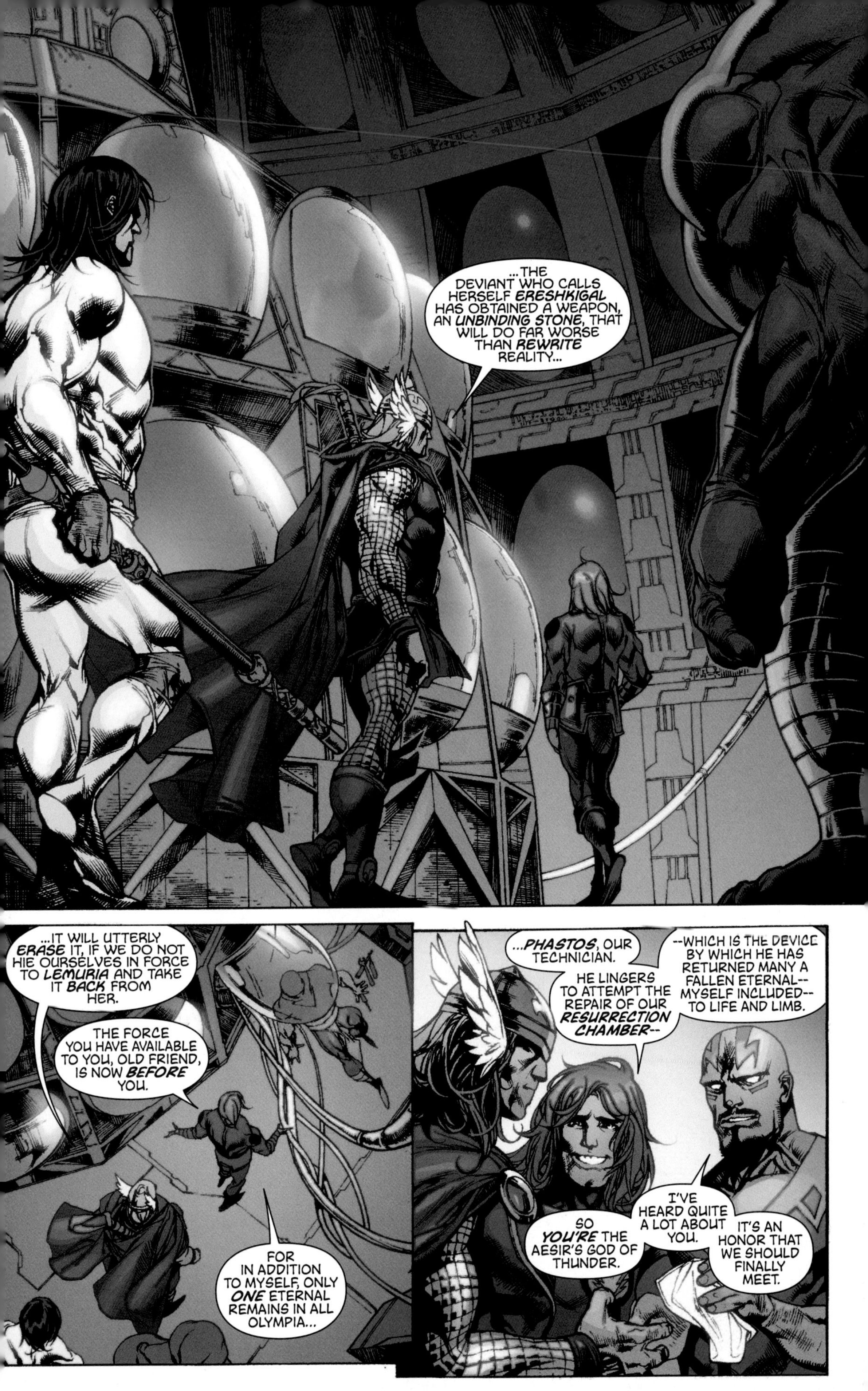
...THE DEVIANT WHO CALLS HERSELF ERESHKIGAL HAS OBTAINED A WEAPON, AN UNBINDING STONE, THAT WILL DO FAR WORSE THAN REWRITE REALITY...
...IT WILL UTTERLY ERASE IT, IF WE DO NOT HIE OURSELVES IN FORCE TO LEMURIA AND TAKE IT BACK FROM HER.
THE FORCE YOU HAVE AVAILABLE TO YOU, OLD FRIEND, IS NOW BEFORE YOU.
FOR IN ADDITION TO MYSELF, ONLY ONE ETERNAL REMAINS IN ALL OLYMPIA...
...PHASTOS, OUR TECHNICIAN.
HE LINGERS TO ATTEMPT THE REPAIR OF OUR RESURRECTION CHAMBER--
--WHICH IS THE DEVICE BY WHICH HE HAS RETURNED MANY A FALLEN ETERNAL-- MYSELF INCLUDED-- TO LIFE AND LIMB.
SO YOU'RE THE AESIR'S GOD OF THUNDER.
I'VE HEARD QUITE A LOT ABOUT YOU.
IT'S AN HONOR THAT WE SHOULD FINALLY MEET.

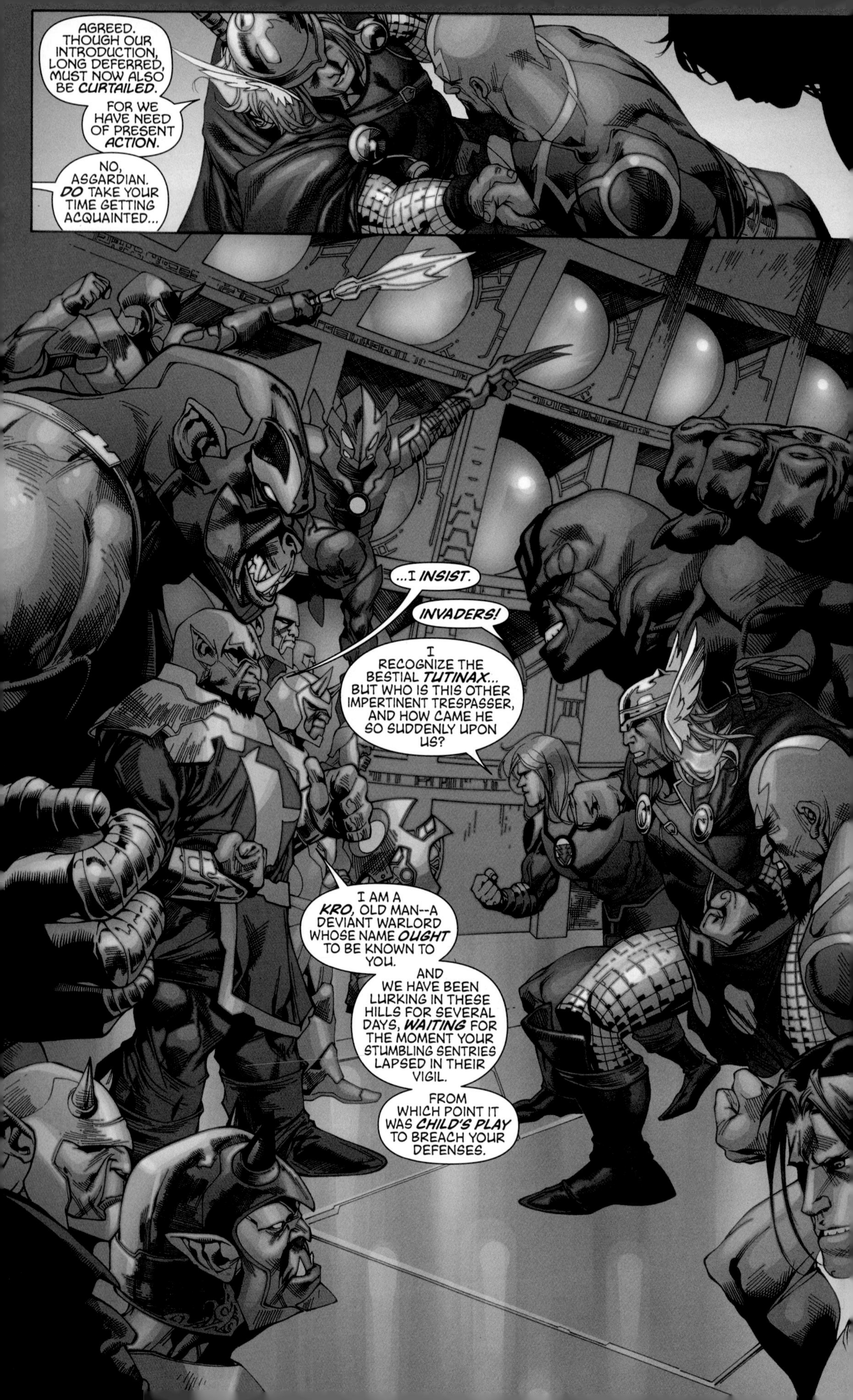
AGREED. THOUGH OUR INTRODUCTION, LONG DEFERRED, MUST NOW ALSO BE CURTAILED.
FOR WE HAVE NEED OF PRESENT ACTION.
NO, ASGARDIAN. DO TAKE YOUR TIME GETTING ACQUAINTED...
...I INSIST.
INVADERS!
I RECOGNIZE THE BESTIAL TUTINAX... BUT WHO IS THIS OTHER IMPERTINENT TRESPASSER, AND HOW CAME HE SO SUDDENLY UPON US?
I AM A KRO, OLD MAN--A DEVIANT WARLORD WHOSE NAME OUGHT TO BE KNOWN TO YOU.
AND WE HAVE BEEN LURKING IN THESE HILLS FOR SEVERAL DAYS, WAITING FOR THE MOMENT YOUR STUMBLING SENTRIES LAPSED IN THEIR VIGIL.
FROM WHICH POINT IT WAS CHILD'S PLAY TO BREACH YOUR DEFENSES.

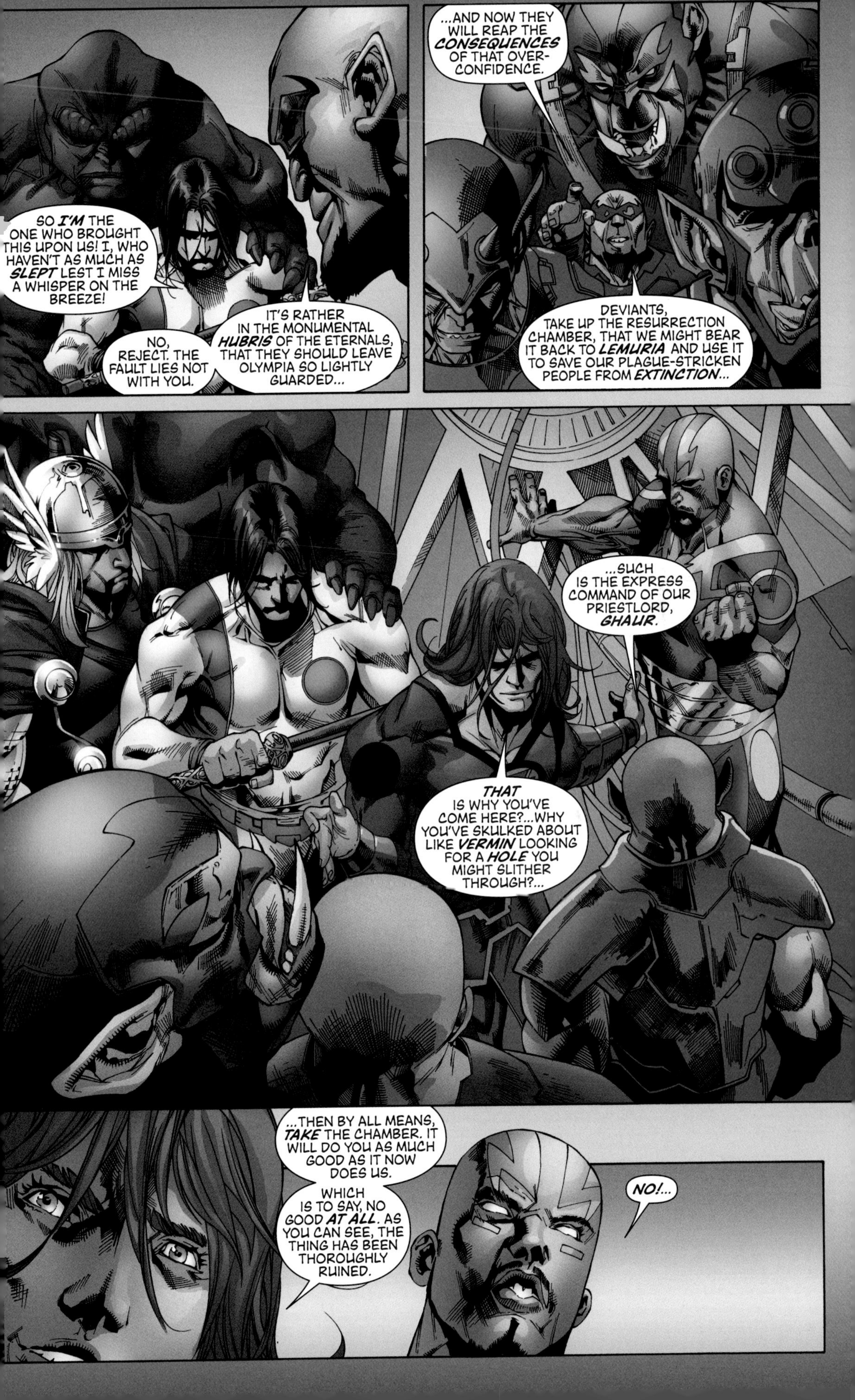
SO I'M THE ONE WHO BROUGHT THIS UPON US! I, WHO HAVEN'T AS MUCH AS SLEPT LEST I MISS A WHISPER ON THE BREEZE!
NO, REJECT. THE FAULT LIES NOT WITH YOU.
IT'S RATHER IN THE MONUMENTAL HUBRIS OF THE ETERNALS, THAT THEY SHOULD LEAVE OLYMPIA SO LIGHTLY GUARDED...
...AND NOW THEY WILL REAP THE CONSEQUENCES OF THAT OVER-CONFIDENCE.
DEVIANTS, TAKE UP THE RESURRECTION CHAMBER, THAT WE MIGHT BEAR IT BACK TO LEMURIA AND USE IT TO SAVE OUR PLAGUE-STRICKEN PEOPLE FROM EXTINCTION...
...SUCH IS THE EXPRESS COMMAND OF OUR PRIESTLORD, GHAUR.
THAT IS WHY YOU'VE COME HERE?...WHY YOU'VE SKULKED ABOUT LIKE VERMIN LOOKING FOR A HOLE YOU MIGHT SLITHER THROUGH?...
...THEN BY ALL MEANS, TAKE THE CHAMBER. IT WILL DO YOU AS MUCH GOOD AS IT NOW DOES US.
WHICH IS TO SAY, NO GOOD AT ALL. AS YOU CAN SEE, THE THING HAS BEEN THOROUGHLY RUINED.
NO!...

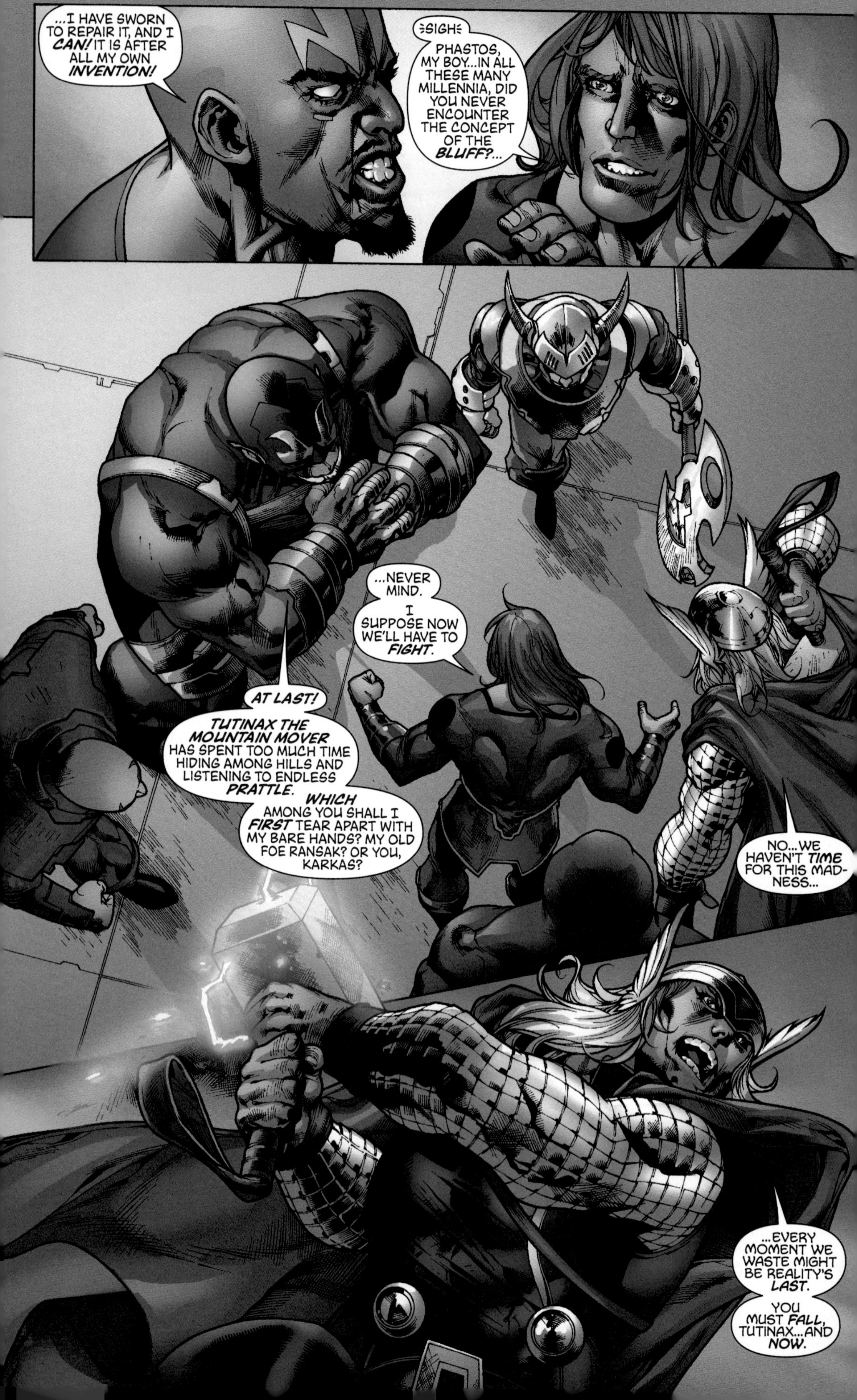
...I HAVE SWORN TO REPAIR IT, AND I CAN! IT IS AFTER ALL MY OWN INVENTION!
SIGH
PHASTOS, MY BOY...IN ALL THESE MANY MILLENNIA, DID YOU NEVER ENCOUNTER THE CONCEPT OF THE BLUFF?...
...NEVER MIND.
I SUPPOSE NOW WE'LL HAVE TO FIGHT.
AT LAST!
TUTINAX THE MOUNTAIN MOVER HAS SPENT TOO MUCH TIME HIDING AMONG HILLS AND LISTENING TO ENDLESS PRATTLE.
WHICH AMONG YOU SHALL I FIRST TEAR APART WITH MY BARE HANDS? MY OLD FOE RANSAK? OR YOU, KARKAS?
NO...WE HAVEN'T TIME FOR THIS MADNESS...
...EVERY MOMENT WE WASTE MIGHT BE REALITY'S LAST.
YOU MUST FALL, TUTINAX...AND NOW.

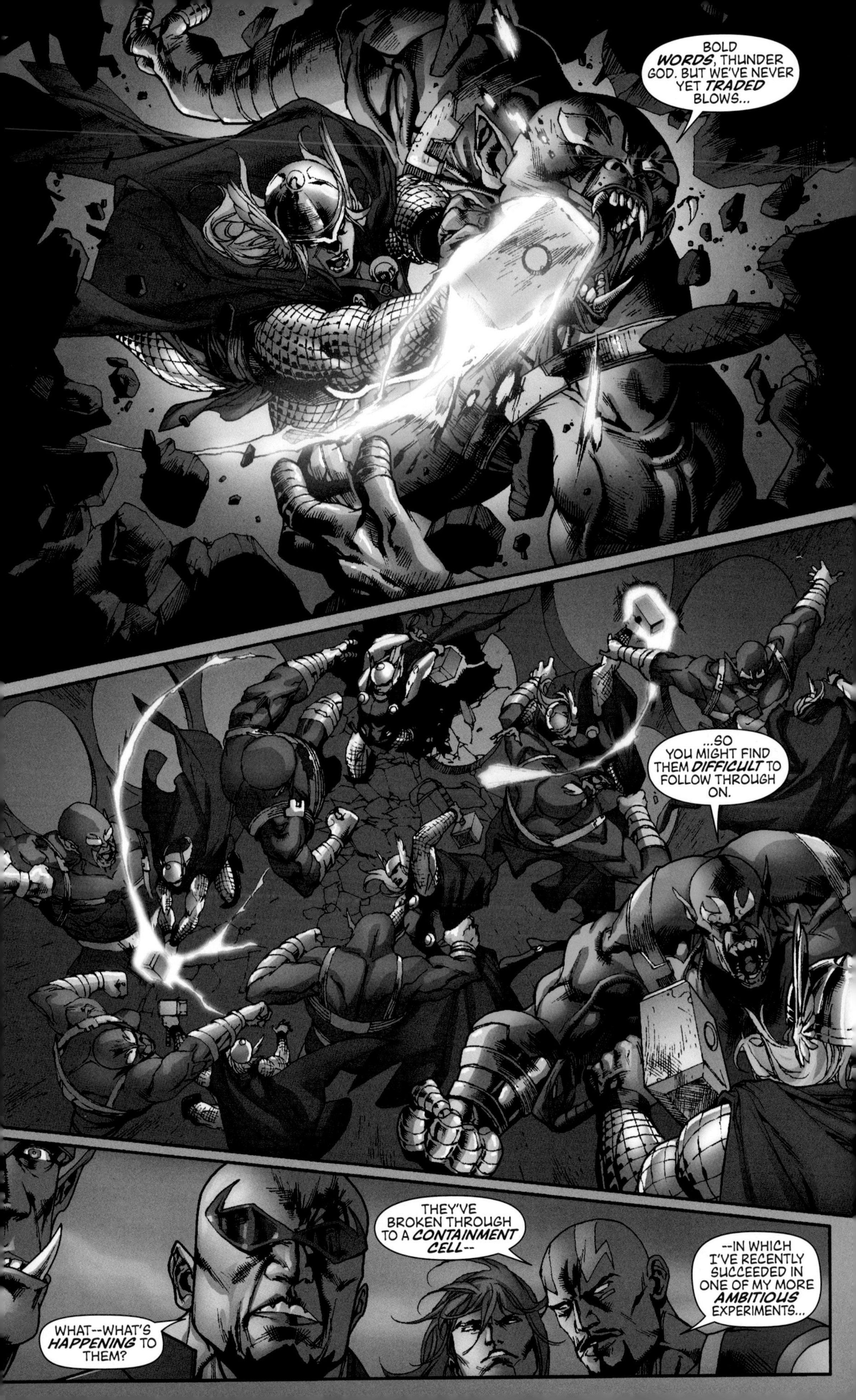
BOLD *WORDS*, THUNDER GOD. BUT WE'VE NEVER YET *TRADED* BLOWS...
...SO YOU MIGHT FIND THEM *DIFFICULT* TO FOLLOW THROUGH ON.
WHAT--WHAT'S *HAPPENING* TO THEM?
THEY'VE BROKEN THROUGH TO A *CONTAINMENT CELL*--
--IN WHICH I'VE RECENTLY SUCCEEDED IN ONE OF MY MORE *AMBITIOUS* EXPERIMENTS...

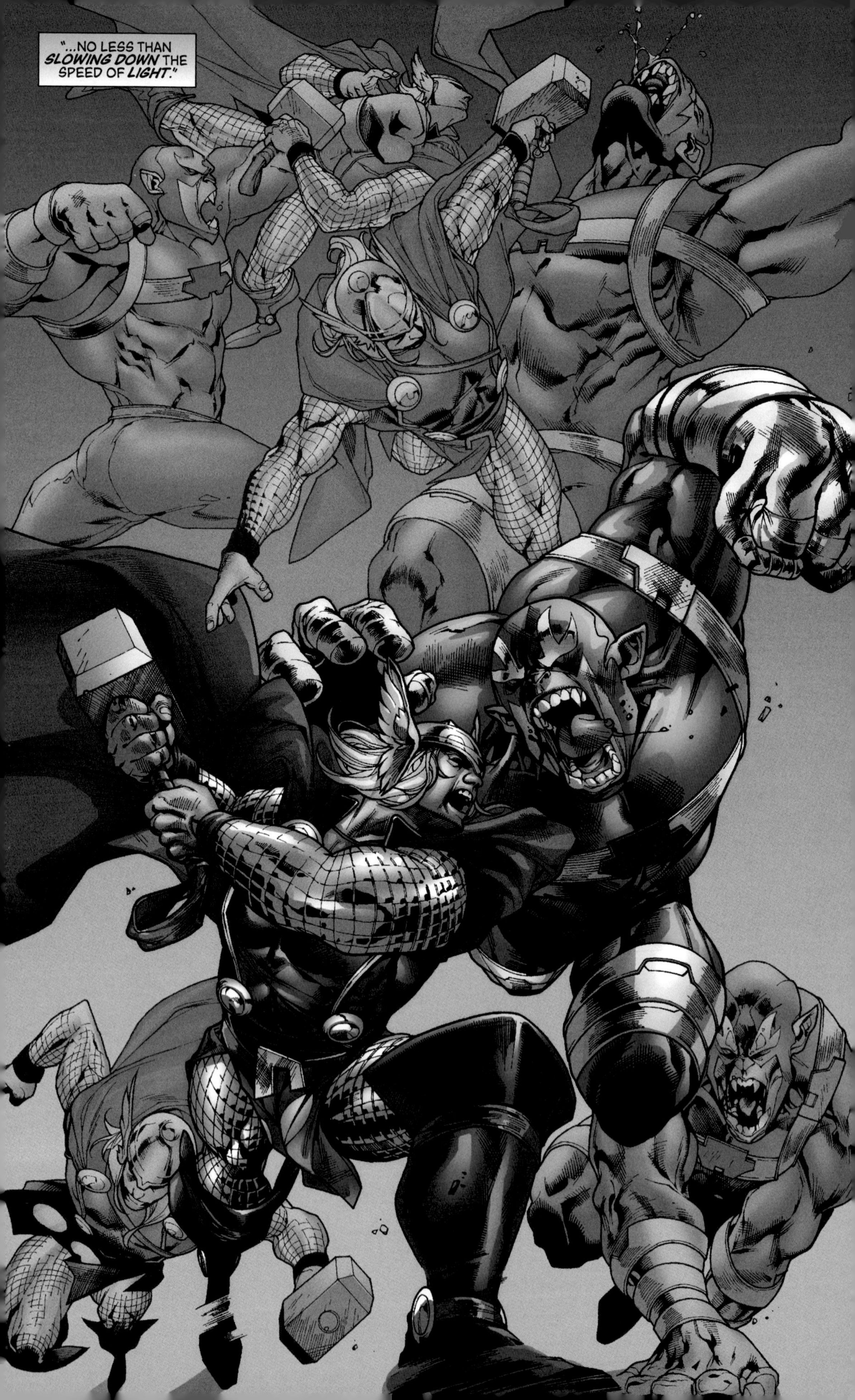
"...NO LESS THAN SLOWING DOWN THE SPEED OF LIGHT."

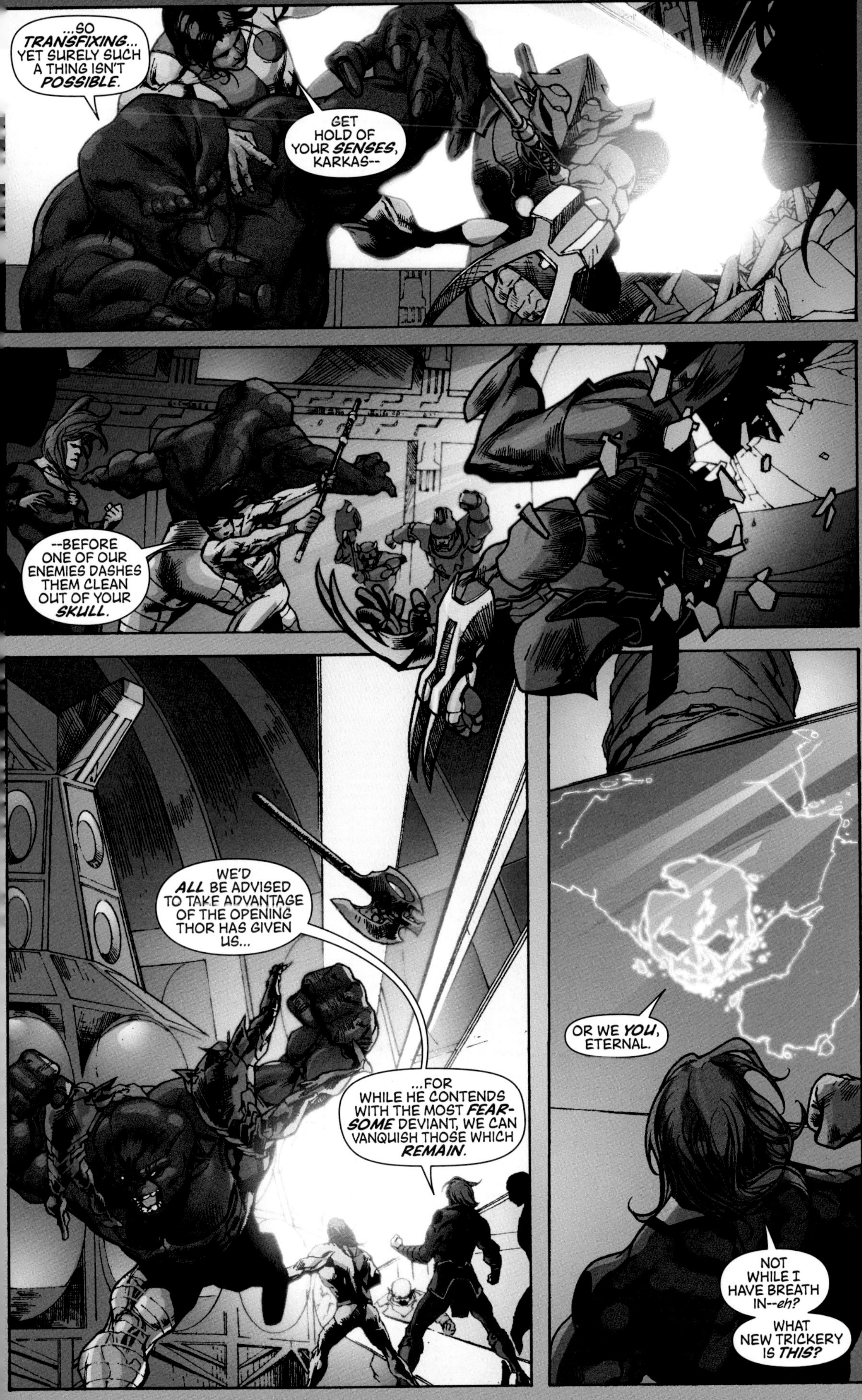
...SO TRANSFIXING... YET SURELY SUCH A THING ISN'T POSSIBLE.
GET HOLD OF YOUR SENSES, KARKAS--
--BEFORE ONE OF OUR ENEMIES DASHES THEM CLEAN OUT OF YOUR SKULL.
WE'D ALL BE ADVISED TO TAKE ADVANTAGE OF THE OPENING THOR HAS GIVEN US...
...FOR WHILE HE CONTENDS WITH THE MOST FEARSOME DEVIANT, WE CAN VANQUISH THOSE WHICH REMAIN.
OR WE YOU, ETERNAL.
NOT WHILE I HAVE BREATH IN--eh?
WHAT NEW TRICKERY IS THIS?

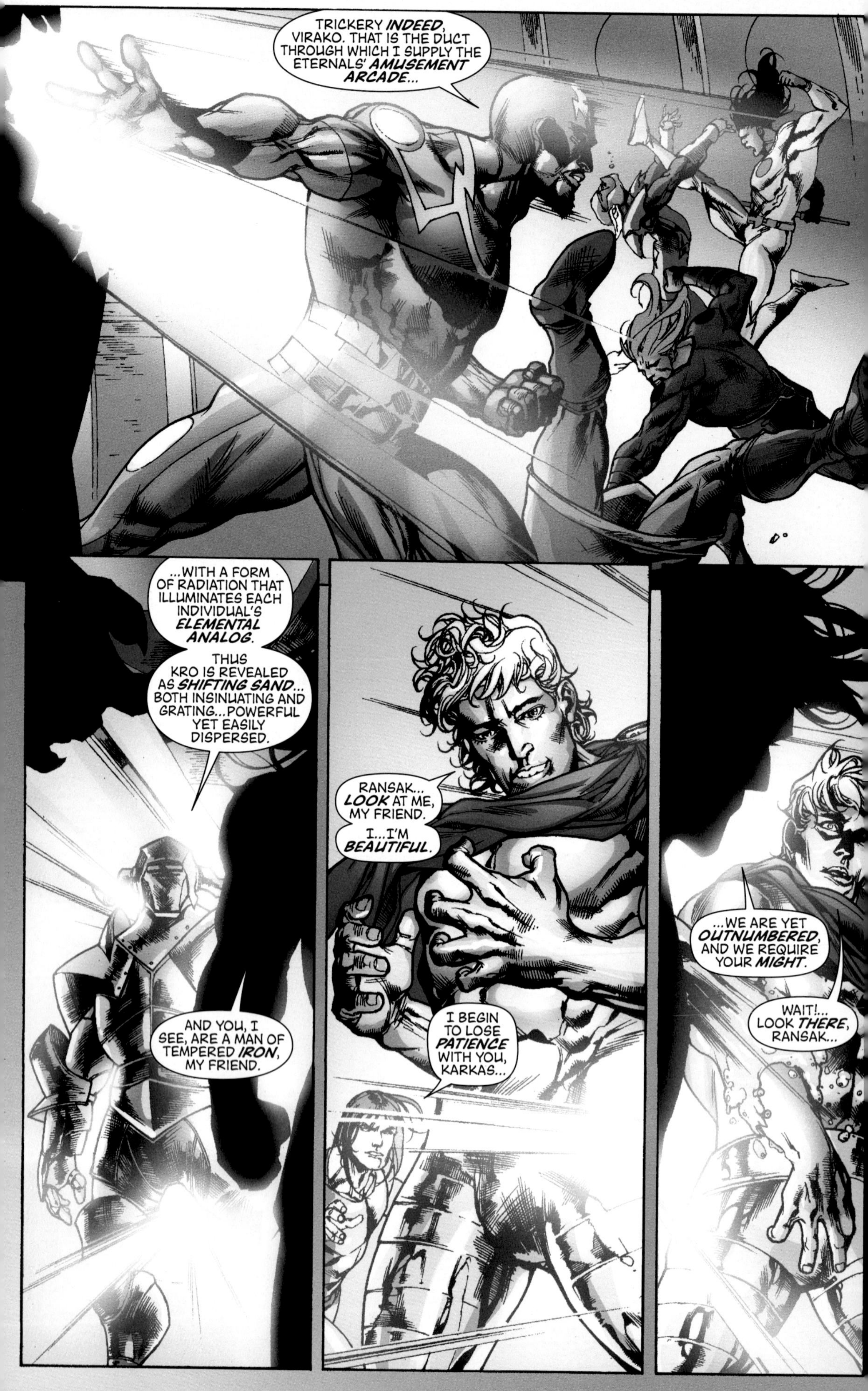

TRICKERY *INDEED*, VIRAKO. THAT IS THE DUCT THROUGH WHICH I SUPPLY THE ETERNALS' *AMUSEMENT ARCADE*...
...WITH A FORM OF RADIATION THAT ILLUMINATES EACH INDIVIDUAL'S *ELEMENTAL ANALOG*.
THUS KRO IS REVEALED AS *SHIFTING SAND*... BOTH INSINUATING AND GRATING...POWERFUL YET EASILY DISPERSED.
AND YOU, I SEE, ARE A MAN OF TEMPERED *IRON*, MY FRIEND.
RANSAK... *LOOK* AT ME, MY FRIEND.
I...I'M *BEAUTIFUL*.
I BEGIN TO LOSE *PATIENCE* WITH YOU, KARKAS...
...WE ARE YET *OUTNUMBERED*, AND WE REQUIRE YOUR *MIGHT*.
WAIT!... LOOK *THERE*, RANSAK...

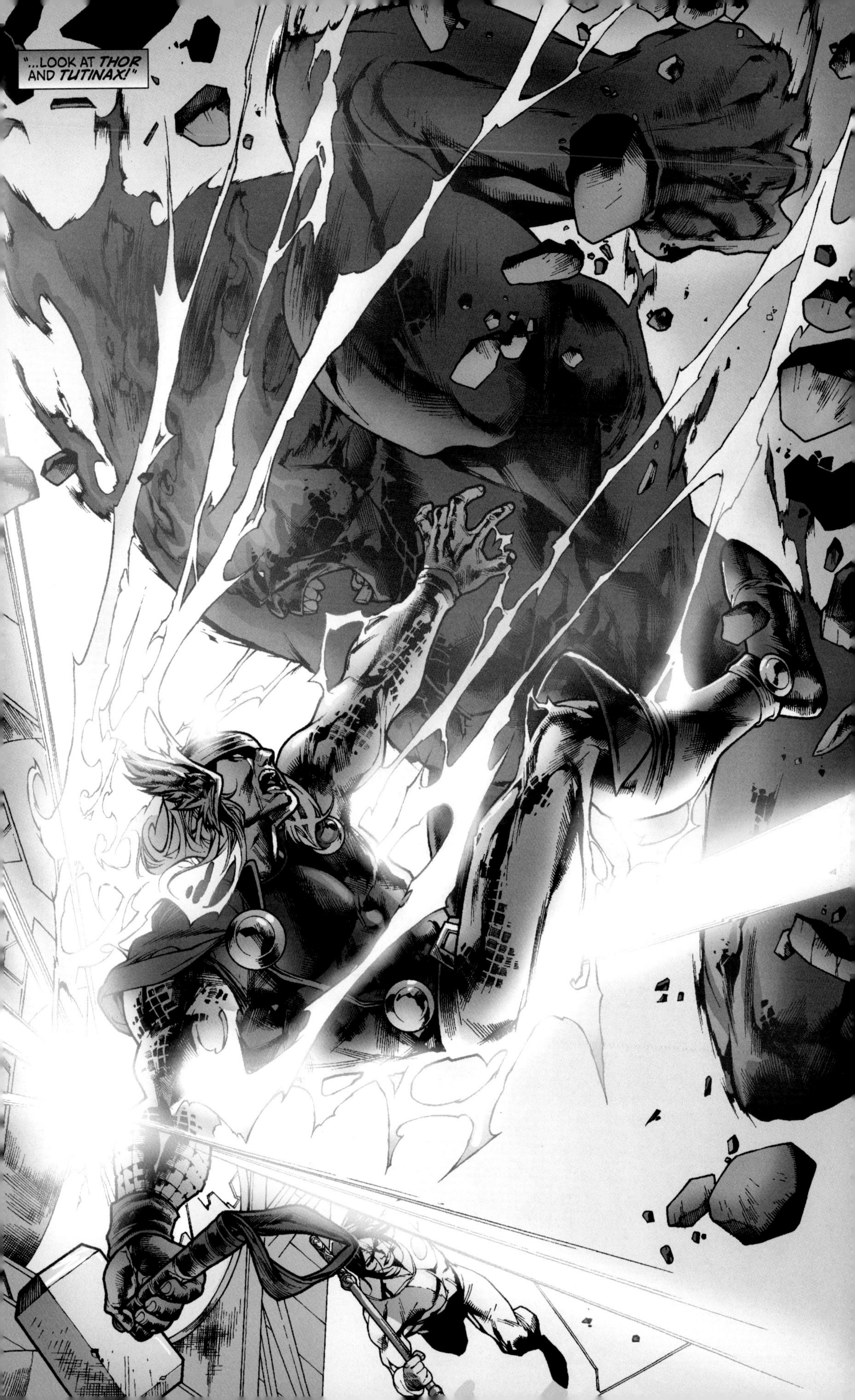
"...LOOK AT THOR AND TUTINAX!"

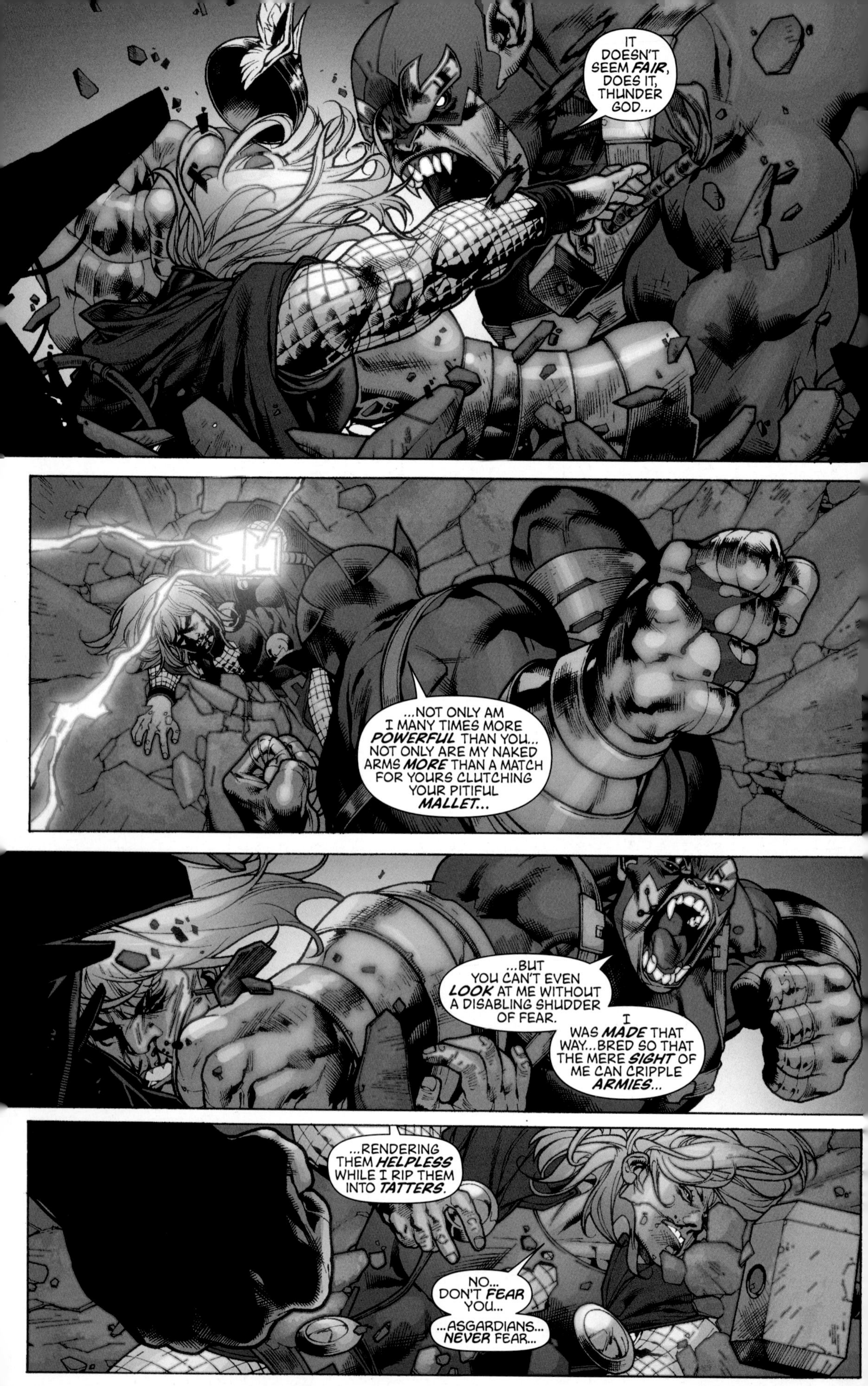
IT DOESN'T SEEM FAIR, DOES IT, THUNDER GOD...
...NOT ONLY AM I MANY TIMES MORE POWERFUL THAN YOU... NOT ONLY ARE MY NAKED ARMS MORE THAN A MATCH FOR YOURS CLUTCHING YOUR PITIFUL MALLET...
...BUT YOU CAN'T EVEN LOOK AT ME WITHOUT A DISABLING SHUDDER OF FEAR.
I WAS MADE THAT WAY...BRED SO THAT THE MERE SIGHT OF ME CAN CRIPPLE ARMIES...
...RENDERING THEM HELPLESS WHILE I RIP THEM INTO TATTERS.
NO... DON'T FEAR YOU...
...ASGARDIANS... NEVER FEAR...

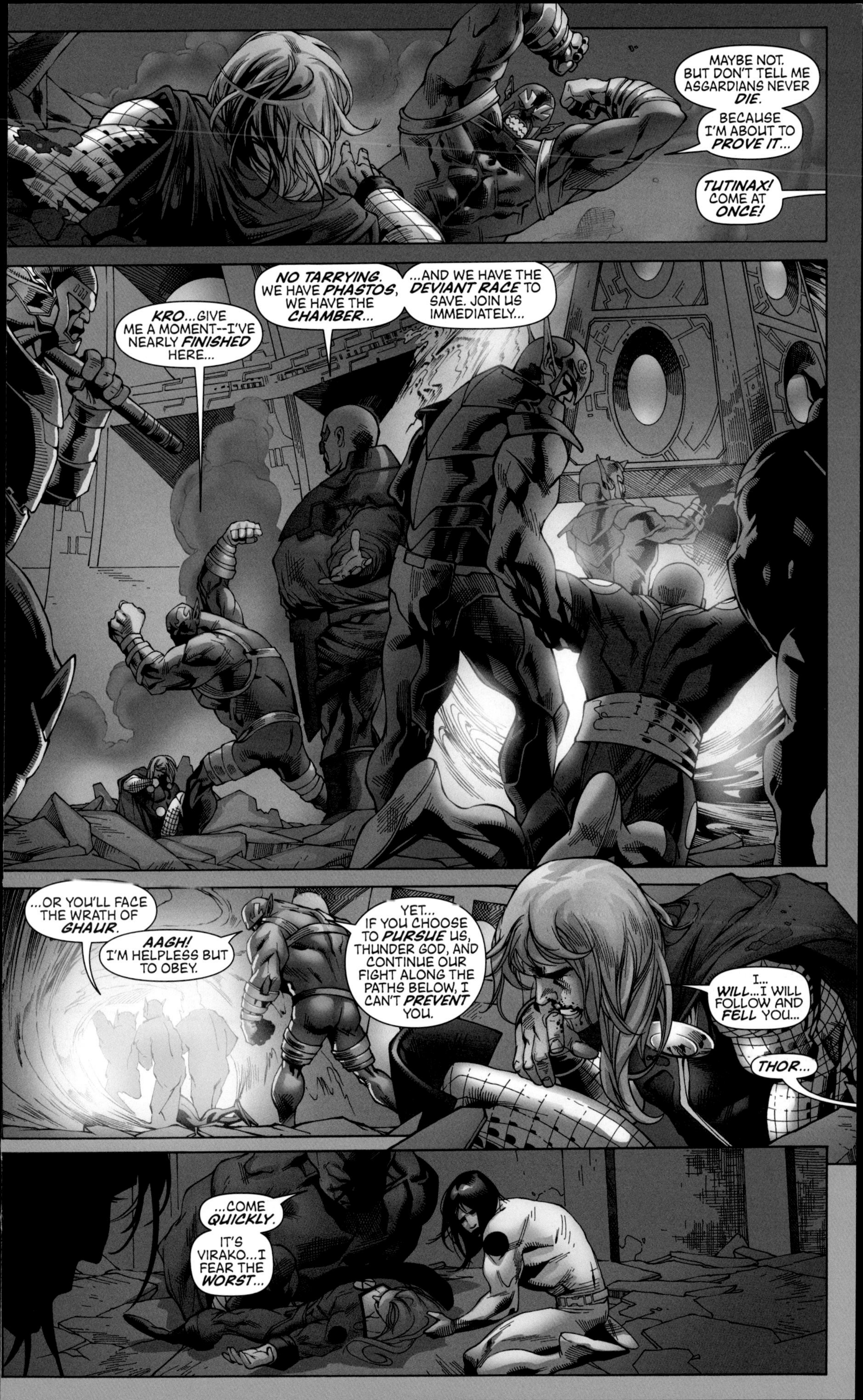

MAYBE NOT. BUT DON'T TELL ME ASGARDIANS NEVER DIE.
BECAUSE I'M ABOUT TO PROVE IT...
TUTINAX! COME AT ONCE!
KRO...GIVE ME A MOMENT--I'VE NEARLY FINISHED HERE...
NO TARRYING. WE HAVE PHASTOS, WE HAVE THE CHAMBER...
...AND WE HAVE THE DEVIANT RACE TO SAVE. JOIN US IMMEDIATELY...
...OR YOU'LL FACE THE WRATH OF GHAUR.
AAGH! I'M HELPLESS BUT TO OBEY.
YET... IF YOU CHOOSE TO PURSUE US, THUNDER GOD, AND CONTINUE OUR FIGHT ALONG THE PATHS BELOW, I CAN'T PREVENT YOU.
I... WILL...I WILL FOLLOW AND FELL YOU...
THOR...
...COME QUICKLY.
IT'S VIRAKO...I FEAR THE WORST...

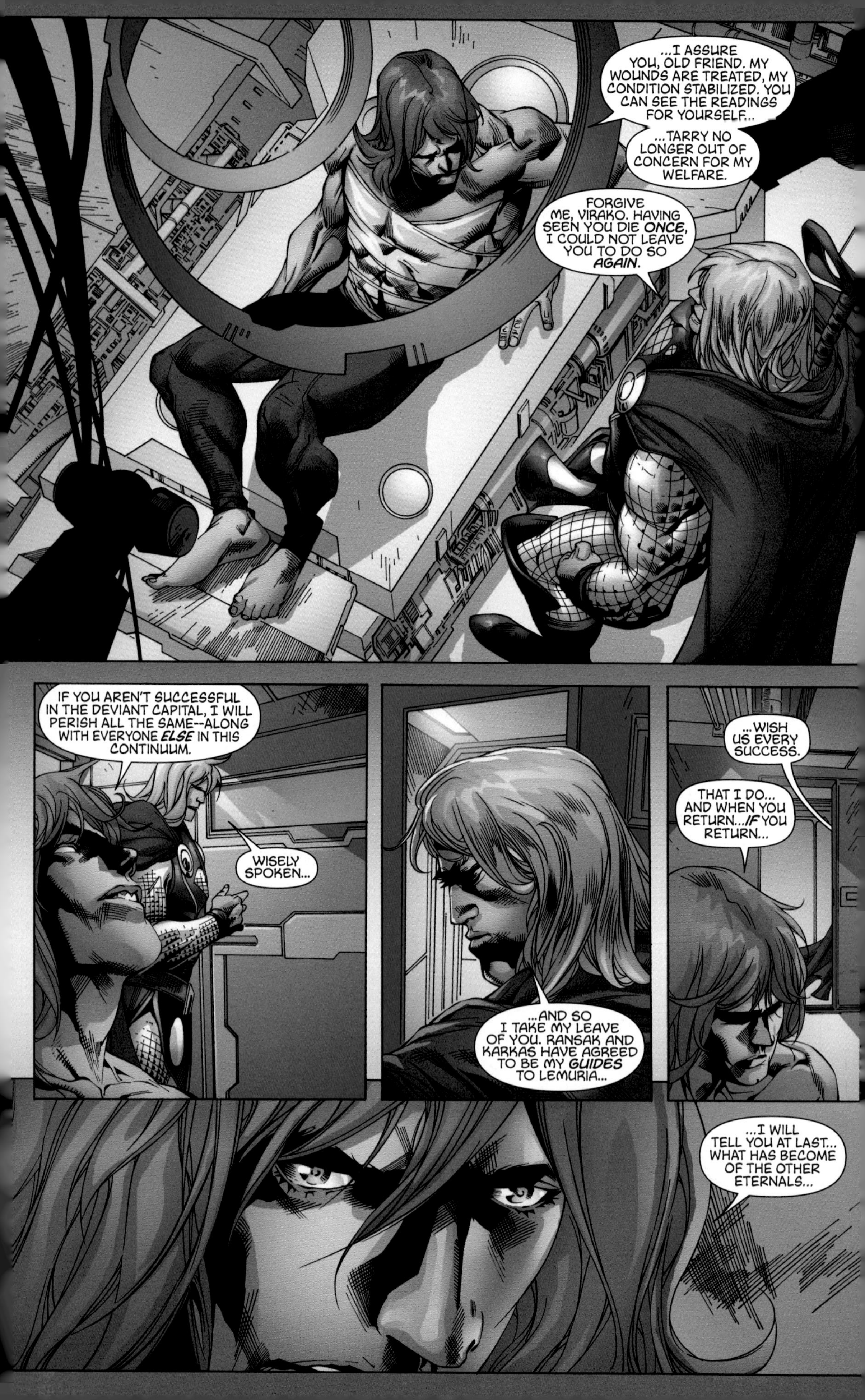
...I ASSURE YOU, OLD FRIEND. MY WOUNDS ARE TREATED, MY CONDITION STABILIZED. YOU CAN SEE THE READINGS FOR YOURSELF...
...TARRY NO LONGER OUT OF CONCERN FOR MY WELFARE.
FORGIVE ME, VIRAKO. HAVING SEEN YOU DIE ONCE, I COULD NOT LEAVE YOU TO DO SO AGAIN.
IF YOU AREN'T SUCCESSFUL IN THE DEVIANT CAPITAL, I WILL PERISH ALL THE SAME--ALONG WITH EVERYONE ELSE IN THIS CONTINUUM.
WISELY SPOKEN...
...AND SO I TAKE MY LEAVE OF YOU. RANSAK AND KARKAS HAVE AGREED TO BE MY GUIDES TO LEMURIA...
...WISH US EVERY SUCCESS.
THAT I DO... AND WHEN YOU RETURN...IF YOU RETURN...
...I WILL TELL YOU AT LAST... WHAT HAS BECOME OF THE OTHER ETERNALS...

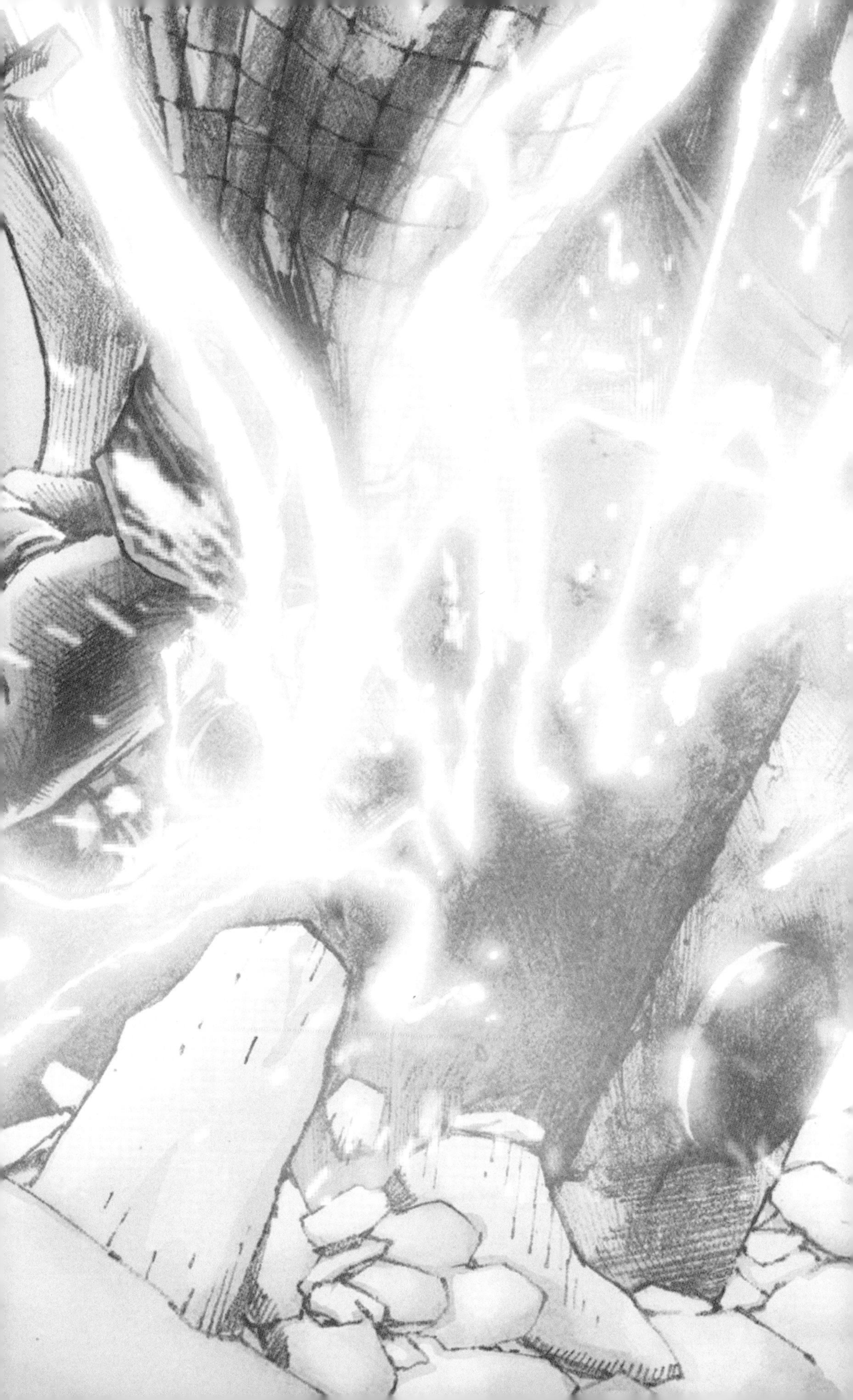

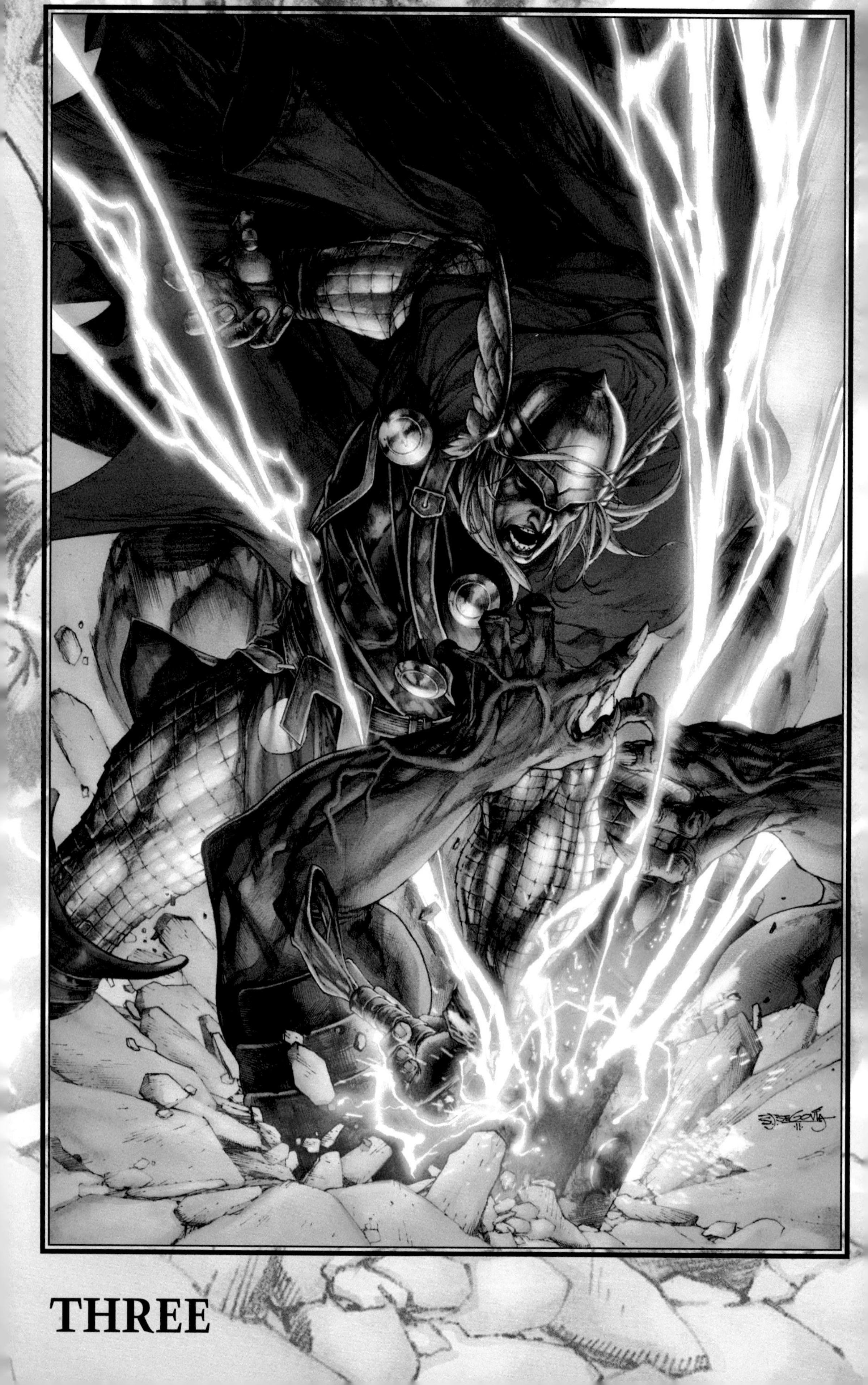

THREE

"MY BIRTH WAS THE CULMINATION OF *CENTURIES* OF EUGENIC CROSS-BREEDING BY THE PRIESTLORDS OF THE DEPTHS-DWELLING *DEVIANT* RACE.

"THEIR GIFT TO ME WAS THAT OF *PSYCHIC MANIPULATION*. I COULD CONTROL THE MIND OF ANY DEVIANT WHOSE GENETIC CODE WAS KNOWN TO ME.

"WHICH I MADE CERTAIN WAS EVERY DEVIANT *ALIVE*... EVEN *ROYALTY*.

"YET THE RULE OF A SINGLE RACE SOON GREW STALE. I SET MY SIGHTS FAR HIGHER...

"...AND FOR A BRIEF MOMENT, ACHIEVED *UNPARALLELED* POWER.

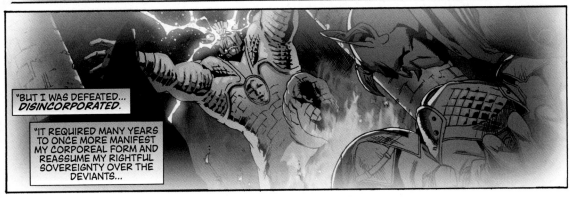

"BUT I WAS DEFEATED... *DISINCORPORATED*.

"IT REQUIRED MANY YEARS TO ONCE MORE MANIFEST MY CORPOREAL FORM AND REASSUME MY RIGHTFUL SOVEREIGNTY OVER THE DEVIANTS...

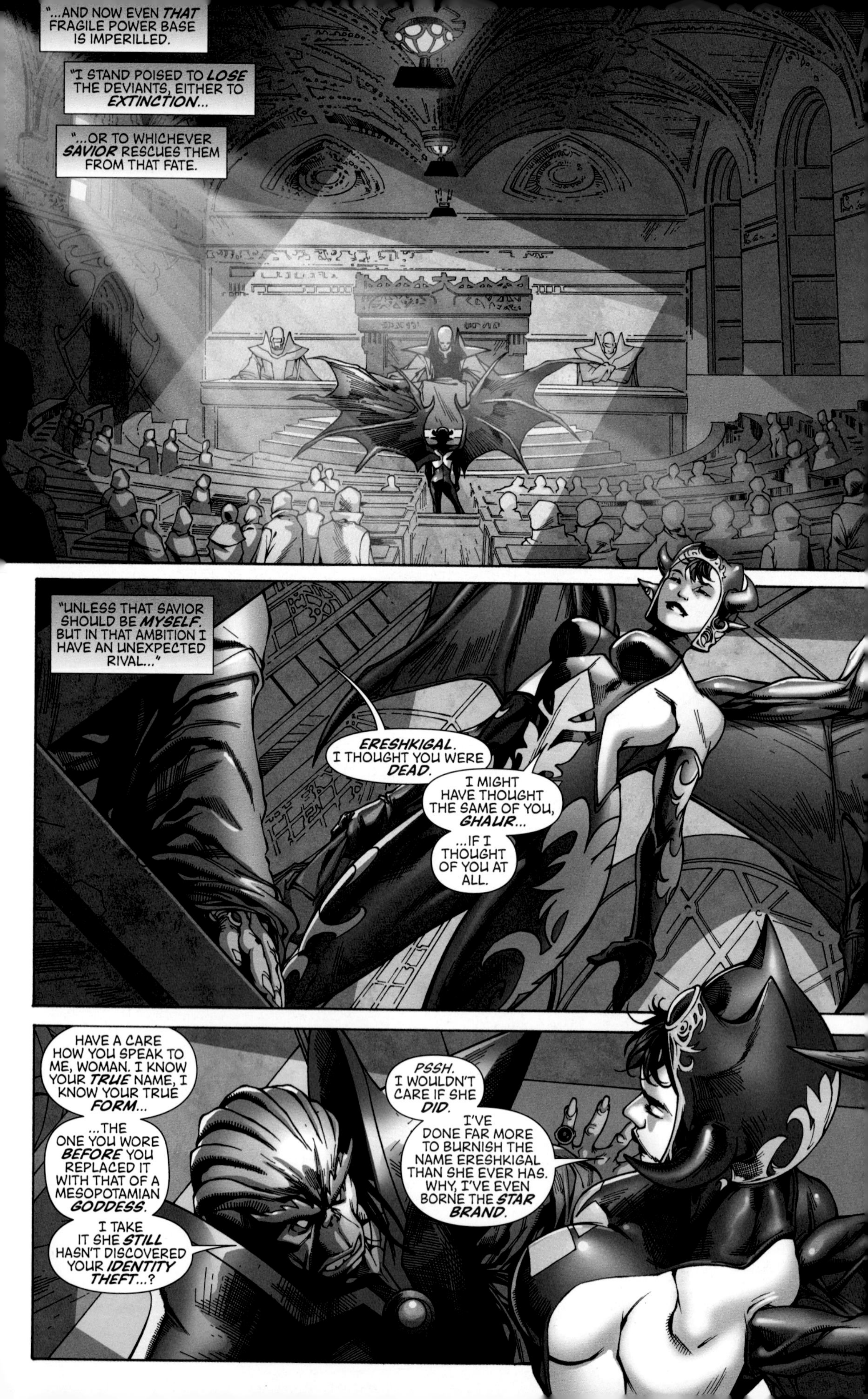
"...AND NOW EVEN THAT FRAGILE POWER BASE IS IMPERILLED.
"I STAND POISED TO LOSE THE DEVIANTS, EITHER TO EXTINCTION...
"...OR TO WHICHEVER SAVIOR RESCUES THEM FROM THAT FATE.
"UNLESS THAT SAVIOR SHOULD BE MYSELF. BUT IN THAT AMBITION I HAVE AN UNEXPECTED RIVAL..."
ERESHKIGAL. I THOUGHT YOU WERE DEAD.
I MIGHT HAVE THOUGHT THE SAME OF YOU, GHAUR...
...IF I THOUGHT OF YOU AT ALL.
HAVE A CARE HOW YOU SPEAK TO ME, WOMAN. I KNOW YOUR TRUE NAME, I KNOW YOUR TRUE FORM...
...THE ONE YOU WORE BEFORE YOU REPLACED IT WITH THAT OF A MESOPOTAMIAN GODDESS.
I TAKE IT SHE STILL HASN'T DISCOVERED YOUR IDENTITY THEFT...?
PSSH. I WOULDN'T CARE IF SHE DID.
I'VE DONE FAR MORE TO BURNISH THE NAME ERESHKIGAL THAN SHE EVER HAS. WHY, I'VE EVEN BORNE THE STAR BRAND.

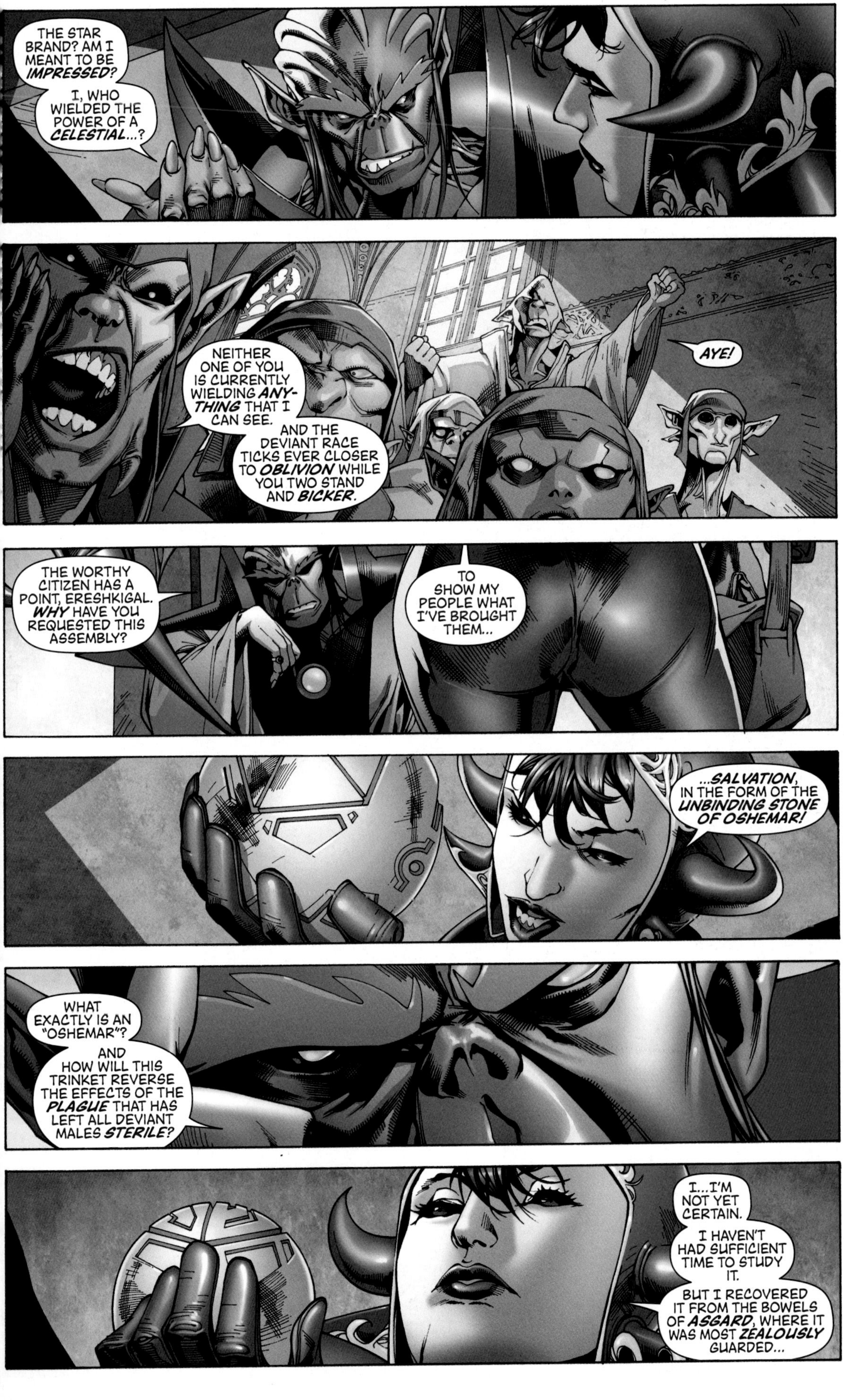
THE STAR BRAND? AM I MEANT TO BE IMPRESSED?
I, WHO WIELDED THE POWER OF A CELESTIAL...?
NEITHER ONE OF YOU IS CURRENTLY WIELDING ANY-THING THAT I CAN SEE.
AND THE DEVIANT RACE TICKS EVER CLOSER TO OBLIVION WHILE YOU TWO STAND AND BICKER.
AYE!
THE WORTHY CITIZEN HAS A POINT, ERESHKIGAL. WHY HAVE YOU REQUESTED THIS ASSEMBLY?
TO SHOW MY PEOPLE WHAT I'VE BROUGHT THEM...
...SALVATION, IN THE FORM OF THE UNBINDING STONE OF OSHEMAR!
WHAT EXACTLY IS AN "OSHEMAR"?
AND HOW WILL THIS TRINKET REVERSE THE EFFECTS OF THE PLAGUE THAT HAS LEFT ALL DEVIANT MALES STERILE?
I...I'M NOT YET CERTAIN.
I HAVEN'T HAD SUFFICIENT TIME TO STUDY IT.
BUT I RECOVERED IT FROM THE BOWELS OF ASGARD, WHERE IT WAS MOST ZEALOUSLY GUARDED...

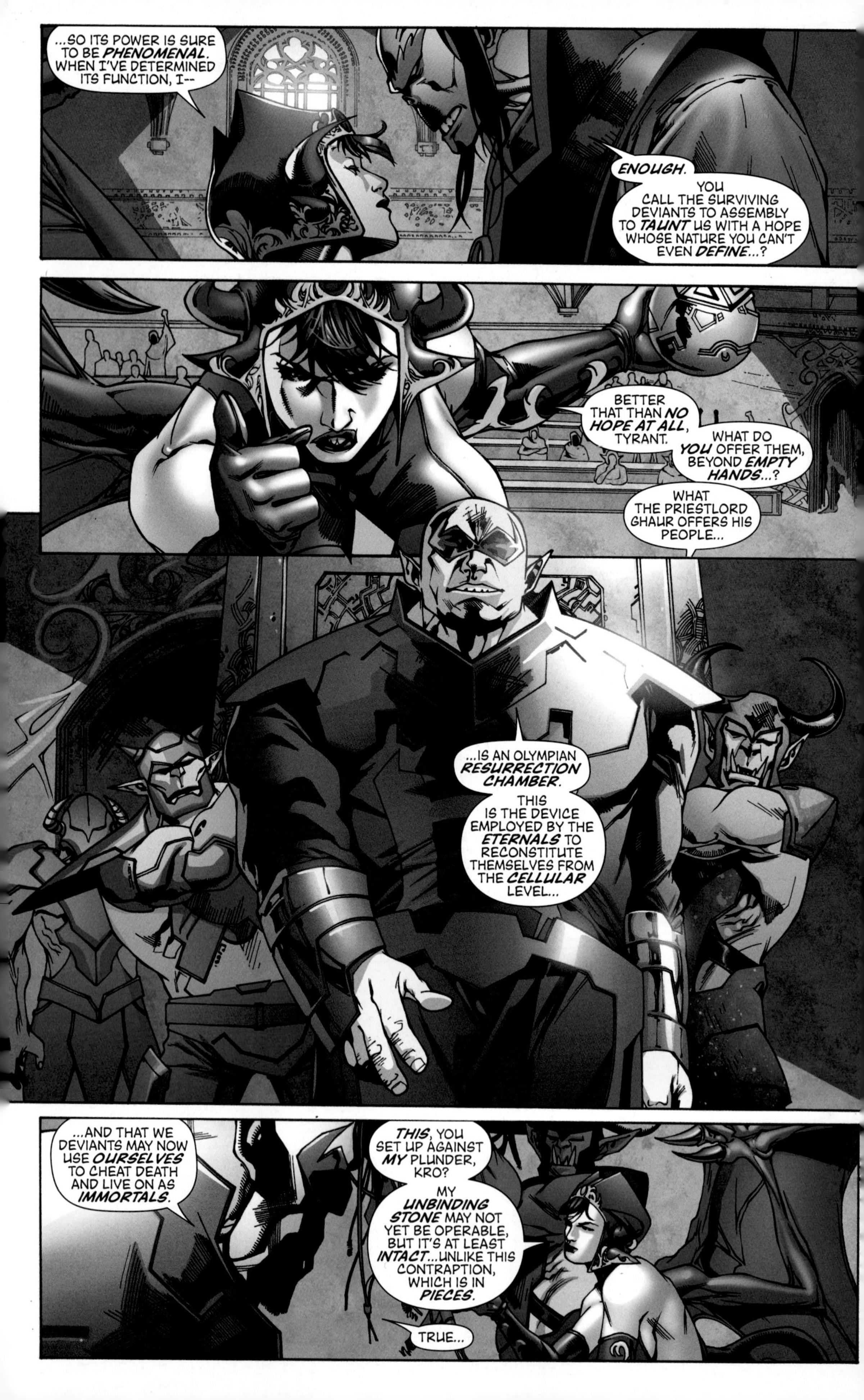
...SO ITS POWER IS SURE TO BE *PHENOMENAL*. WHEN I'VE DETERMINED ITS FUNCTION, I--
ENOUGH.
YOU CALL THE SURVIVING DEVIANTS TO ASSEMBLY TO *TAUNT* US WITH A HOPE WHOSE NATURE YOU CAN'T EVEN *DEFINE*...?
BETTER THAT THAN *NO HOPE AT ALL*, TYRANT.
WHAT DO *YOU* OFFER THEM, BEYOND *EMPTY HANDS*...?
WHAT THE PRIESTLORD GHAUR OFFERS HIS PEOPLE...
...IS AN OLYMPIAN *RESURRECTION CHAMBER*.
THIS IS THE DEVICE EMPLOYED BY THE *ETERNALS* TO RECONSTITUTE THEMSELVES FROM THE *CELLULAR* LEVEL...
...AND THAT WE DEVIANTS MAY NOW USE *OURSELVES* TO CHEAT DEATH AND LIVE ON AS *IMMORTALS*.
THIS, YOU SET UP AGAINST *MY* PLUNDER, KRO?
MY *UNBINDING STONE* MAY NOT YET BE OPERABLE, BUT IT'S AT LEAST *INTACT*...UNLIKE THIS CONTRAPTION, WHICH IS IN *PIECES*.
TRUE...

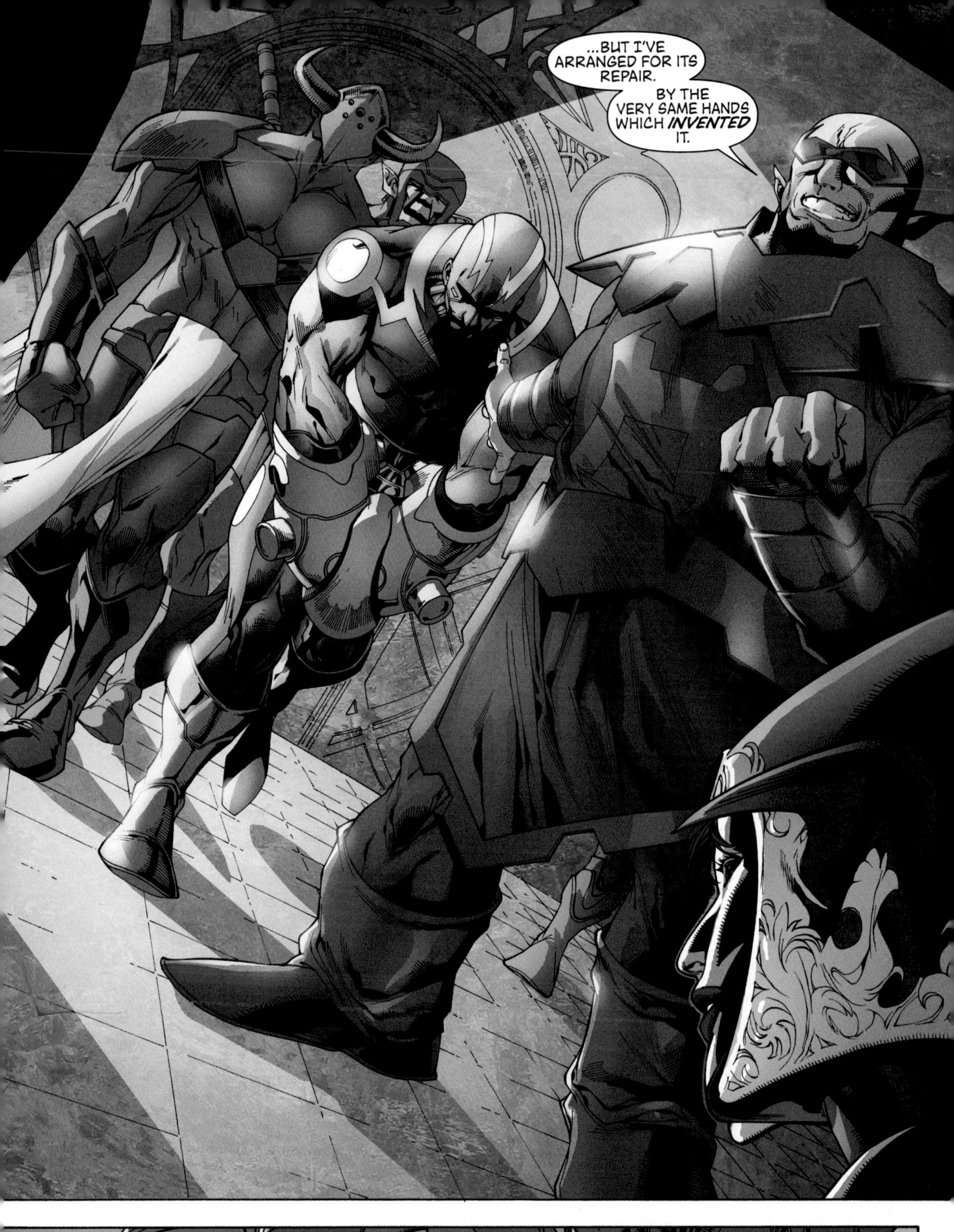
...BUT I'VE ARRANGED FOR ITS REPAIR.
BY THE VERY SAME HANDS WHICH *INVENTED* IT.

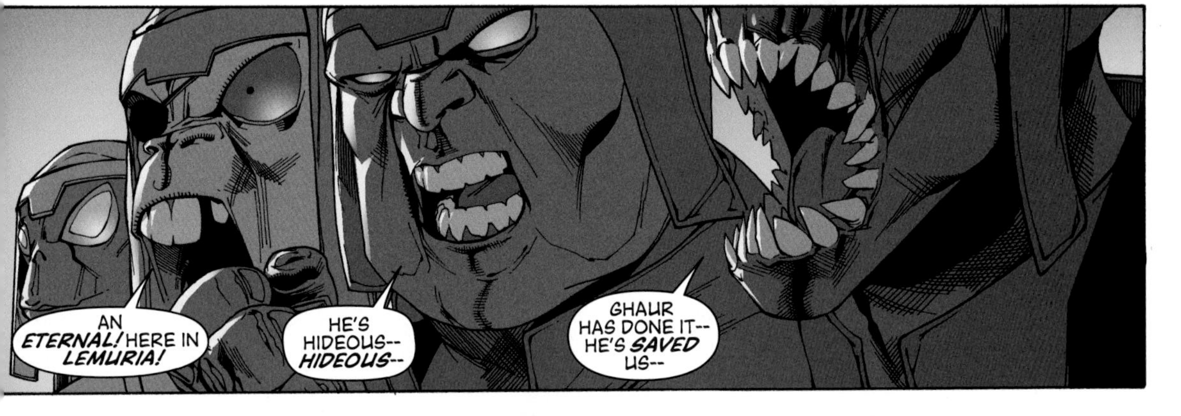
AN *ETERNAL!* HERE IN *LEMURIA!*
HE'S HIDEOUS-- *HIDEOUS*--
GHAUR HAS DONE IT-- HE'S *SAVED* US--

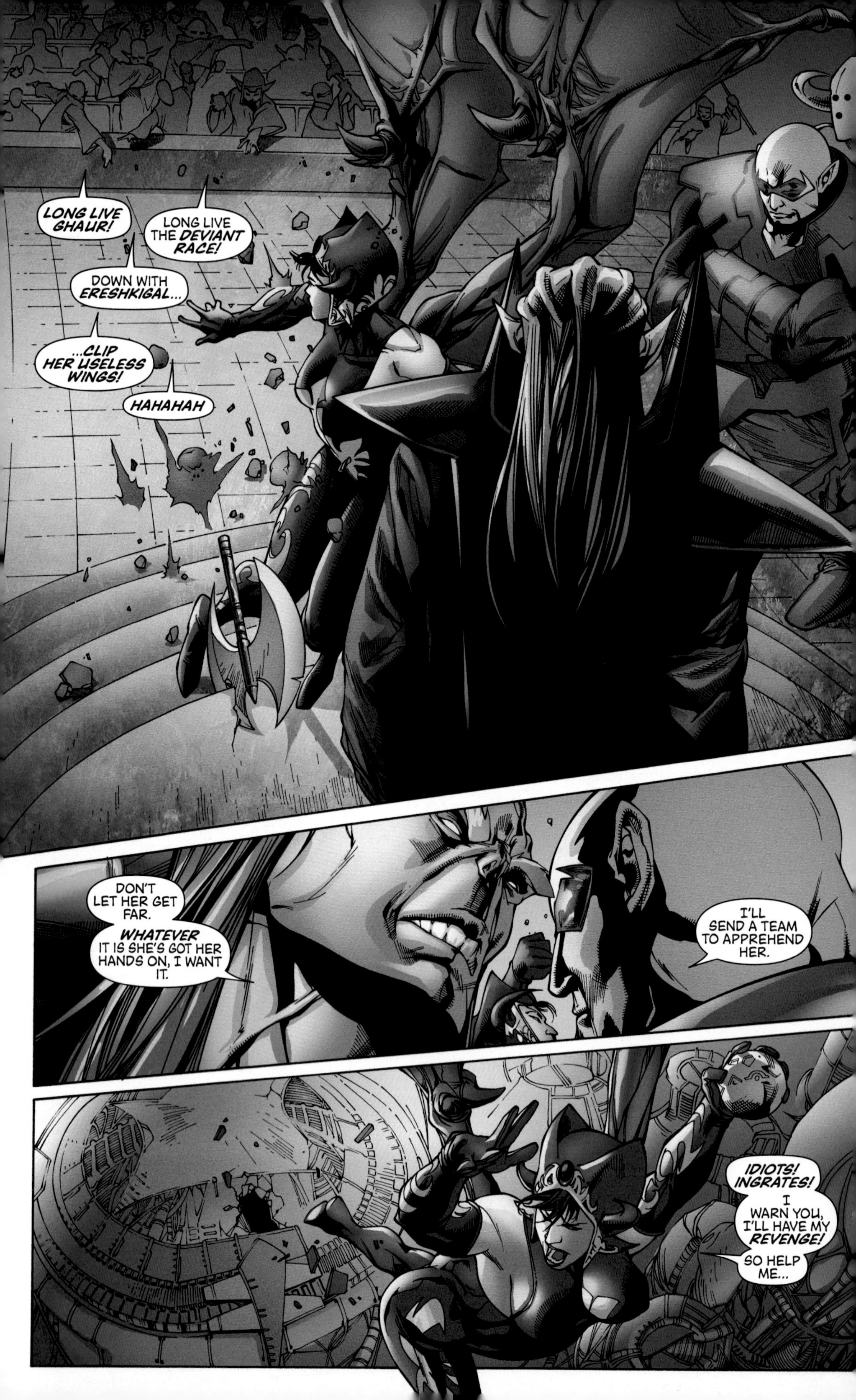
LONG LIVE GHAUR!
LONG LIVE THE DEVIANT RACE!
DOWN WITH ERESHKIGAL...
...CLIP HER USELESS WINGS!
HAHAHAH
DON'T LET HER GET FAR. WHATEVER IT IS SHE'S GOT HER HANDS ON, I WANT IT.
I'LL SEND A TEAM TO APPREHEND HER.
IDIOTS! INGRATES!
I WARN YOU, I'LL HAVE MY REVENGE!
SO HELP ME...

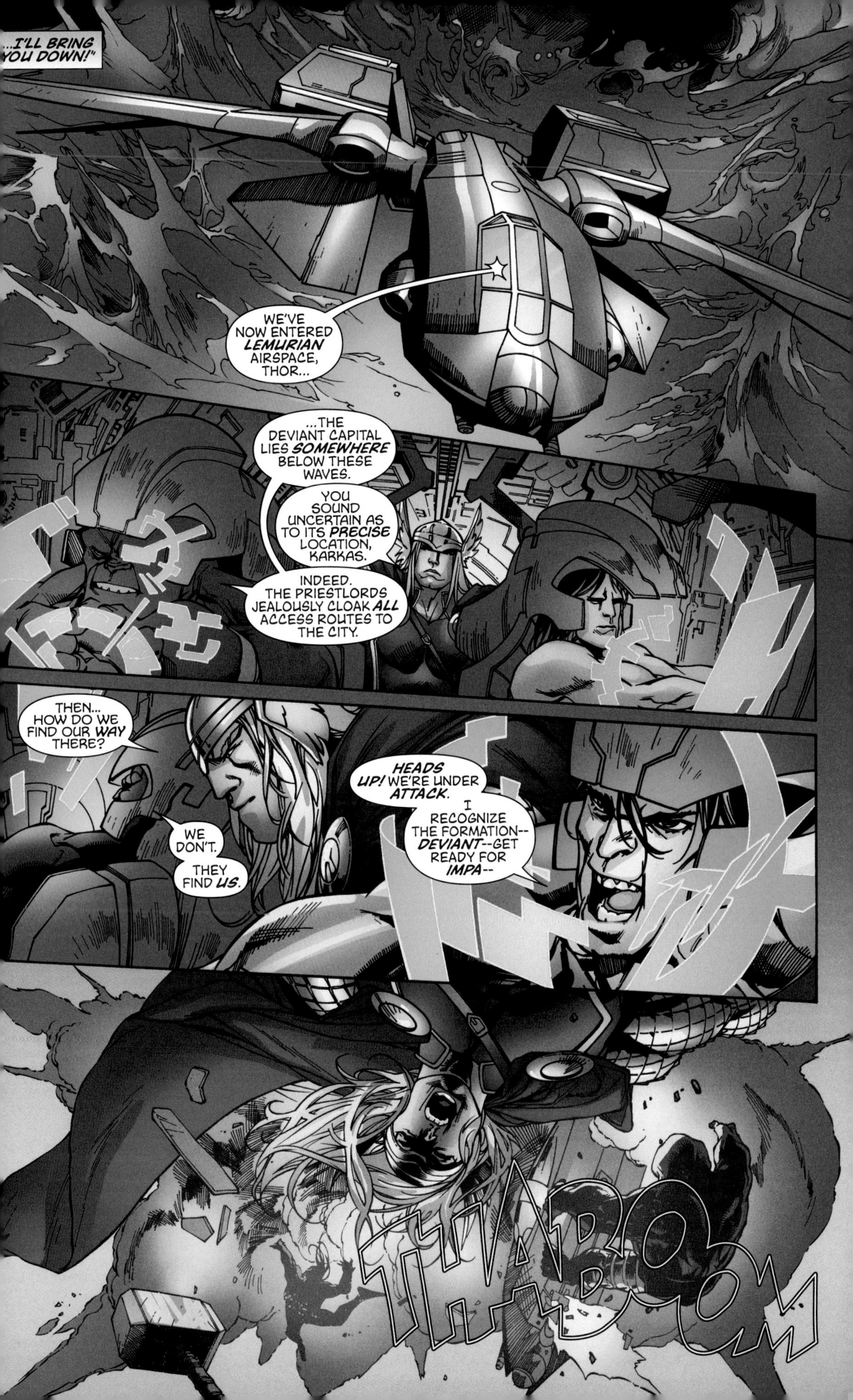

"...I'LL BRING YOU DOWN!"
WE'VE NOW ENTERED LEMURIAN AIRSPACE, THOR...
...THE DEVIANT CAPITAL LIES SOMEWHERE BELOW THESE WAVES.
YOU SOUND UNCERTAIN AS TO ITS PRECISE LOCATION, KARKAS.
INDEED. THE PRIESTLORDS JEALOUSLY CLOAK ALL ACCESS ROUTES TO THE CITY.
THEN... HOW DO WE FIND OUR WAY THERE?
WE DON'T.
THEY FIND US.
HEADS UP! WE'RE UNDER ATTACK.
I RECOGNIZE THE FORMATION--DEVIANT--GET READY FOR IMPA--
THABOOM

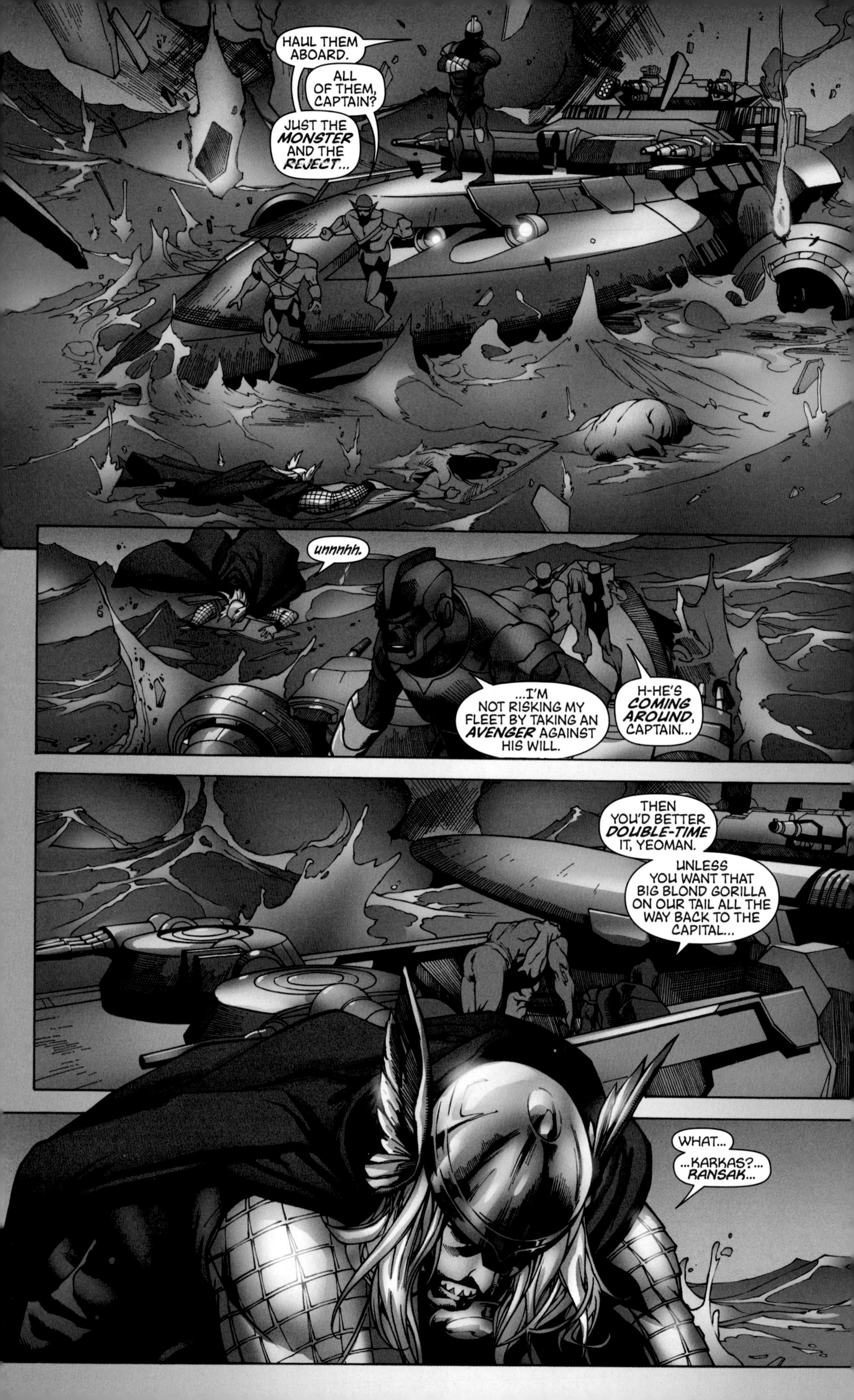
HAUL THEM ABOARD.
ALL OF THEM, CAPTAIN?
JUST THE MONSTER AND THE REJECT...
unnnhh.
...I'M NOT RISKING MY FLEET BY TAKING AN AVENGER AGAINST HIS WILL.
H-HE'S COMING AROUND, CAPTAIN...
THEN YOU'D BETTER DOUBLE-TIME IT, YEOMAN.
UNLESS YOU WANT THAT BIG BLOND GORILLA ON OUR TAIL ALL THE WAY BACK TO THE CAPITAL...
WHAT...
...KARKAS?... RANSAK...

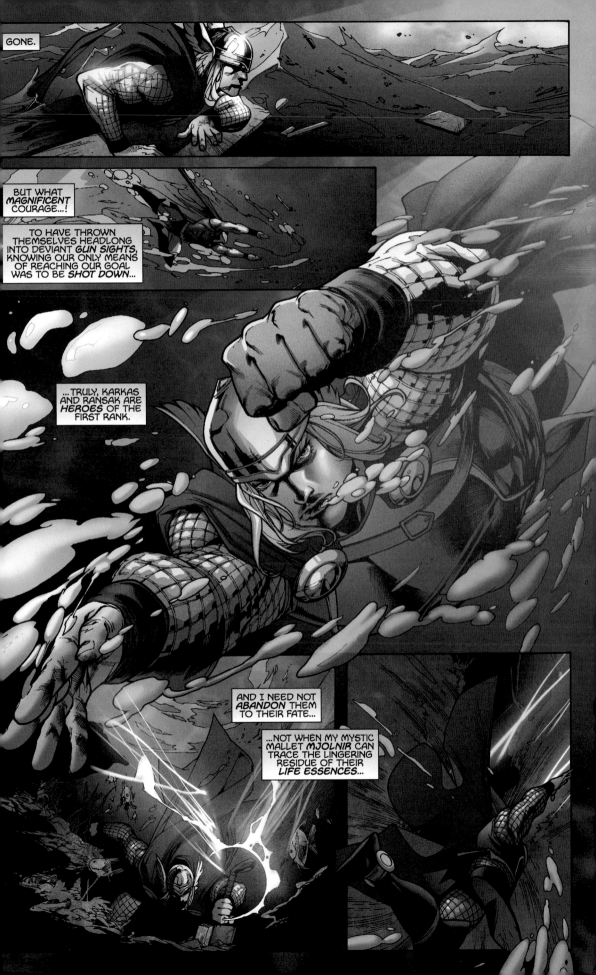

GONE.

BUT WHAT *MAGNIFICENT* COURAGE...!

TO HAVE THROWN THEMSELVES HEADLONG INTO DEVIANT *GUN SIGHTS*, KNOWING OUR ONLY MEANS OF REACHING OUR GOAL WAS TO BE *SHOT DOWN*...

...TRULY, KARKAS AND RANSAK ARE *HEROES* OF THE FIRST RANK.

AND I NEED NOT *ABANDON* THEM TO THEIR FATE...

...NOT WHEN MY MYSTIC MALLET *MJOLNIR* CAN TRACE THE LINGERING RESIDUE OF THEIR *LIFE ESSENCES*...

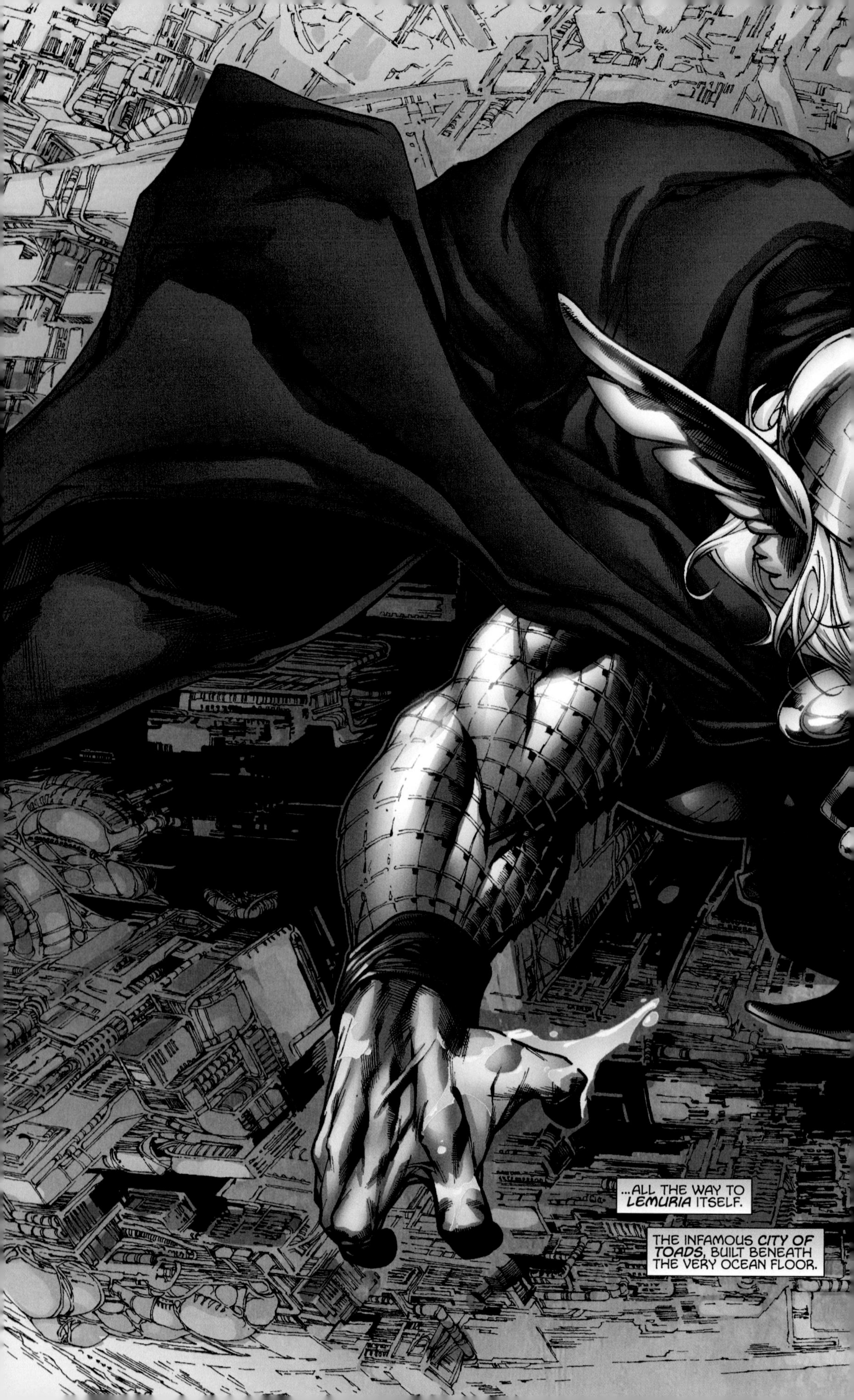
...ALL THE WAY TO LEMURIA ITSELF.
THE INFAMOUS CITY OF TOADS, BUILT BENEATH THE VERY OCEAN FLOOR.

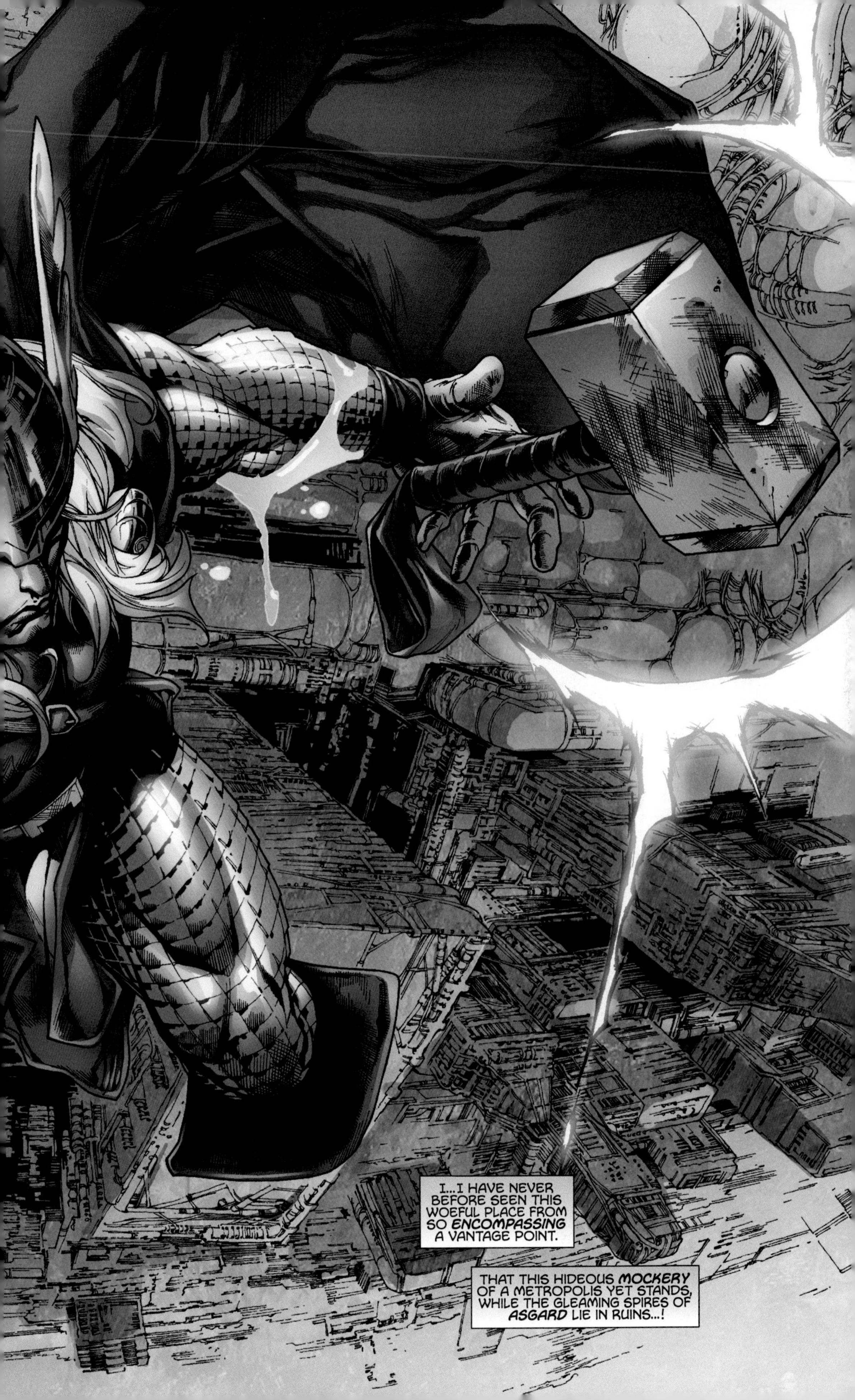
I...I HAVE NEVER BEFORE SEEN THIS WOEFUL PLACE FROM SO *ENCOMPASSING* A VANTAGE POINT.
THAT THIS HIDEOUS *MOCKERY* OF A METROPOLIS YET STANDS, WHILE THE GLEAMING SPIRES OF *ASGARD* LIE IN RUINS...!

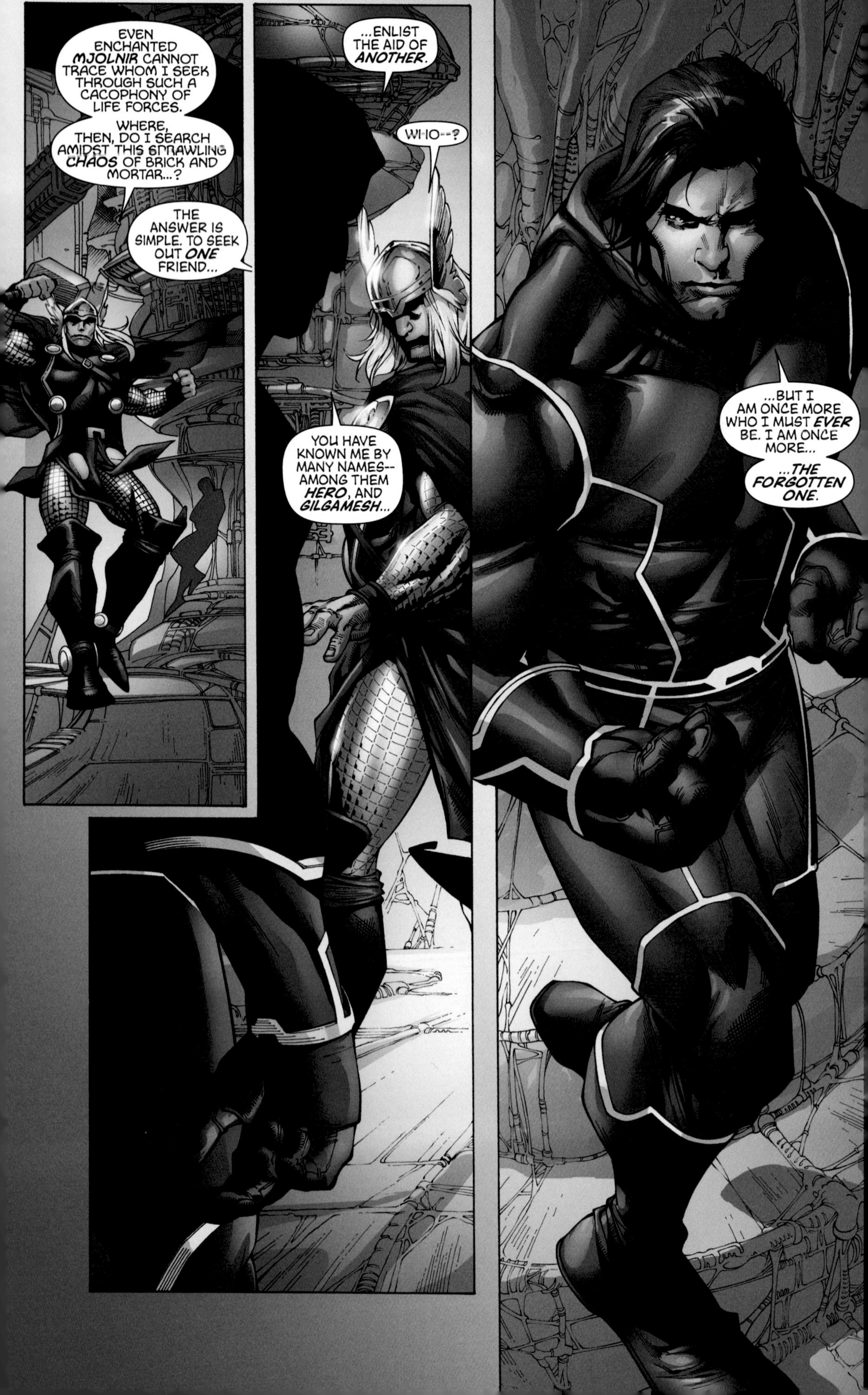
EVEN ENCHANTED MJOLNIR CANNOT TRACE WHOM I SEEK THROUGH SUCH A CACOPHONY OF LIFE FORCES.
WHERE, THEN, DO I SEARCH AMIDST THIS SPRAWLING CHAOS OF BRICK AND MORTAR...?
THE ANSWER IS SIMPLE. TO SEEK OUT ONE FRIEND...
...ENLIST THE AID OF ANOTHER.
WHO--?
YOU HAVE KNOWN ME BY MANY NAMES--AMONG THEM HERO, AND GILGAMESH...
...BUT I AM ONCE MORE WHO I MUST EVER BE. I AM ONCE MORE...
...THE FORGOTTEN ONE.

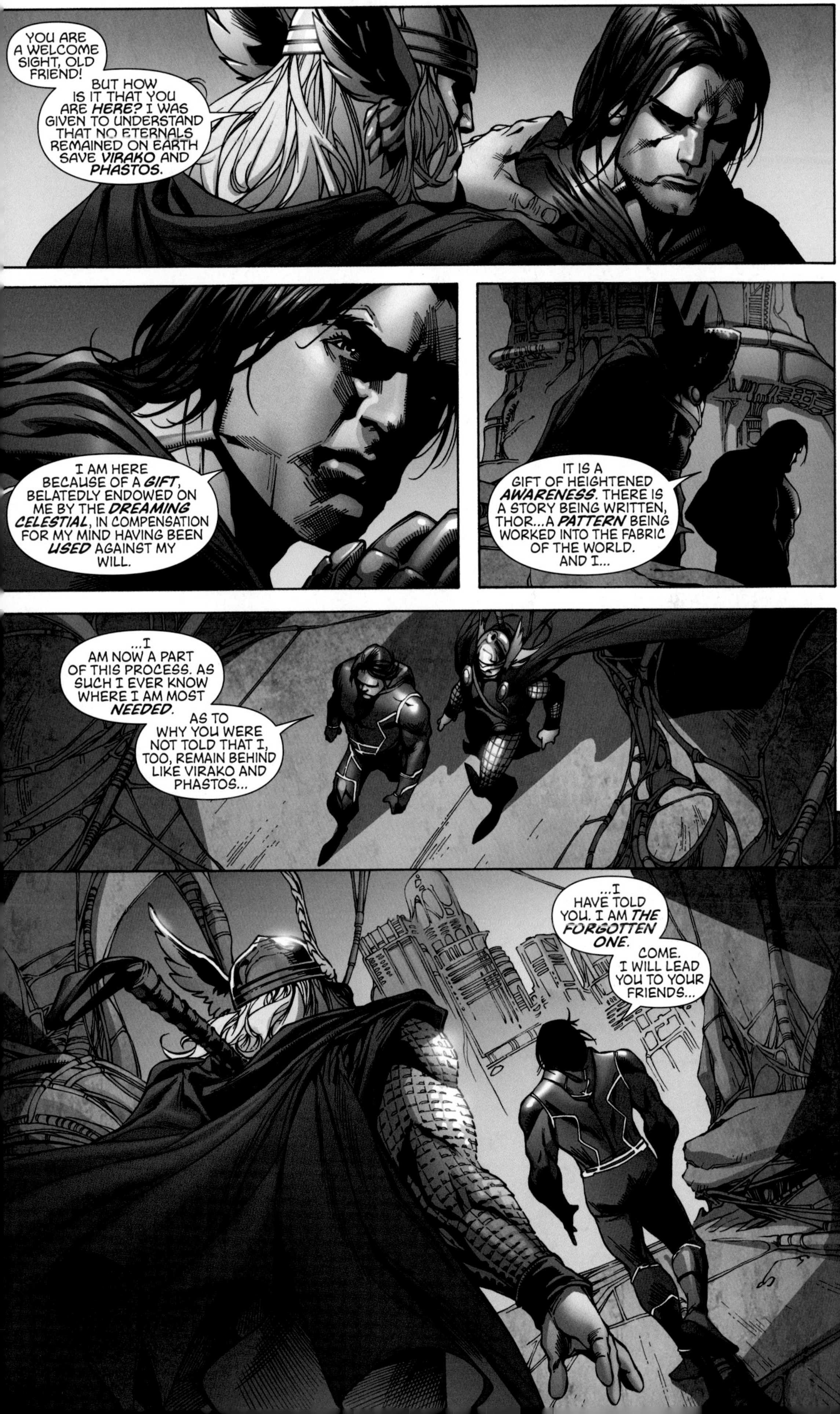
YOU ARE A WELCOME SIGHT, OLD FRIEND!
BUT HOW IS IT THAT YOU ARE *HERE?* I WAS GIVEN TO UNDERSTAND THAT NO ETERNALS REMAINED ON EARTH SAVE *VIRAKO* AND *PHASTOS*.
I AM HERE BECAUSE OF A *GIFT*, BELATEDLY ENDOWED ON ME BY THE *DREAMING CELESTIAL*, IN COMPENSATION FOR MY MIND HAVING BEEN *USED* AGAINST MY WILL.
IT IS A GIFT OF HEIGHTENED *AWARENESS*. THERE IS A STORY BEING WRITTEN, THOR...A *PATTERN* BEING WORKED INTO THE FABRIC OF THE WORLD. AND I...
...I AM NOW A PART OF THIS PROCESS. AS SUCH I EVER KNOW WHERE I AM MOST *NEEDED*.
AS TO WHY YOU WERE NOT TOLD THAT I, TOO, REMAIN BEHIND LIKE VIRAKO AND PHASTOS...
...I HAVE TOLD YOU. I AM *THE FORGOTTEN ONE*.
COME. I WILL LEAD YOU TO YOUR FRIENDS...

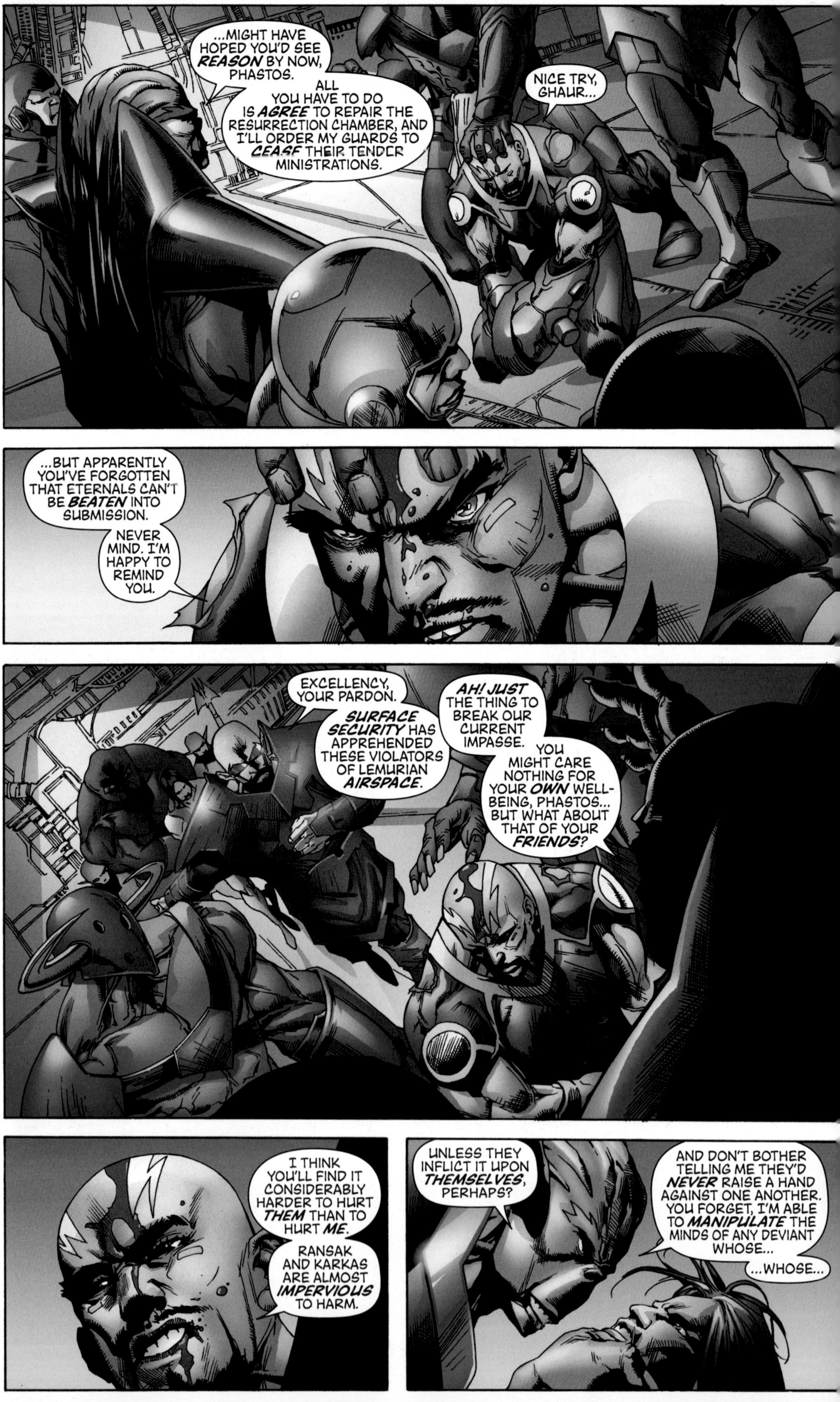
...MIGHT HAVE HOPED YOU'D SEE REASON BY NOW, PHASTOS.
ALL YOU HAVE TO DO IS AGREE TO REPAIR THE RESURRECTION CHAMBER, AND I'LL ORDER MY GUARDS TO CEASE THEIR TENDER MINISTRATIONS.
NICE TRY, GHAUR...
...BUT APPARENTLY YOU'VE FORGOTTEN THAT ETERNALS CAN'T BE BEATEN INTO SUBMISSION.
NEVER MIND. I'M HAPPY TO REMIND YOU.
EXCELLENCY, YOUR PARDON.
SURFACE SECURITY HAS APPREHENDED THESE VIOLATORS OF LEMURIAN AIRSPACE.
AH! JUST THE THING TO BREAK OUR CURRENT IMPASSE.
YOU MIGHT CARE NOTHING FOR YOUR OWN WELL-BEING, PHASTOS... BUT WHAT ABOUT THAT OF YOUR FRIENDS?
I THINK YOU'LL FIND IT CONSIDERABLY HARDER TO HURT THEM THAN TO HURT ME.
RANSAK AND KARKAS ARE ALMOST IMPERVIOUS TO HARM.
UNLESS THEY INFLICT IT UPON THEMSELVES, PERHAPS?
AND DON'T BOTHER TELLING ME THEY'D NEVER RAISE A HAND AGAINST ONE ANOTHER. YOU FORGET, I'M ABLE TO MANIPULATE THE MINDS OF ANY DEVIANT WHOSE...
...WHOSE...

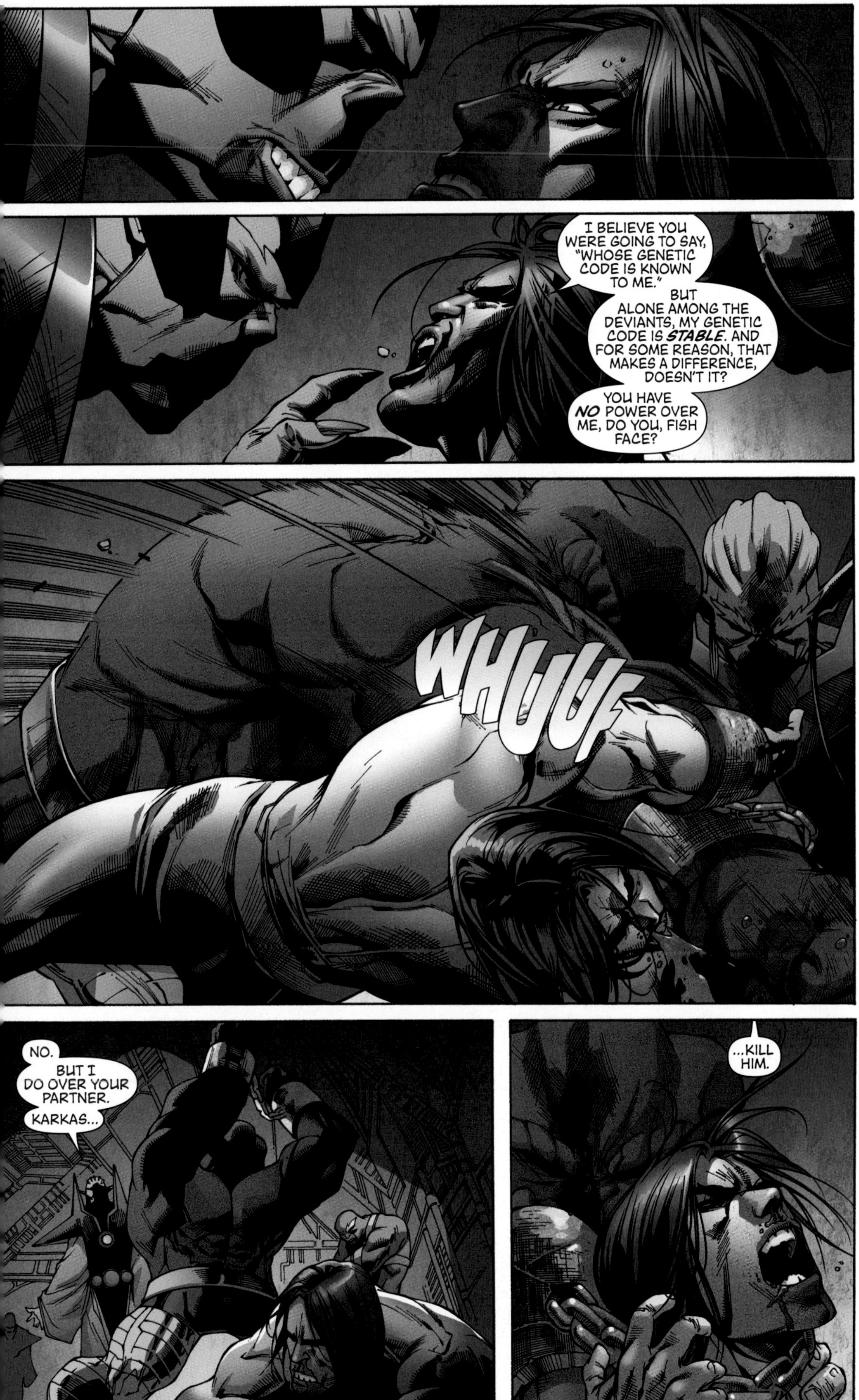
I BELIEVE YOU WERE GOING TO SAY, "WHOSE GENETIC CODE IS KNOWN TO ME."
BUT ALONE AMONG THE DEVIANTS, MY GENETIC CODE IS *STABLE*. AND FOR SOME REASON, THAT MAKES A DIFFERENCE, DOESN'T IT?
YOU HAVE *NO* POWER OVER ME, DO YOU, FISH FACE?
WHUUF
NO.
BUT I DO OVER YOUR PARTNER.
KARKAS...
...KILL HIM.

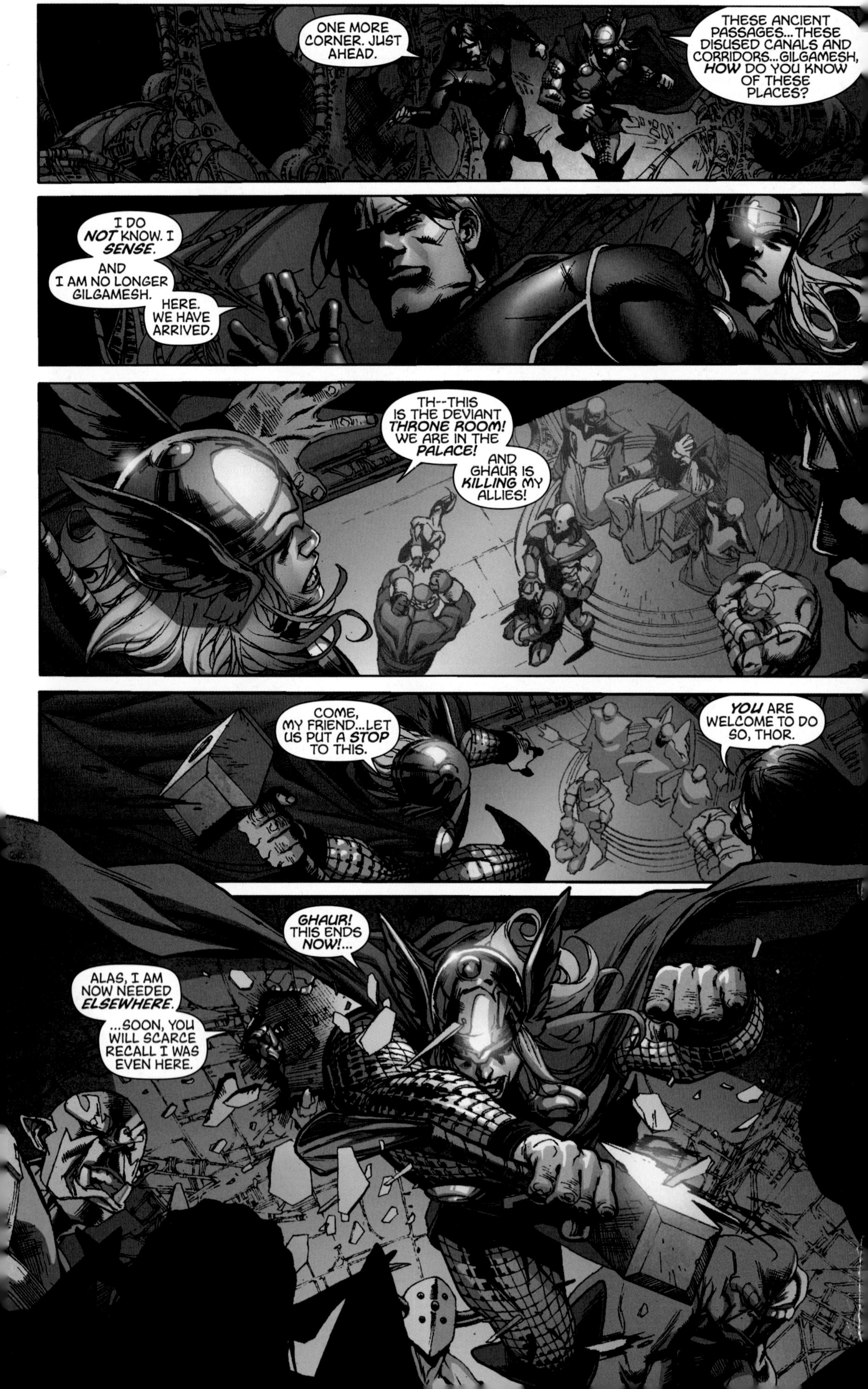
ONE MORE CORNER. JUST AHEAD.
THESE ANCIENT PASSAGES...THESE DISUSED CANALS AND CORRIDORS...GILGAMESH, HOW DO YOU KNOW OF THESE PLACES?
I DO NOT KNOW. I SENSE.
AND I AM NO LONGER GILGAMESH.
HERE. WE HAVE ARRIVED.
TH--THIS IS THE DEVIANT THRONE ROOM! WE ARE IN THE PALACE!
AND GHAUR IS KILLING MY ALLIES!
COME, MY FRIEND...LET US PUT A STOP TO THIS.
YOU ARE WELCOME TO DO SO, THOR.
GHAUR! THIS ENDS NOW!...
ALAS, I AM NOW NEEDED ELSEWHERE.
...SOON, YOU WILL SCARCE RECALL I WAS EVEN HERE.

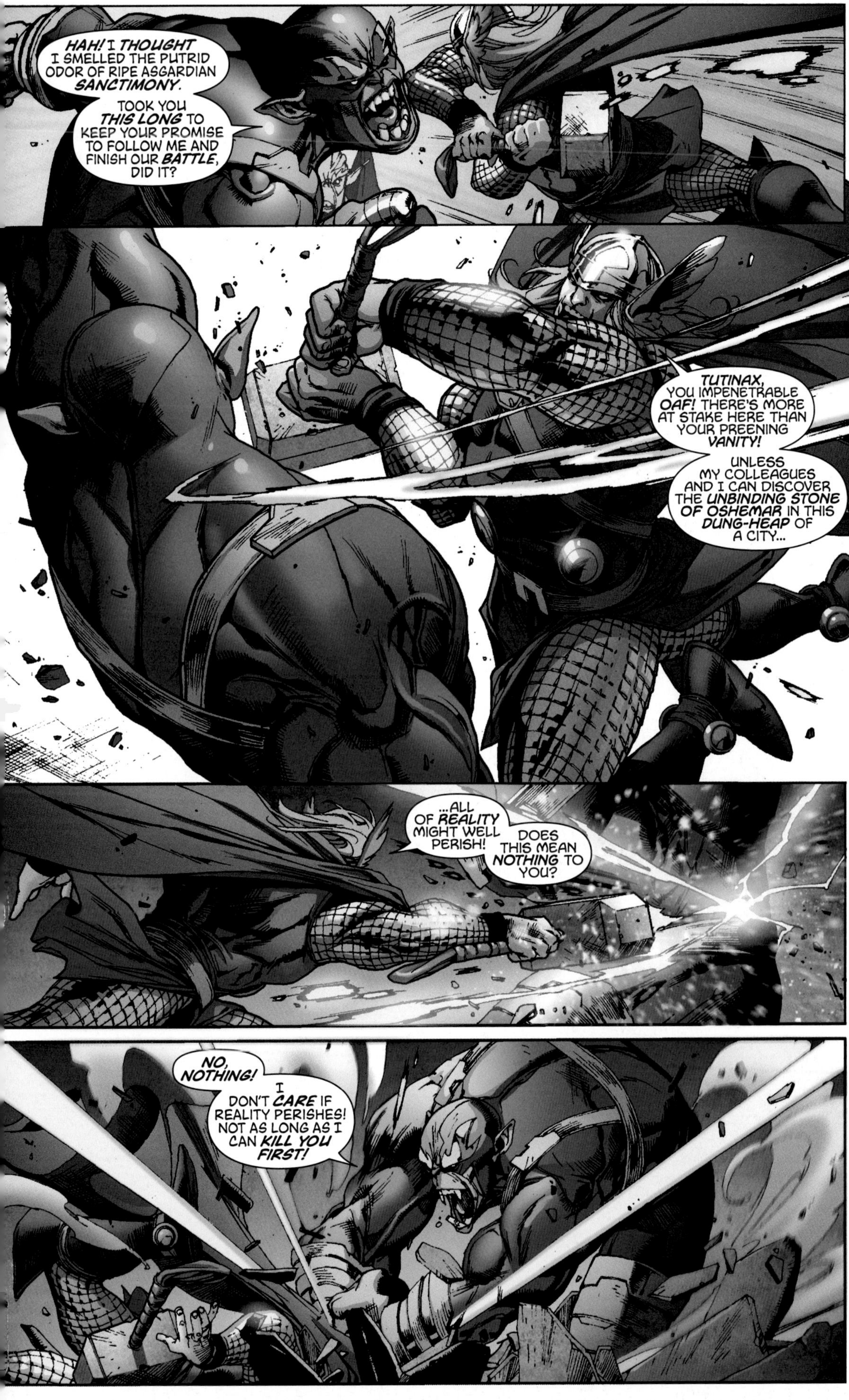
HAH! I THOUGHT I SMELLED THE PUTRID ODOR OF RIPE ASGARDIAN SANCTIMONY.
TOOK YOU THIS LONG TO KEEP YOUR PROMISE TO FOLLOW ME AND FINISH OUR BATTLE, DID IT?
TUTINAX, YOU IMPENETRABLE OAF! THERE'S MORE AT STAKE HERE THAN YOUR PREENING VANITY!
UNLESS MY COLLEAGUES AND I CAN DISCOVER THE UNBINDING STONE OF OSHEMAR IN THIS DUNG-HEAP OF A CITY...
...ALL OF REALITY MIGHT WELL PERISH!
DOES THIS MEAN NOTHING TO YOU?
NO, NOTHING!
I DON'T CARE IF REALITY PERISHES! NOT AS LONG AS I CAN KILL YOU FIRST!

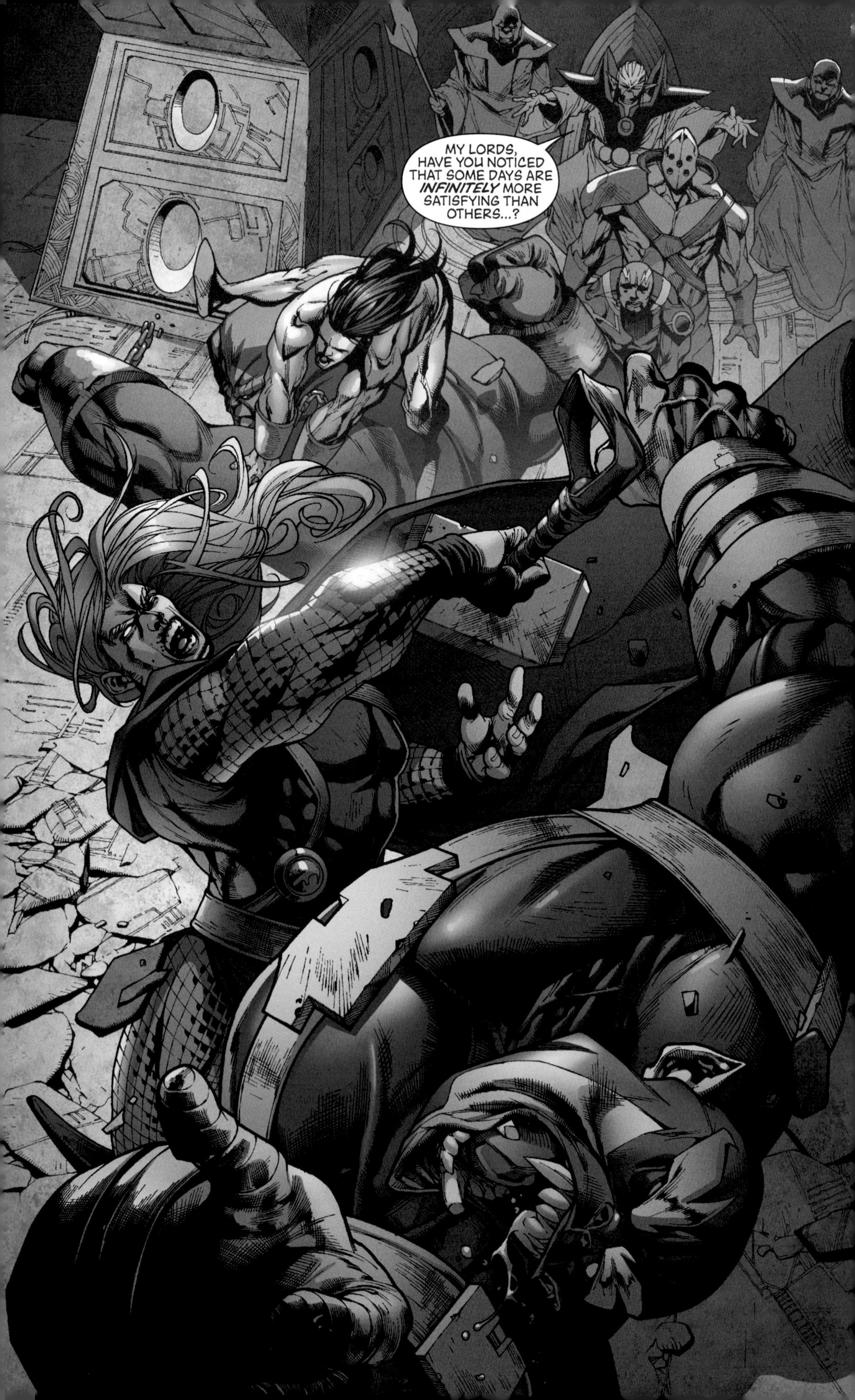
MY LORDS, HAVE YOU NOTICED THAT SOME DAYS ARE *INFINITELY* MORE SATISFYING THAN OTHERS...?

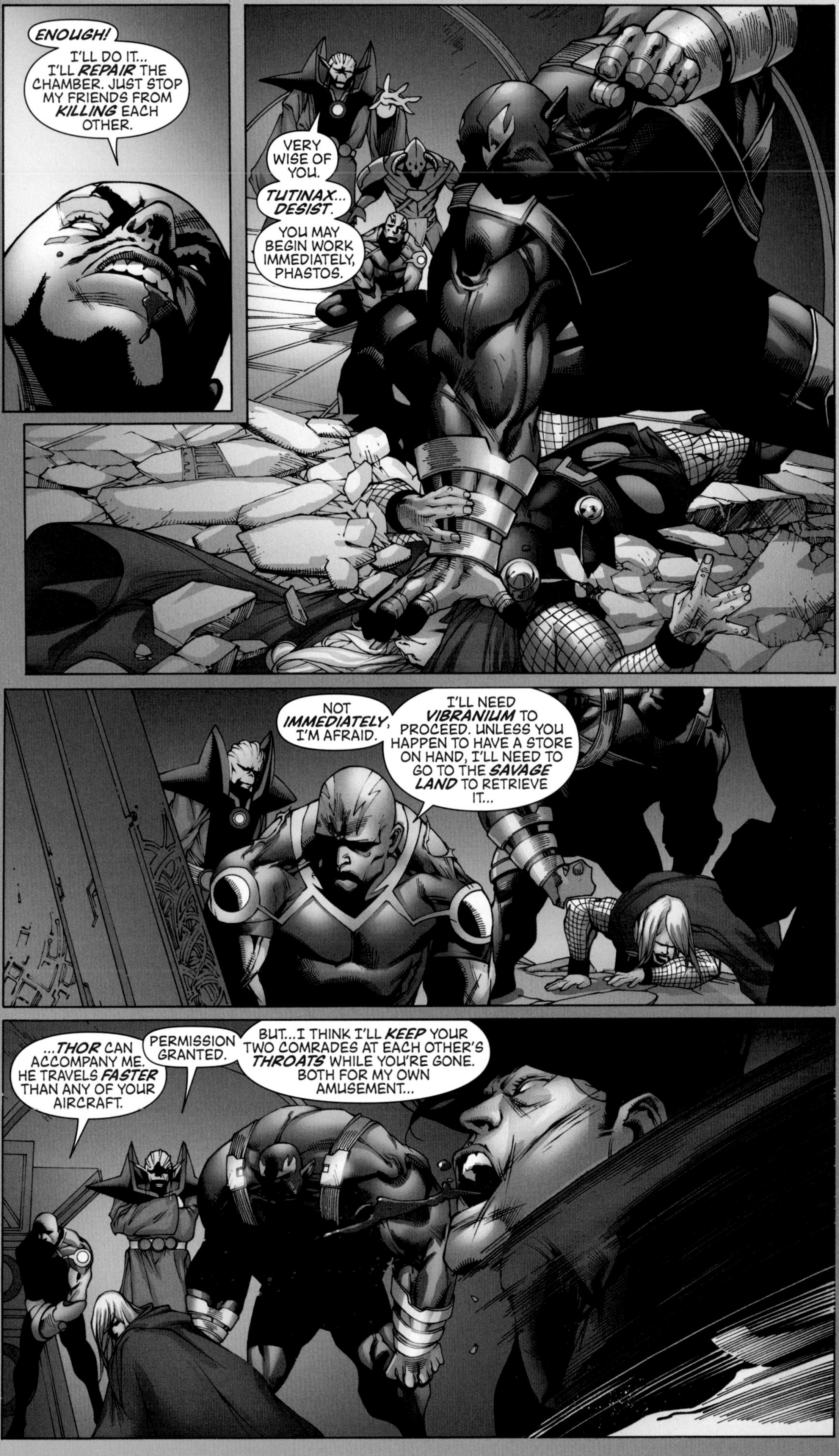
ENOUGH!
I'LL DO IT... I'LL REPAIR THE CHAMBER. JUST STOP MY FRIENDS FROM KILLING EACH OTHER.
VERY WISE OF YOU.
TUTINAX... DESIST.
YOU MAY BEGIN WORK IMMEDIATELY, PHASTOS.
NOT IMMEDIATELY, I'M AFRAID.
I'LL NEED VIBRANIUM TO PROCEED. UNLESS YOU HAPPEN TO HAVE A STORE ON HAND, I'LL NEED TO GO TO THE SAVAGE LAND TO RETRIEVE IT...
...THOR CAN ACCOMPANY ME. HE TRAVELS FASTER THAN ANY OF YOUR AIRCRAFT.
PERMISSION GRANTED.
BUT...I THINK I'LL KEEP YOUR TWO COMRADES AT EACH OTHER'S THROATS WHILE YOU'RE GONE. BOTH FOR MY OWN AMUSEMENT...

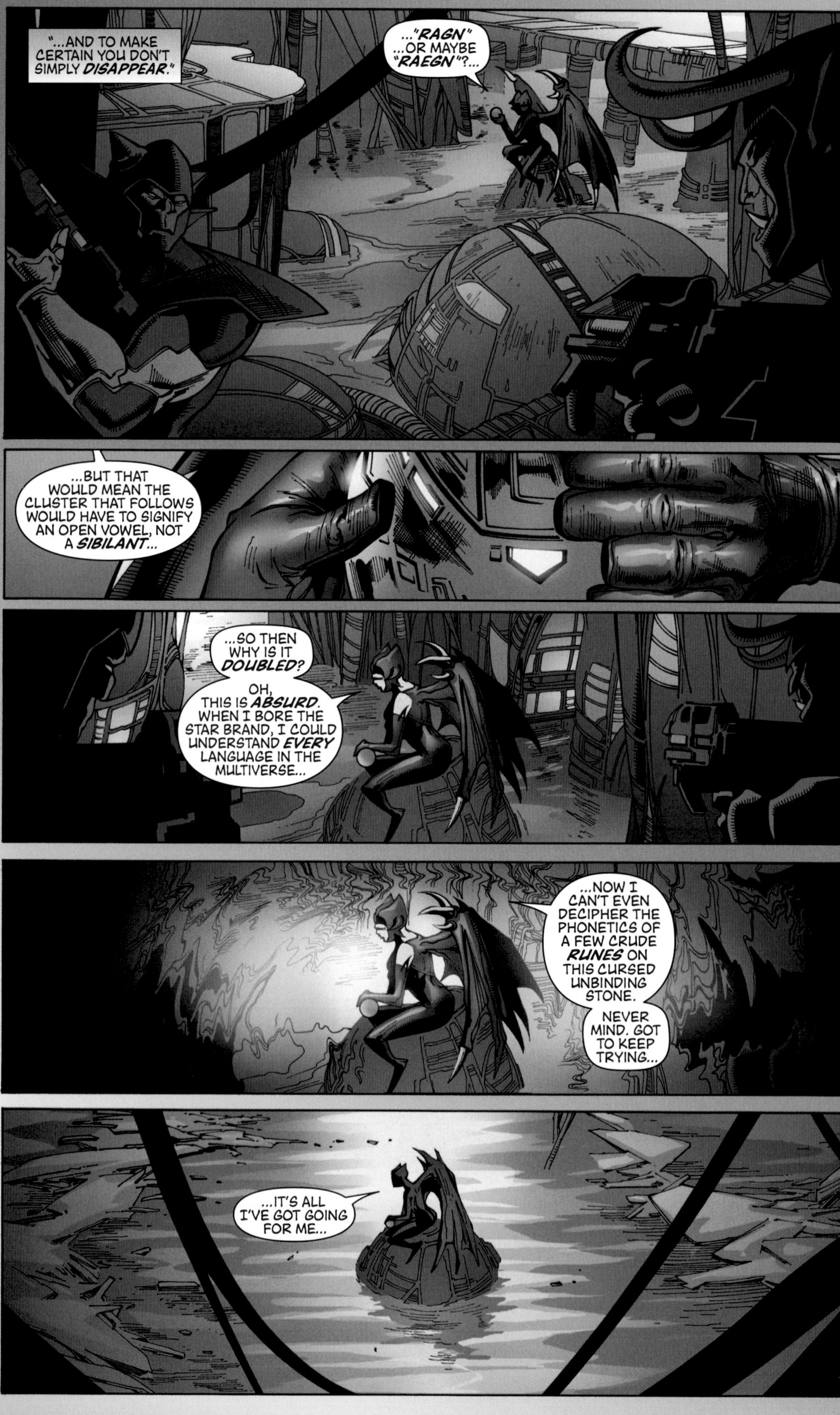
"...AND TO MAKE CERTAIN YOU DON'T SIMPLY *DISAPPEAR*."
..."*RAGN*" ...OR MAYBE "*RAEGN*"?...
...BUT THAT WOULD MEAN THE CLUSTER THAT FOLLOWS WOULD HAVE TO SIGNIFY AN OPEN VOWEL, NOT A *SIBILANT*...
...SO THEN WHY IS IT *DOUBLED*?
OH, THIS IS *ABSURD*. WHEN I BORE THE STAR BRAND, I COULD UNDERSTAND *EVERY* LANGUAGE IN THE MULTIVERSE...
...NOW I CAN'T EVEN DECIPHER THE PHONETICS OF A FEW CRUDE *RUNES* ON THIS CURSED UNBINDING STONE.
NEVER MIND. GOT TO KEEP TRYING...
...IT'S ALL I'VE GOT GOING FOR ME...

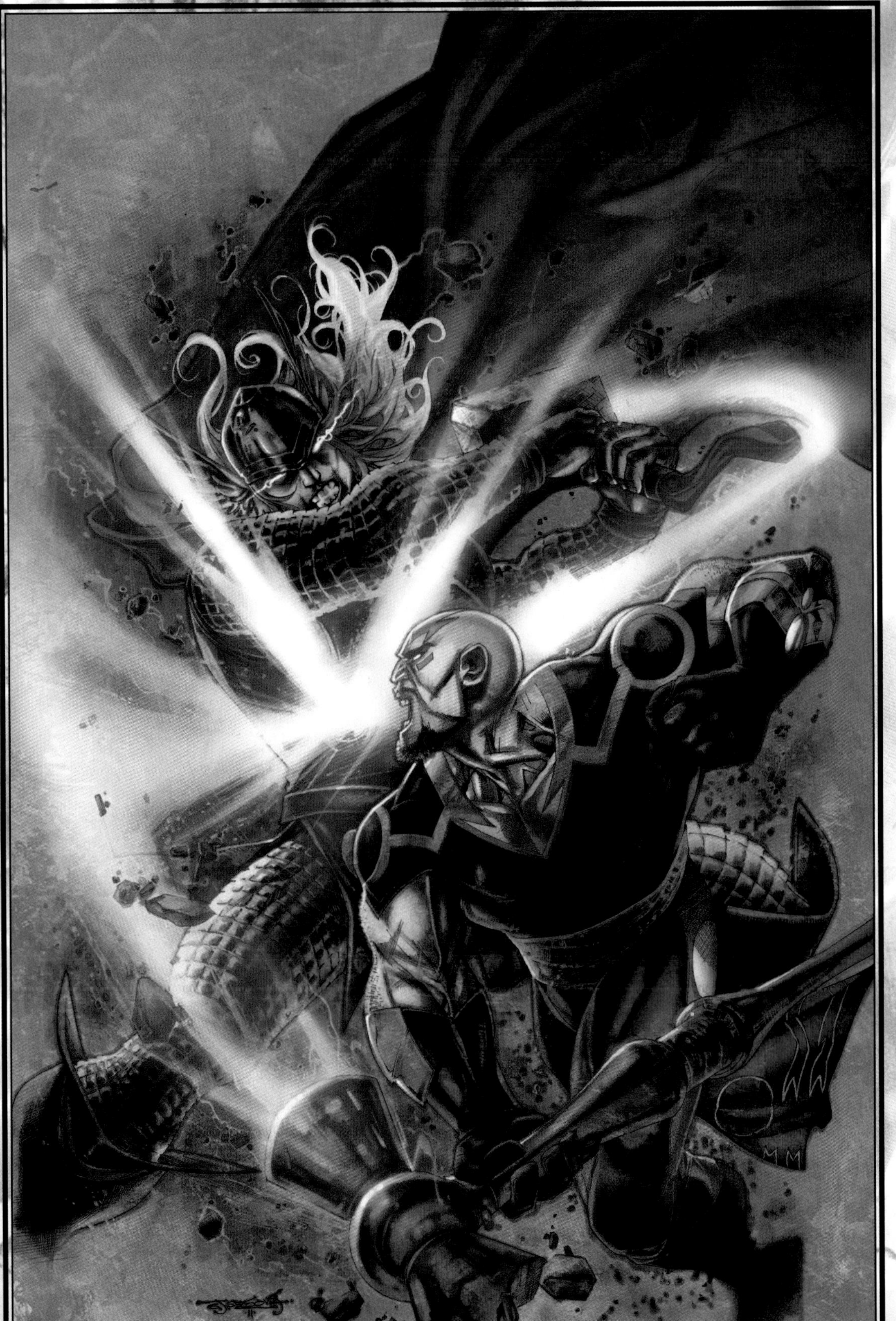

FOUR

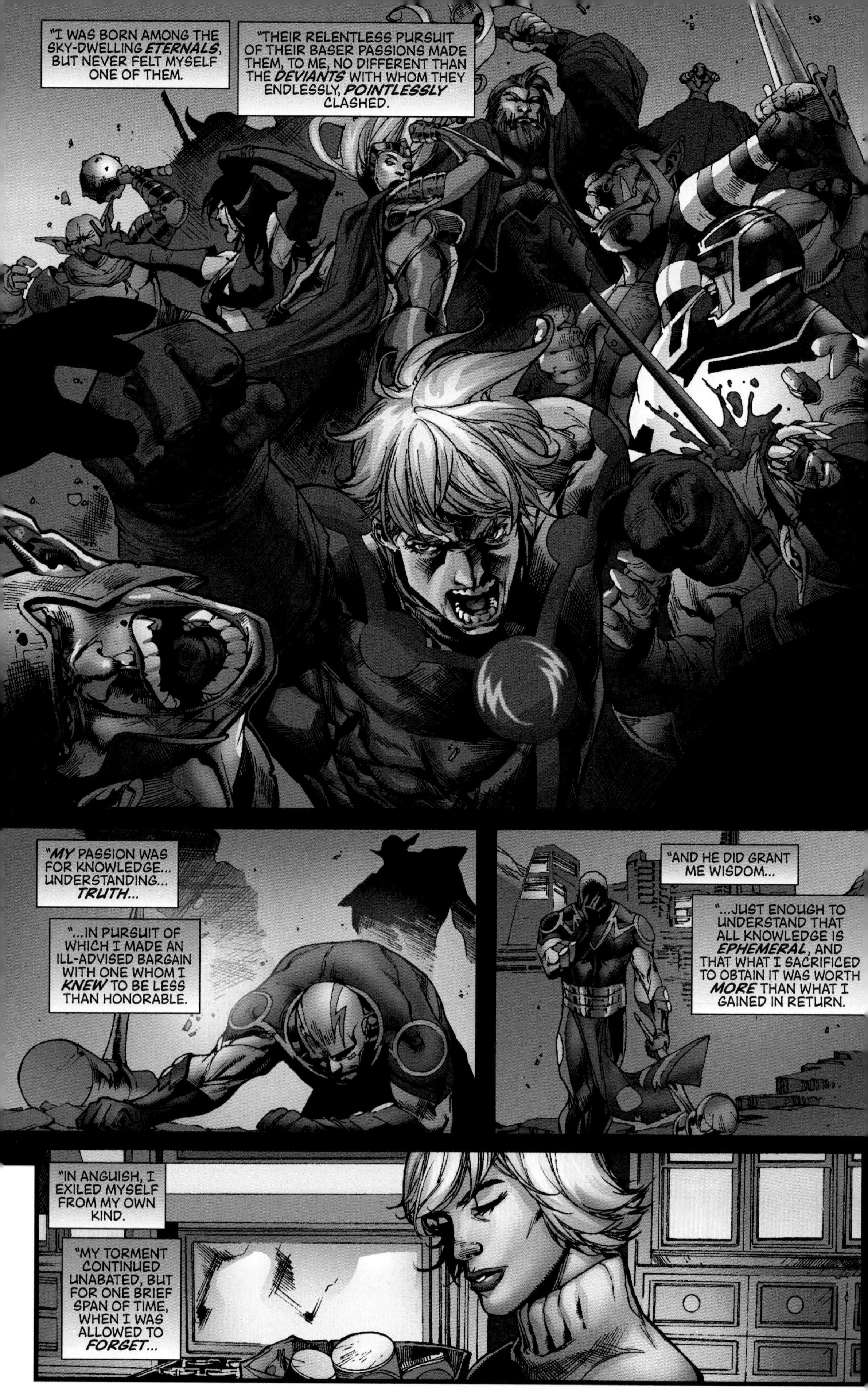
"I WAS BORN AMONG THE SKY-DWELLING *ETERNALS*, BUT NEVER FELT MYSELF ONE OF THEM.
"THEIR RELENTLESS PURSUIT OF THEIR BASER PASSIONS MADE THEM, TO ME, NO DIFFERENT THAN THE *DEVIANTS* WITH WHOM THEY ENDLESSLY, *POINTLESSLY* CLASHED.
"*MY* PASSION WAS FOR KNOWLEDGE... UNDERSTANDING... *TRUTH*...
"...IN PURSUIT OF WHICH I MADE AN ILL-ADVISED BARGAIN WITH ONE WHOM I *KNEW* TO BE LESS THAN HONORABLE.
"AND HE DID GRANT ME WISDOM...
"...JUST ENOUGH TO UNDERSTAND THAT ALL KNOWLEDGE IS *EPHEMERAL*, AND THAT WHAT I SACRIFICED TO OBTAIN IT WAS WORTH *MORE* THAN WHAT I GAINED IN RETURN.
"IN ANGUISH, I EXILED MYSELF FROM MY OWN KIND.
"MY TORMENT CONTINUED UNABATED, BUT FOR ONE BRIEF SPAN OF TIME, WHEN I WAS ALLOWED TO *FORGET*...

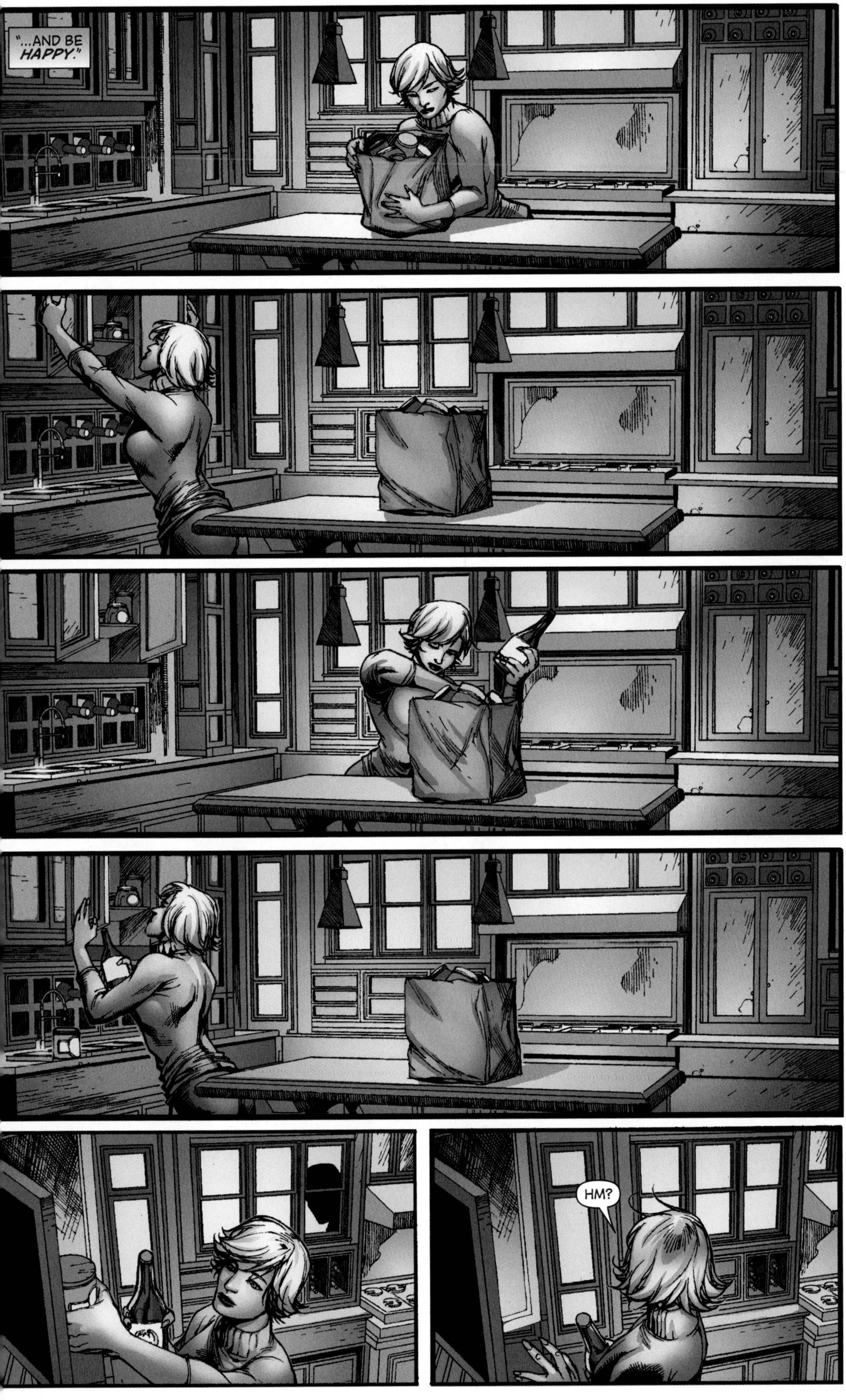
"...AND BE HAPPY."
HM?

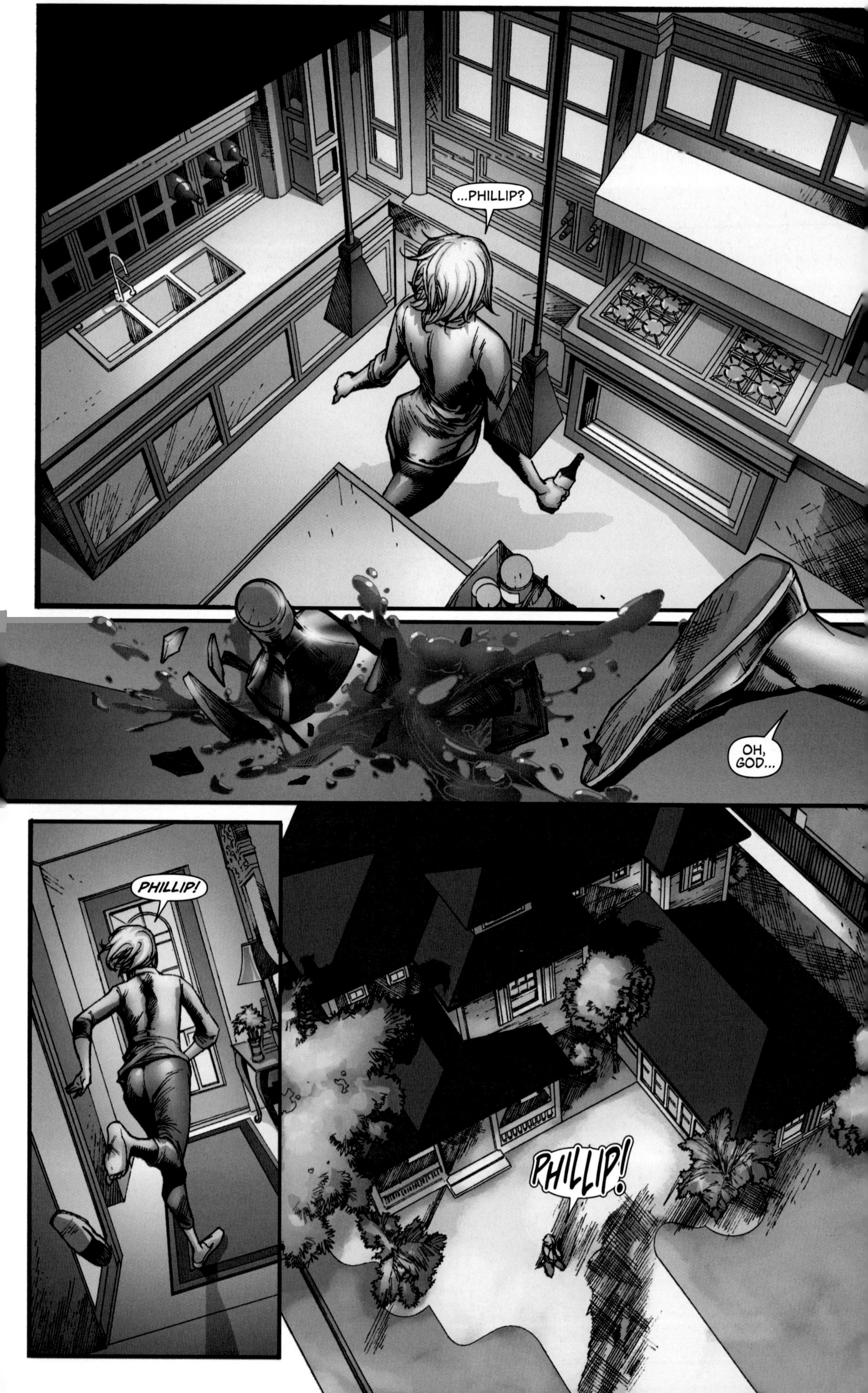
...PHILLIP?
OH, GOD...
PHILLIP!
PHILLIP!

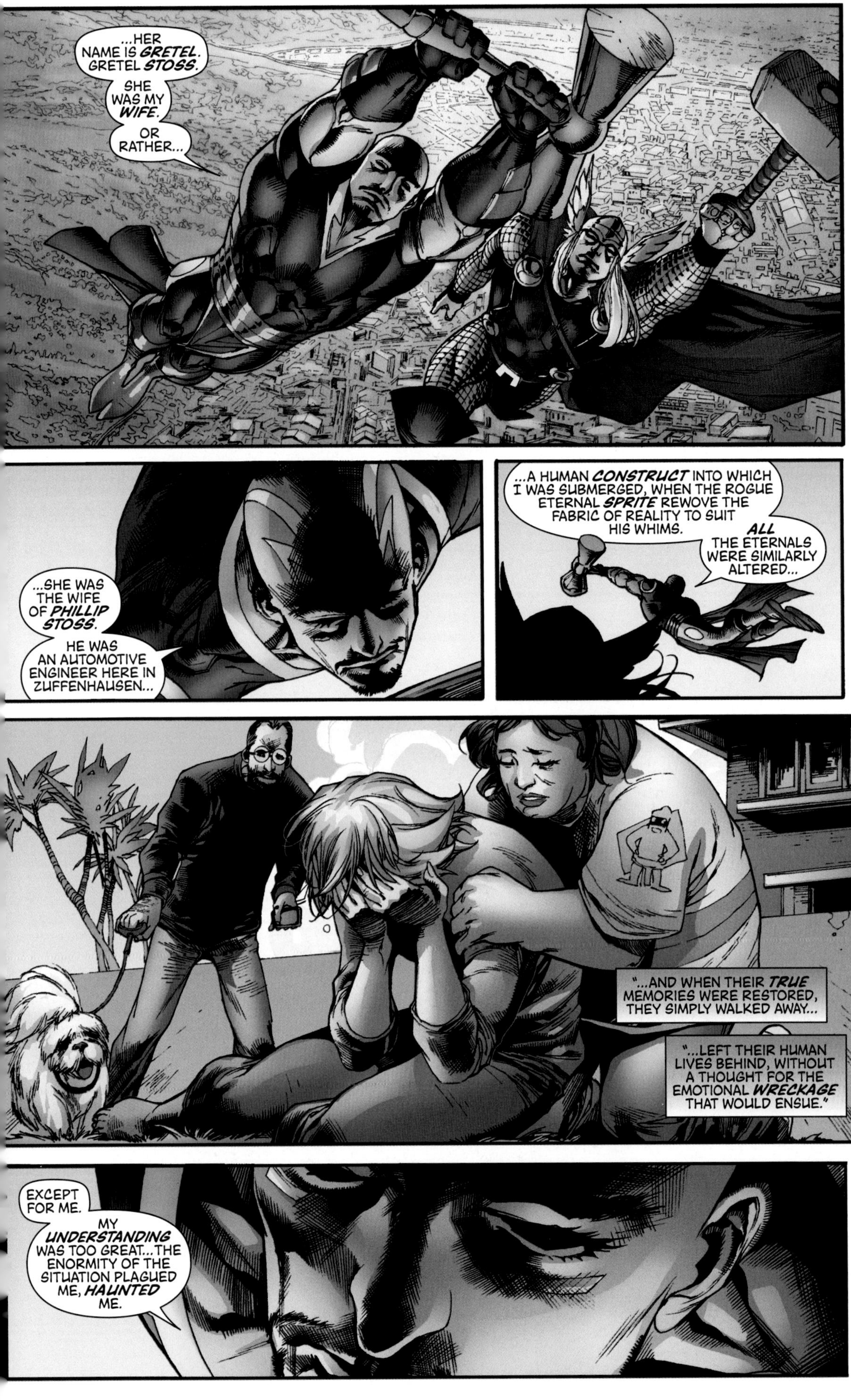
...HER NAME IS GRETEL. GRETEL STOSS.
SHE WAS MY WIFE.
OR RATHER...
...SHE WAS THE WIFE OF PHILLIP STOSS.
HE WAS AN AUTOMOTIVE ENGINEER HERE IN ZUFFENHAUSEN...
...A HUMAN CONSTRUCT INTO WHICH I WAS SUBMERGED, WHEN THE ROGUE ETERNAL SPRITE REWOVE THE FABRIC OF REALITY TO SUIT HIS WHIMS.
ALL THE ETERNALS WERE SIMILARLY ALTERED...
"...AND WHEN THEIR TRUE MEMORIES WERE RESTORED, THEY SIMPLY WALKED AWAY...
"...LEFT THEIR HUMAN LIVES BEHIND, WITHOUT A THOUGHT FOR THE EMOTIONAL WRECKAGE THAT WOULD ENSUE."
EXCEPT FOR ME.
MY UNDERSTANDING WAS TOO GREAT...THE ENORMITY OF THE SITUATION PLAGUED ME, HAUNTED ME.

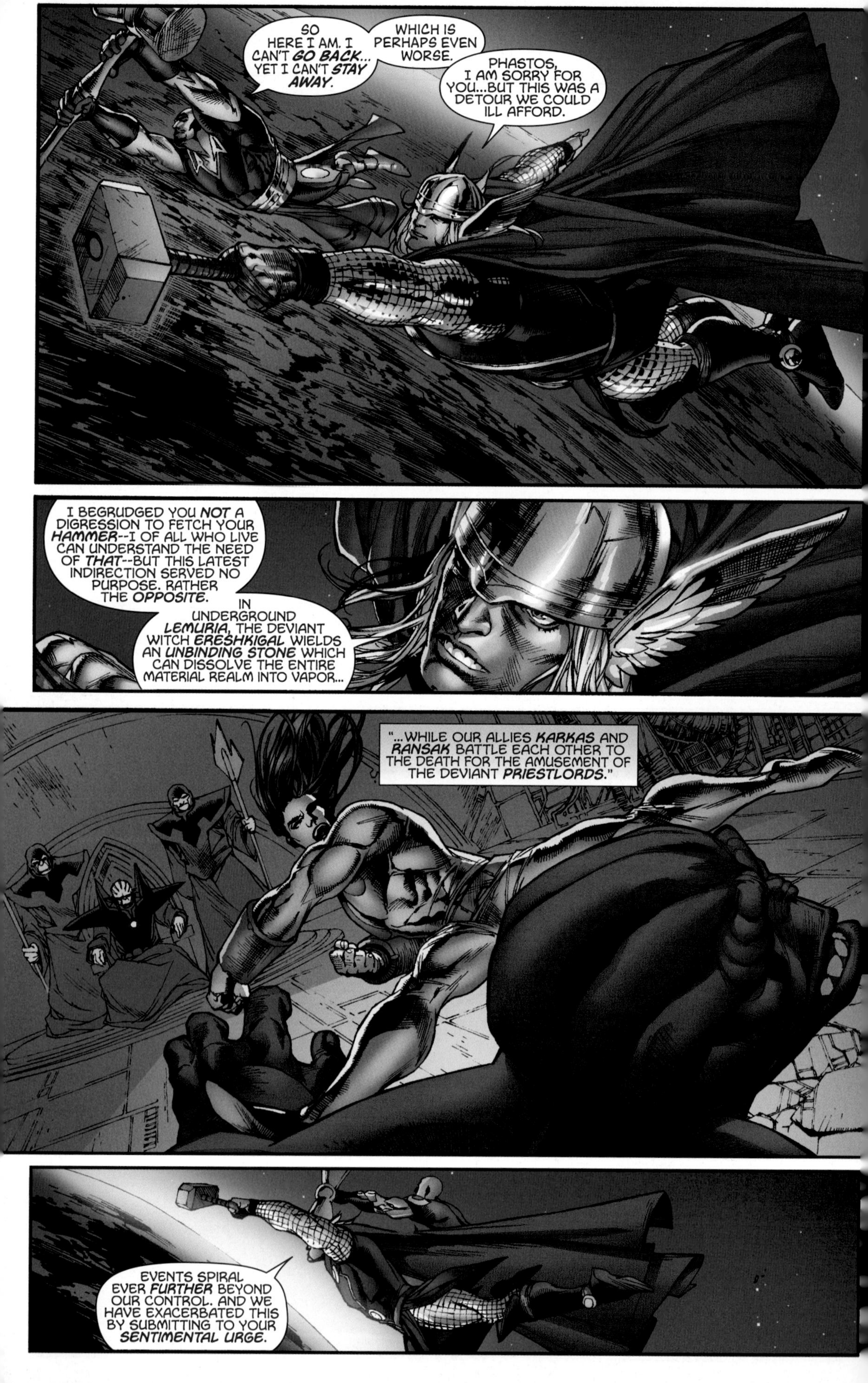
SO HERE I AM. I CAN'T GO BACK... YET I CAN'T STAY AWAY.
WHICH IS PERHAPS EVEN WORSE.
PHASTOS, I AM SORRY FOR YOU...BUT THIS WAS A DETOUR WE COULD ILL AFFORD.
I BEGRUDGED YOU NOT A DIGRESSION TO FETCH YOUR HAMMER--I OF ALL WHO LIVE CAN UNDERSTAND THE NEED OF THAT--BUT THIS LATEST INDIRECTION SERVED NO PURPOSE. RATHER THE OPPOSITE.
IN UNDERGROUND LEMURIA, THE DEVIANT WITCH ERESHKIGAL WIELDS AN UNBINDING STONE WHICH CAN DISSOLVE THE ENTIRE MATERIAL REALM INTO VAPOR...
"...WHILE OUR ALLIES KARKAS AND RANSAK BATTLE EACH OTHER TO THE DEATH FOR THE AMUSEMENT OF THE DEVIANT PRIESTLORDS."
EVENTS SPIRAL EVER FURTHER BEYOND OUR CONTROL. AND WE HAVE EXACERBATED THIS BY SUBMITTING TO YOUR SENTIMENTAL URGE.

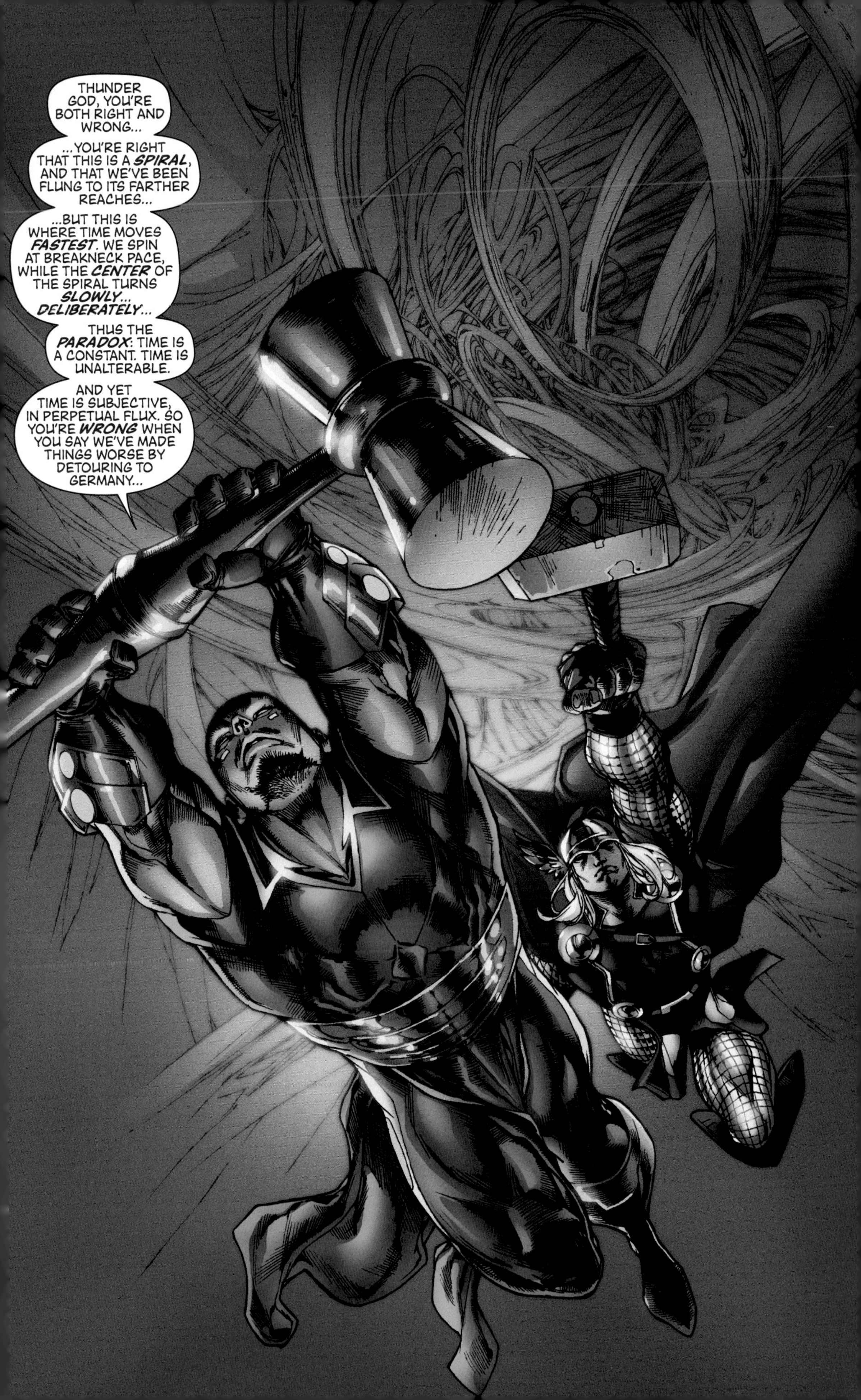
THUNDER GOD, YOU'RE BOTH RIGHT AND WRONG...
...YOU'RE RIGHT THAT THIS IS A *SPIRAL*, AND THAT WE'VE BEEN FLUNG TO ITS FARTHER REACHES...
...BUT THIS IS WHERE TIME MOVES *FASTEST*. WE SPIN AT BREAKNECK PACE, WHILE THE *CENTER* OF THE SPIRAL TURNS *SLOWLY*... *DELIBERATELY*...
THUS THE *PARADOX*: TIME IS A CONSTANT. TIME IS UNALTERABLE.
AND YET TIME IS SUBJECTIVE, IN PERPETUAL FLUX. SO YOU'RE *WRONG* WHEN YOU SAY WE'VE MADE THINGS WORSE BY DETOURING TO GERMANY...

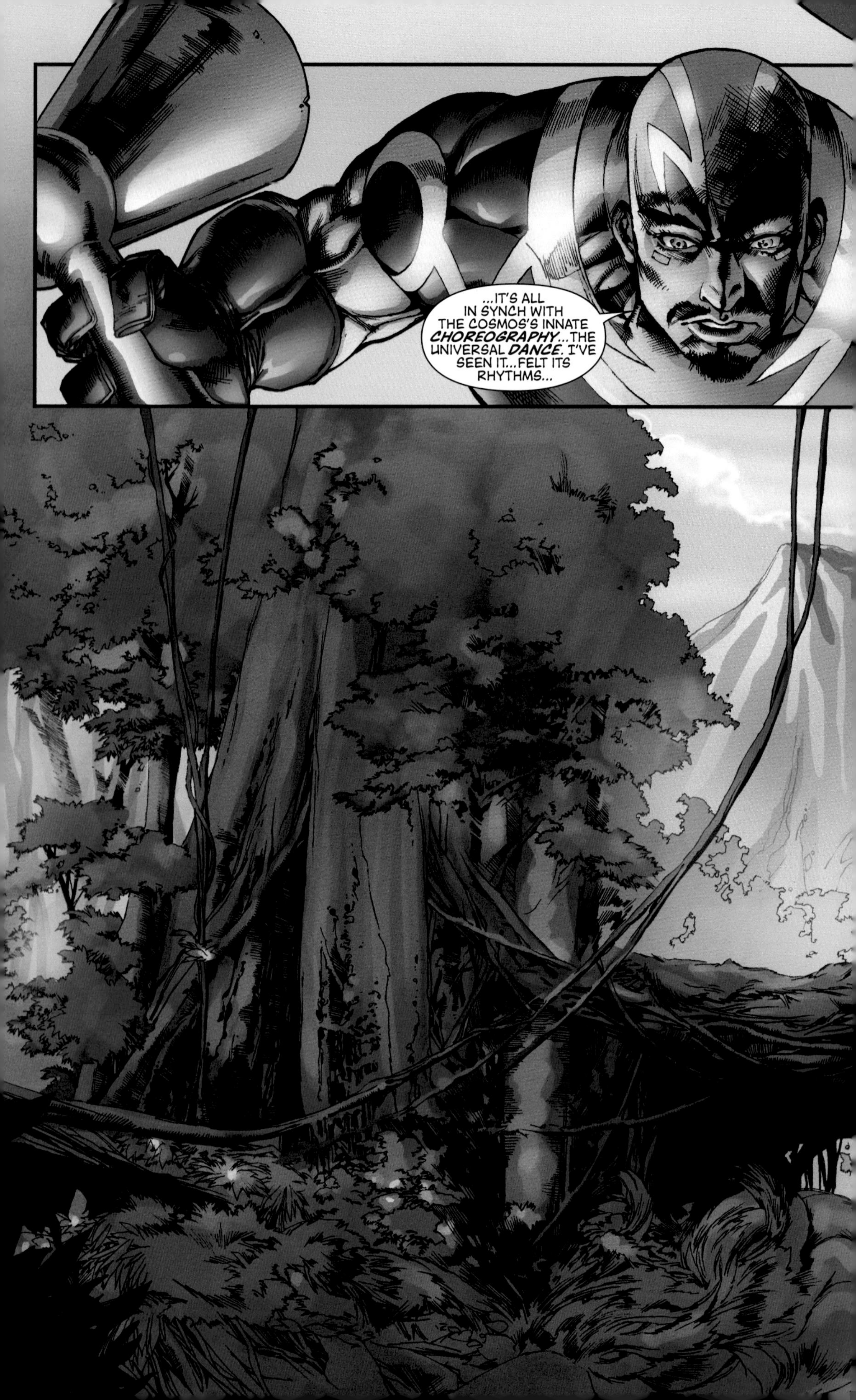
...IT'S ALL IN SYNCH WITH THE COSMOS'S INNATE CHOREOGRAPHY...THE UNIVERSAL DANCE. I'VE SEEN IT...FELT ITS RHYTHMS...

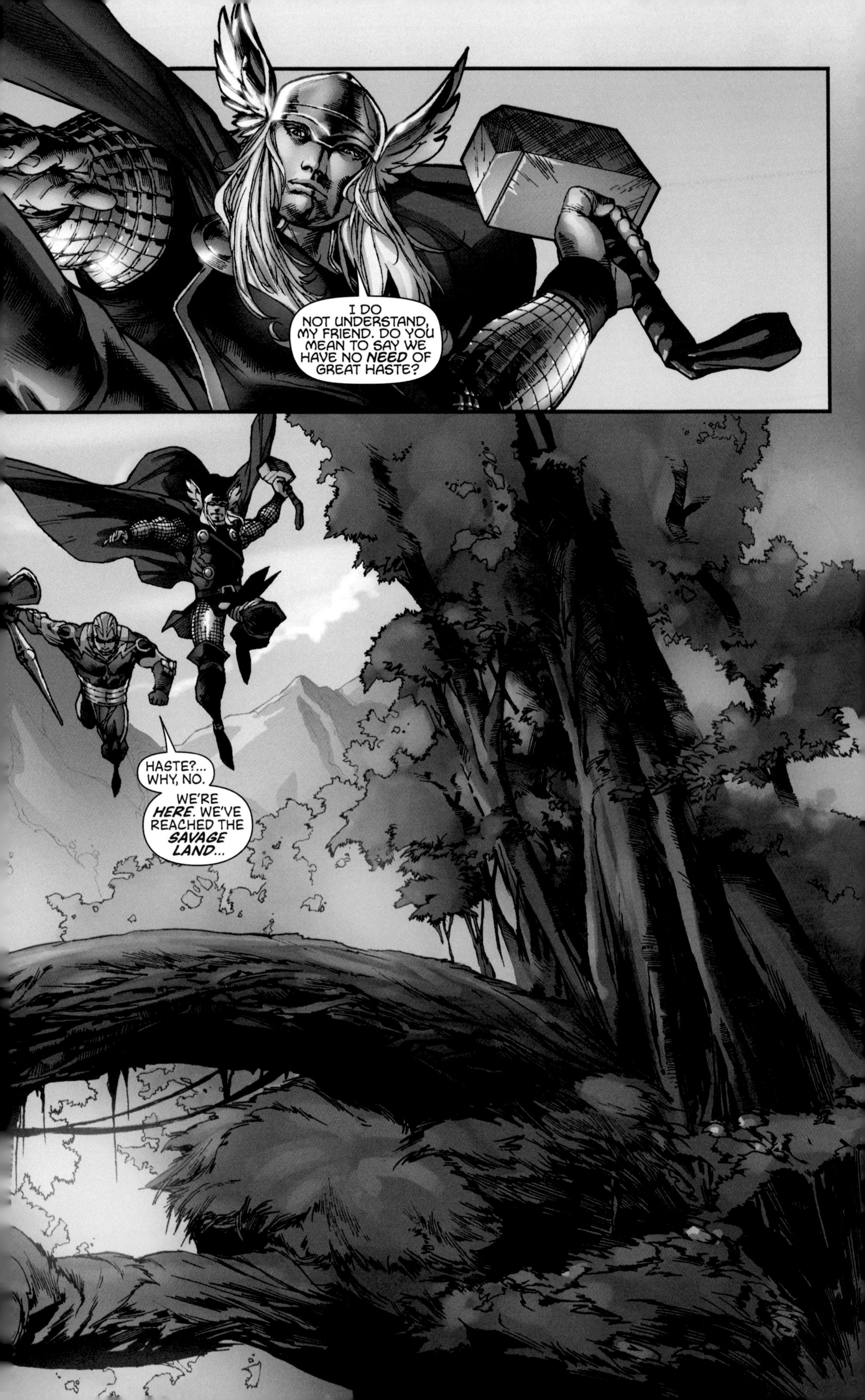
I DO NOT UNDERSTAND, MY FRIEND. DO YOU MEAN TO SAY WE HAVE NO NEED OF GREAT HASTE?
HASTE?... WHY, NO.
WE'RE HERE. WE'VE REACHED THE SAVAGE LAND...

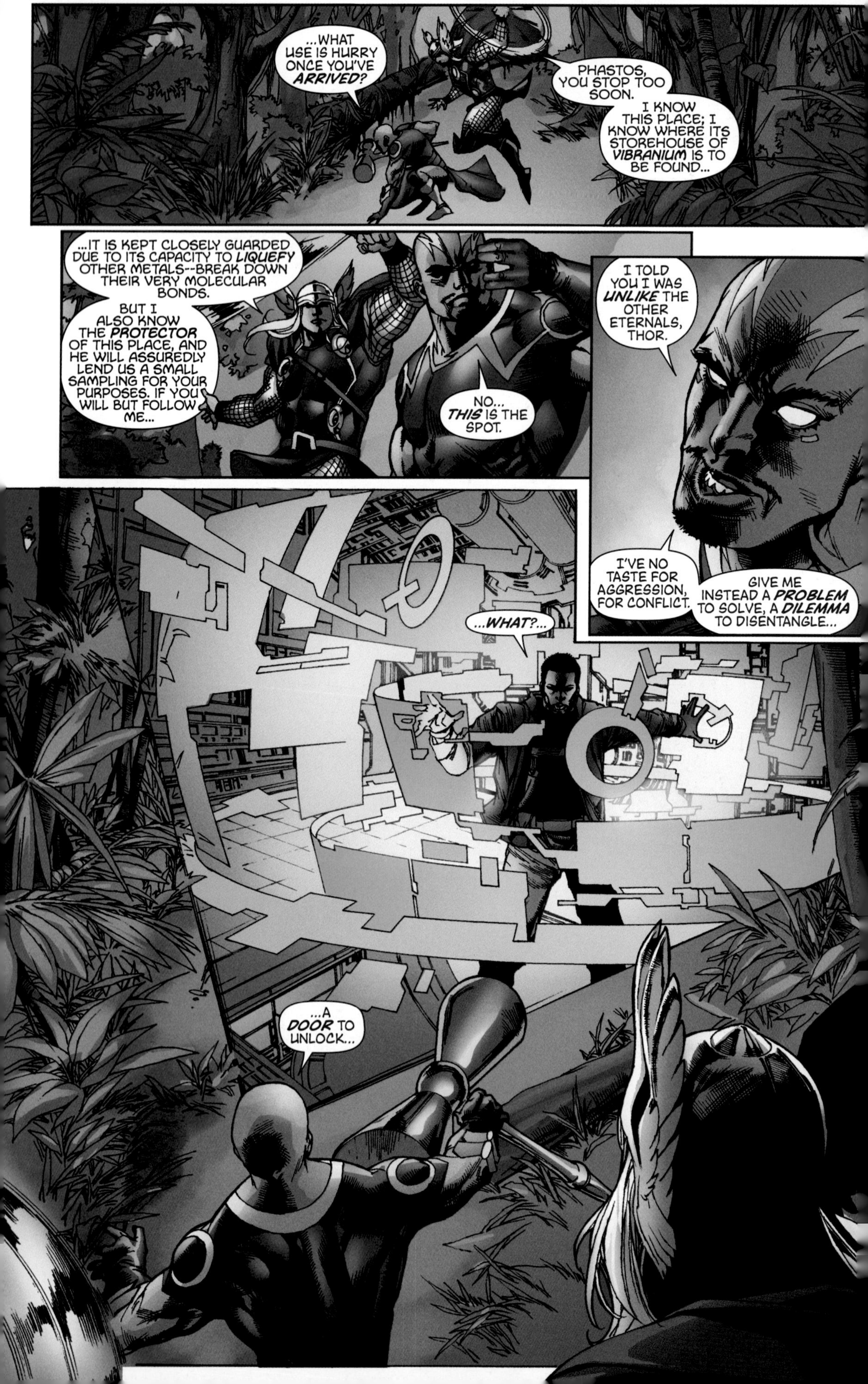
...WHAT USE IS HURRY ONCE YOU'VE ARRIVED?
PHASTOS, YOU STOP TOO SOON.
I KNOW THIS PLACE; I KNOW WHERE ITS STOREHOUSE OF VIBRANIUM IS TO BE FOUND...
...IT IS KEPT CLOSELY GUARDED DUE TO ITS CAPACITY TO LIQUEFY OTHER METALS--BREAK DOWN THEIR VERY MOLECULAR BONDS.
BUT I ALSO KNOW THE PROTECTOR OF THIS PLACE, AND HE WILL ASSUREDLY LEND US A SMALL SAMPLING FOR YOUR PURPOSES. IF YOU WILL BUT FOLLOW ME...
NO... THIS IS THE SPOT.
I TOLD YOU I WAS UNLIKE THE OTHER ETERNALS, THOR.
I'VE NO TASTE FOR AGGRESSION, FOR CONFLICT.
GIVE ME INSTEAD A PROBLEM TO SOLVE, A DILEMMA TO DISENTANGLE...
...WHAT?...
...A DOOR TO UNLOCK...

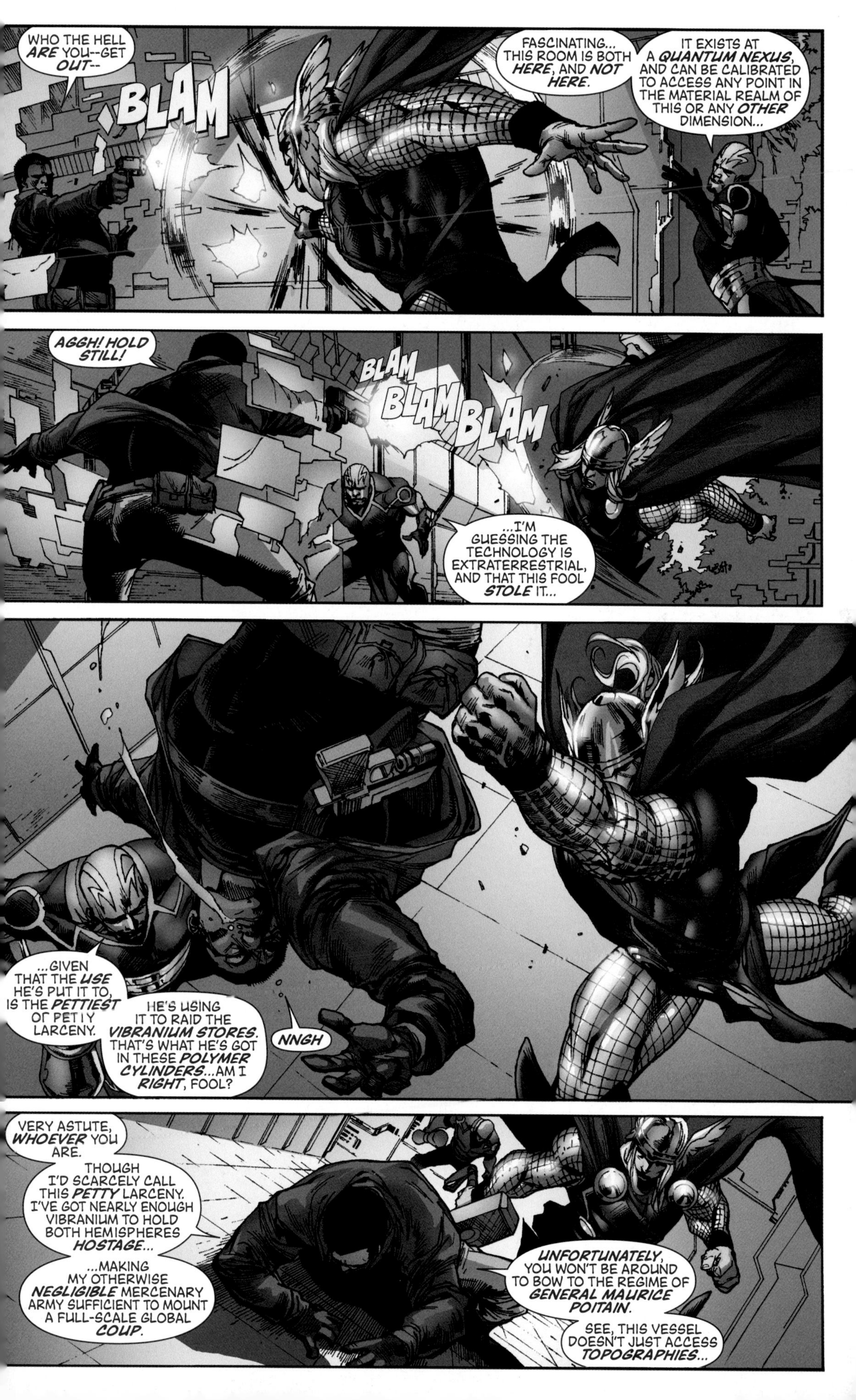
WHO THE HELL ARE YOU--GET OUT--
BLAM
FASCINATING... THIS ROOM IS BOTH HERE, AND NOT HERE.
IT EXISTS AT A QUANTUM NEXUS, AND CAN BE CALIBRATED TO ACCESS ANY POINT IN THE MATERIAL REALM OF THIS OR ANY OTHER DIMENSION...
AGGH! HOLD STILL!
BLAM BLAM BLAM
...I'M GUESSING THE TECHNOLOGY IS EXTRATERRESTRIAL, AND THAT THIS FOOL STOLE IT...
...GIVEN THAT THE USE HE'S PUT IT TO, IS THE PETTIEST OF PETTY LARCENY.
HE'S USING IT TO RAID THE VIBRANIUM STORES. THAT'S WHAT HE'S GOT IN THESE POLYMER CYLINDERS...AM I RIGHT, FOOL?
NNGH
VERY ASTUTE, WHOEVER YOU ARE.
THOUGH I'D SCARCELY CALL THIS PETTY LARCENY. I'VE GOT NEARLY ENOUGH VIBRANIUM TO HOLD BOTH HEMISPHERES HOSTAGE...
...MAKING MY OTHERWISE NEGLIGIBLE MERCENARY ARMY SUFFICIENT TO MOUNT A FULL-SCALE GLOBAL COUP.
UNFORTUNATELY, YOU WON'T BE AROUND TO BOW TO THE REGIME OF GENERAL MAURICE POITAIN.
SEE, THIS VESSEL DOESN'T JUST ACCESS TOPOGRAPHIES...

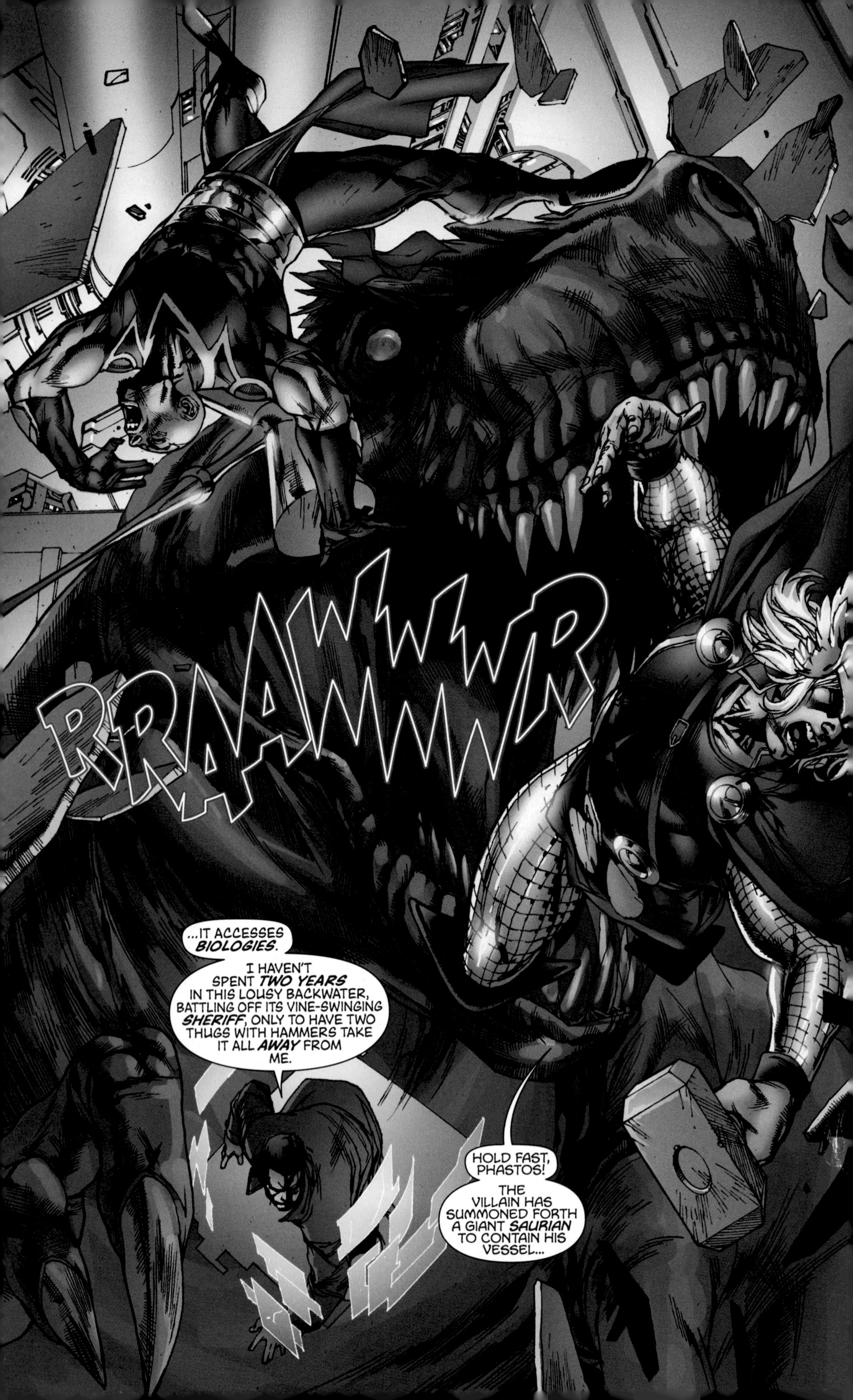
RRAAWWWR
...IT ACCESSES BIOLOGIES.
I HAVEN'T SPENT TWO YEARS IN THIS LOUSY BACKWATER, BATTLING OFF ITS VINE-SWINGING SHERIFF, ONLY TO HAVE TWO THUGS WITH HAMMERS TAKE IT ALL AWAY FROM ME.
HOLD FAST, PHASTOS!
THE VILLAIN HAS SUMMONED FORTH A GIANT SAURIAN TO CONTAIN HIS VESSEL...

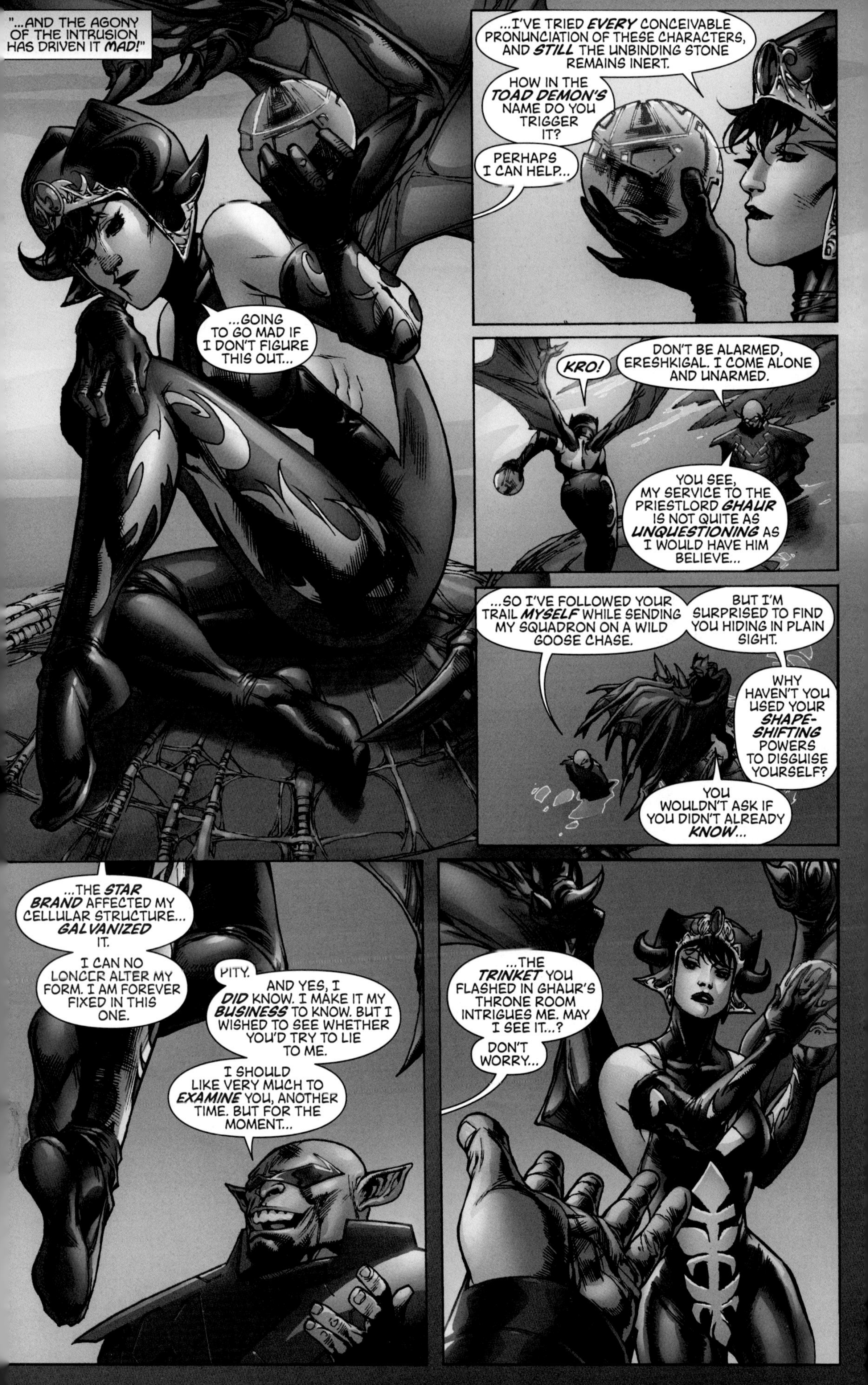
"...AND THE AGONY OF THE INTRUSION HAS DRIVEN IT MAD!"
...GOING TO GO MAD IF I DON'T FIGURE THIS OUT...
...I'VE TRIED EVERY CONCEIVABLE PRONUNCIATION OF THESE CHARACTERS, AND STILL THE UNBINDING STONE REMAINS INERT.
HOW IN THE TOAD DEMON'S NAME DO YOU TRIGGER IT?
PERHAPS I CAN HELP...
KRO!
DON'T BE ALARMED, ERESHKIGAL. I COME ALONE AND UNARMED.
YOU SEE, MY SERVICE TO THE PRIESTLORD GHAUR IS NOT QUITE AS UNQUESTIONING AS I WOULD HAVE HIM BELIEVE...
...SO I'VE FOLLOWED YOUR TRAIL MYSELF WHILE SENDING MY SQUADRON ON A WILD GOOSE CHASE.
BUT I'M SURPRISED TO FIND YOU HIDING IN PLAIN SIGHT.
WHY HAVEN'T YOU USED YOUR SHAPE-SHIFTING POWERS TO DISGUISE YOURSELF?
YOU WOULDN'T ASK IF YOU DIDN'T ALREADY KNOW...
...THE STAR BRAND AFFECTED MY CELLULAR STRUCTURE... GALVANIZED IT.
I CAN NO LONGER ALTER MY FORM. I AM FOREVER FIXED IN THIS ONE.
PITY.
AND YES, I DID KNOW. I MAKE IT MY BUSINESS TO KNOW. BUT I WISHED TO SEE WHETHER YOU'D TRY TO LIE TO ME.
I SHOULD LIKE VERY MUCH TO EXAMINE YOU, ANOTHER TIME. BUT FOR THE MOMENT...
...THE TRINKET YOU FLASHED IN GHAUR'S THRONE ROOM INTRIGUES ME. MAY I SEE IT...?
DON'T WORRY...

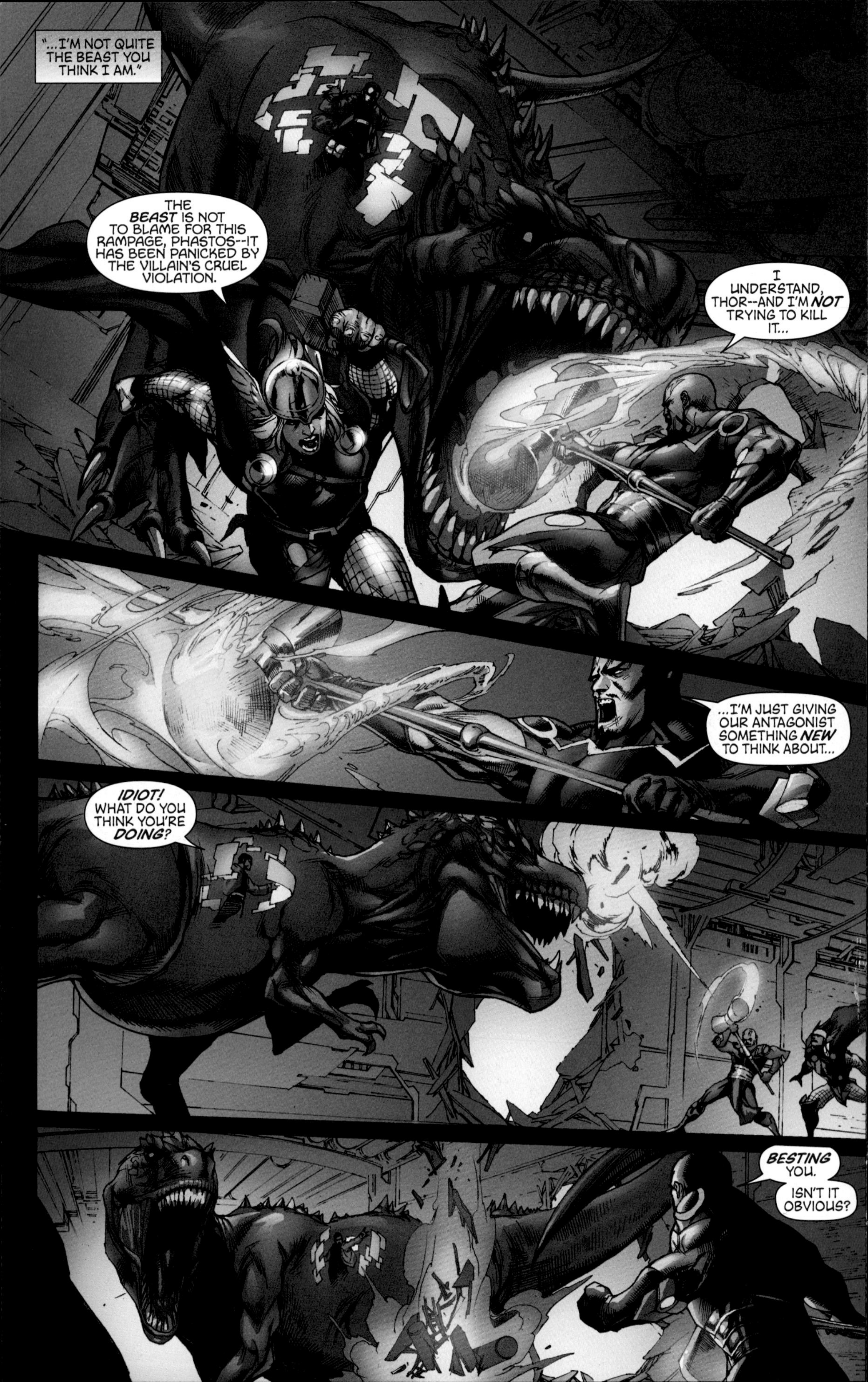
"...I'M NOT QUITE THE BEAST YOU THINK I AM."
THE BEAST IS NOT TO BLAME FOR THIS RAMPAGE, PHASTOS--IT HAS BEEN PANICKED BY THE VILLAIN'S CRUEL VIOLATION.
I UNDERSTAND, THOR--AND I'M NOT TRYING TO KILL IT...
...I'M JUST GIVING OUR ANTAGONIST SOMETHING NEW TO THINK ABOUT...
IDIOT! WHAT DO YOU THINK YOU'RE DOING?
BESTING YOU.
ISN'T IT OBVIOUS?

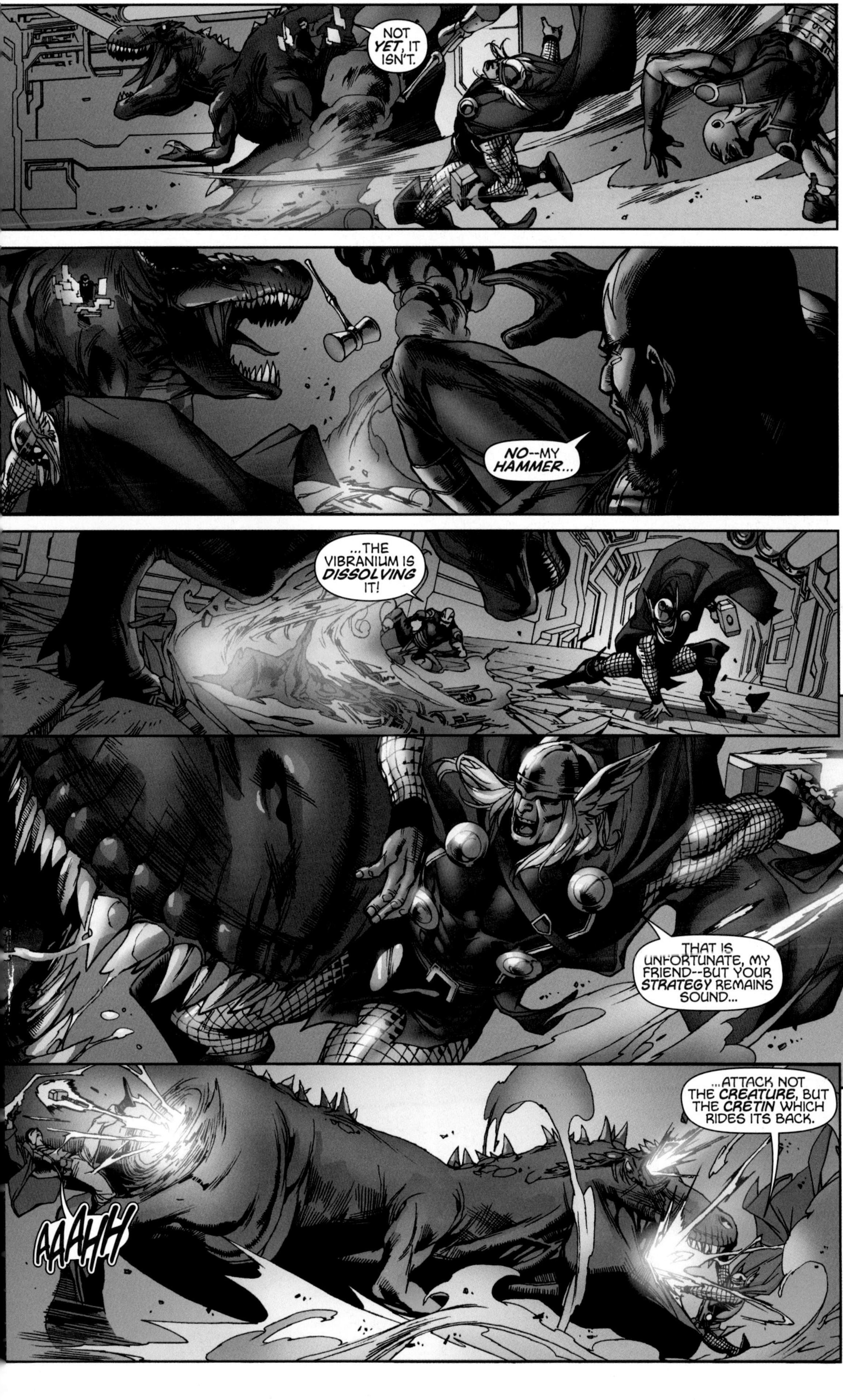
NOT YET, IT ISN'T.
NO--MY HAMMER...
...THE VIBRANIUM IS DISSOLVING IT!
THAT IS UNFORTUNATE, MY FRIEND--BUT YOUR STRATEGY REMAINS SOUND...
...ATTACK NOT THE CREATURE, BUT THE CRETIN WHICH RIDES ITS BACK.
AAAHH

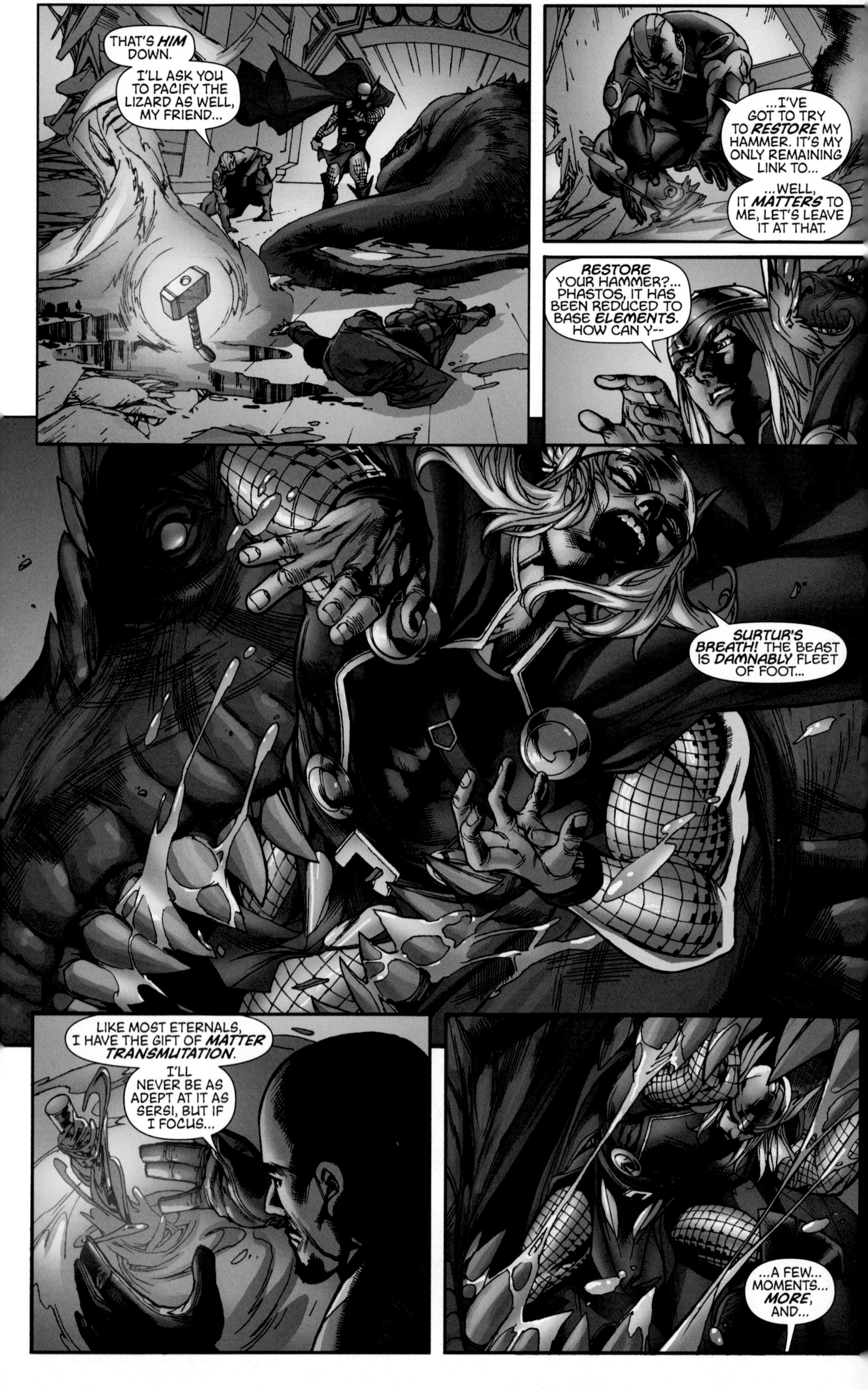
THAT'S HIM DOWN.
I'LL ASK YOU TO PACIFY THE LIZARD AS WELL, MY FRIEND...
...I'VE GOT TO TRY TO RESTORE MY HAMMER. IT'S MY ONLY REMAINING LINK TO...
...WELL, IT MATTERS TO ME, LET'S LEAVE IT AT THAT.
RESTORE YOUR HAMMER?... PHASTOS, IT HAS BEEN REDUCED TO BASE ELEMENTS. HOW CAN Y--
SURTUR'S BREATH! THE BEAST IS DAMNABLY FLEET OF FOOT...
LIKE MOST ETERNALS, I HAVE THE GIFT OF MATTER TRANSMUTATION.
I'LL NEVER BE AS ADEPT AT IT AS SERSI, BUT IF I FOCUS...
...A FEW... MOMENTS... MORE, AND...

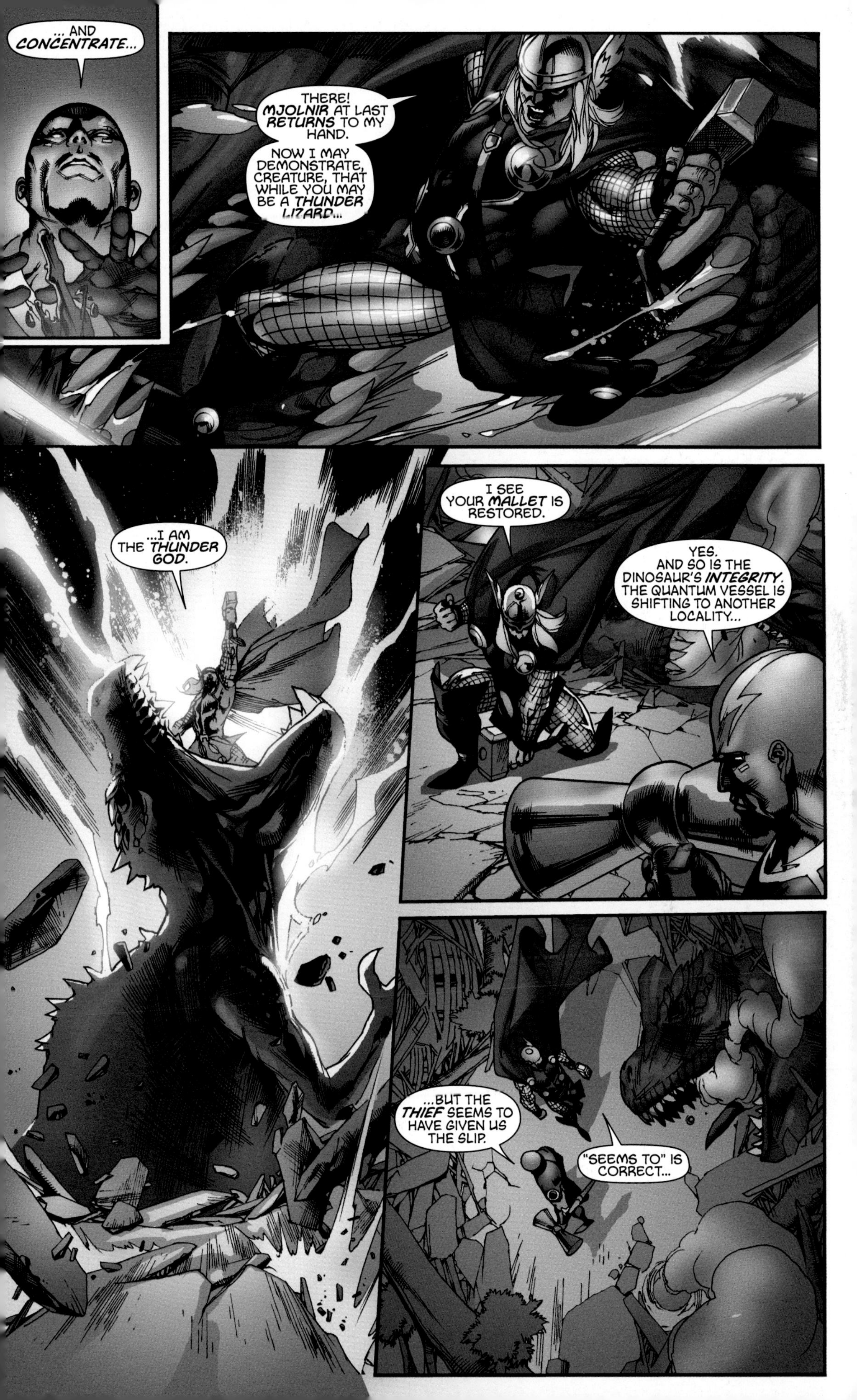
... AND CONCENTRATE...
THERE! MJOLNIR AT LAST RETURNS TO MY HAND.
NOW I MAY DEMONSTRATE, CREATURE, THAT WHILE YOU MAY BE A THUNDER LIZARD...
...I AM THE THUNDER GOD.
I SEE YOUR MALLET IS RESTORED.
YES. AND SO IS THE DINOSAUR'S INTEGRITY. THE QUANTUM VESSEL IS SHIFTING TO ANOTHER LOCALITY...
...BUT THE THIEF SEEMS TO HAVE GIVEN US THE SLIP.
"SEEMS TO" IS CORRECT...

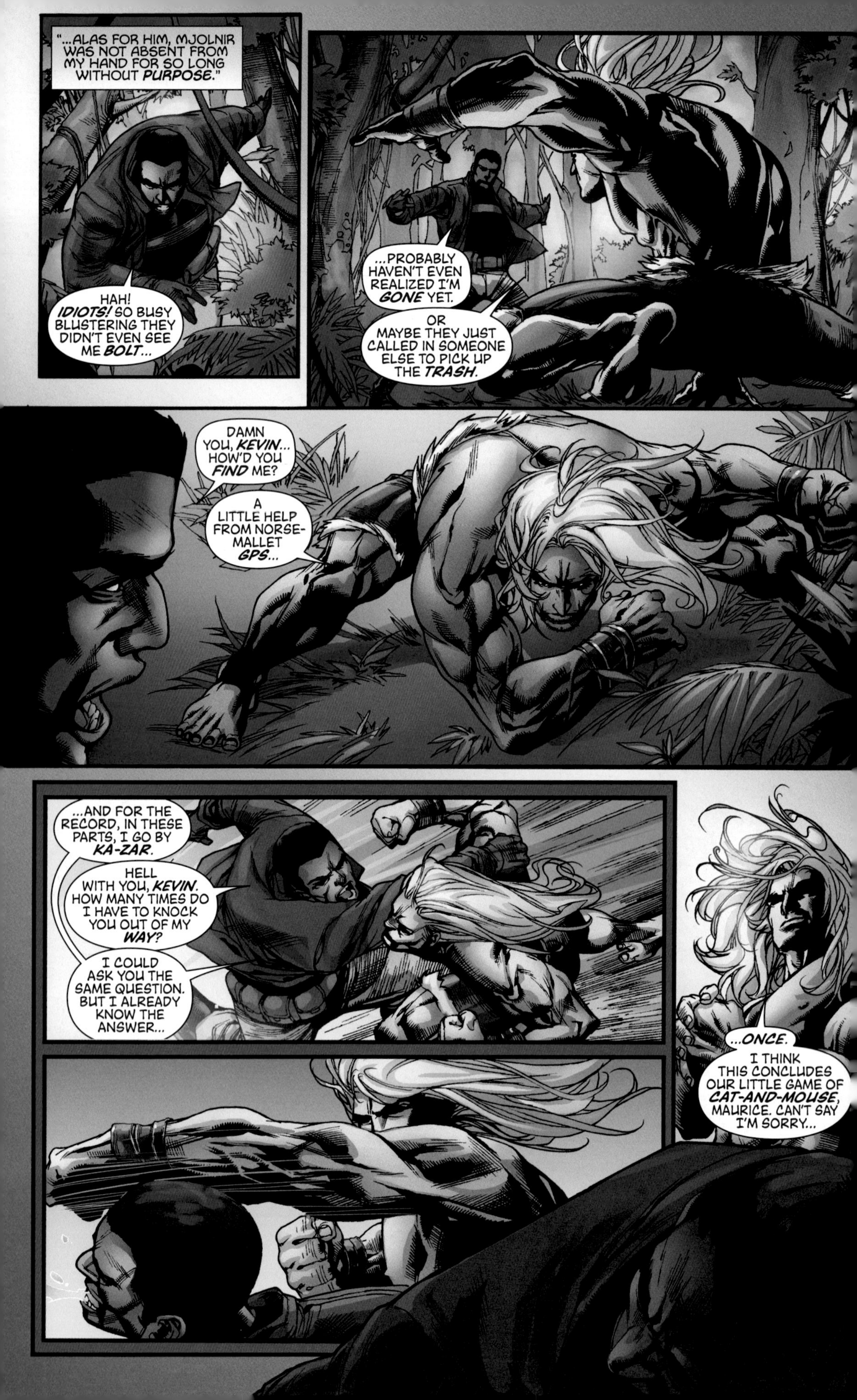
"...ALAS FOR HIM, MJOLNIR WAS NOT ABSENT FROM MY HAND FOR SO LONG WITHOUT *PURPOSE*."
HAH! *IDIOTS!* SO BUSY BLUSTERING THEY DIDN'T EVEN SEE ME *BOLT*...
...PROBABLY HAVEN'T EVEN REALIZED I'M *GONE* YET.
OR MAYBE THEY JUST CALLED IN SOMEONE ELSE TO PICK UP THE *TRASH*.
DAMN YOU, *KEVIN*... HOW'D YOU *FIND* ME?
A LITTLE HELP FROM NORSE-MALLET *GPS*...
...AND FOR THE RECORD, IN THESE PARTS, I GO BY *KA-ZAR*.
HELL WITH YOU, *KEVIN*. HOW MANY TIMES DO I HAVE TO KNOCK YOU OUT OF MY *WAY*?
I COULD ASK YOU THE SAME QUESTION. BUT I ALREADY KNOW THE ANSWER...
...*ONCE*.
I THINK THIS CONCLUDES OUR LITTLE GAME OF *CAT-AND-MOUSE*, MAURICE. CAN'T SAY I'M SORRY...

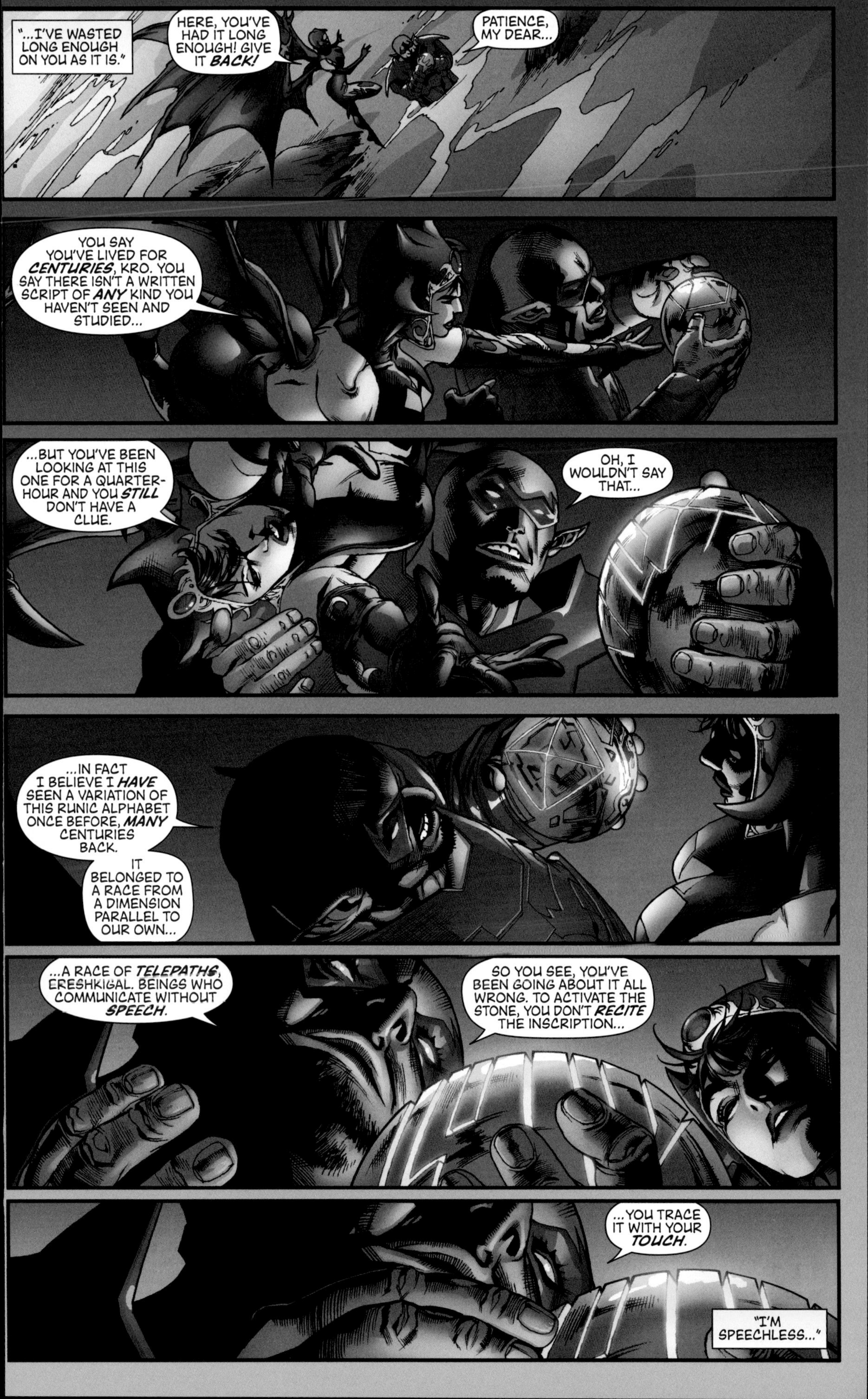
"...I'VE WASTED LONG ENOUGH ON YOU AS IT IS."
HERE, YOU'VE HAD IT LONG ENOUGH! GIVE IT BACK!
PATIENCE, MY DEAR...
YOU SAY YOU'VE LIVED FOR CENTURIES, KRO. YOU SAY THERE ISN'T A WRITTEN SCRIPT OF ANY KIND YOU HAVEN'T SEEN AND STUDIED...
...BUT YOU'VE BEEN LOOKING AT THIS ONE FOR A QUARTER-HOUR AND YOU STILL DON'T HAVE A CLUE.
OH, I WOULDN'T SAY THAT...
...IN FACT I BELIEVE I HAVE SEEN A VARIATION OF THIS RUNIC ALPHABET ONCE BEFORE, MANY CENTURIES BACK.
IT BELONGED TO A RACE FROM A DIMENSION PARALLEL TO OUR OWN...
...A RACE OF TELEPATHS, ERESHKIGAL. BEINGS WHO COMMUNICATE WITHOUT SPEECH.
SO YOU SEE, YOU'VE BEEN GOING ABOUT IT ALL WRONG. TO ACTIVATE THE STONE, YOU DON'T RECITE THE INSCRIPTION...
...YOU TRACE IT WITH YOUR TOUCH.
"I'M SPEECHLESS..."

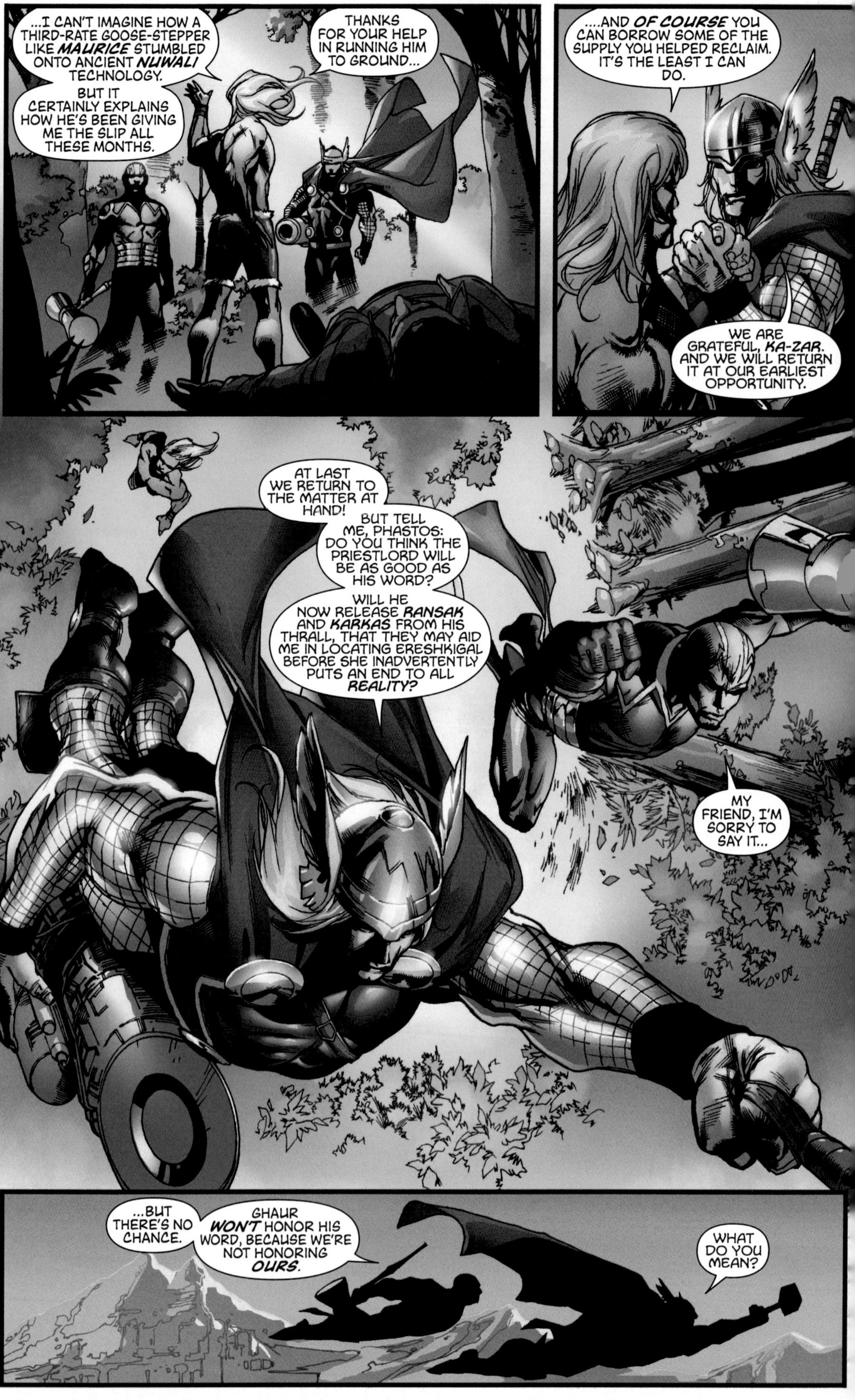

...I CAN'T IMAGINE HOW A THIRD-RATE GOOSE-STEPPER LIKE MAURICE STUMBLED ONTO ANCIENT NUWALI TECHNOLOGY.
BUT IT CERTAINLY EXPLAINS HOW HE'S BEEN GIVING ME THE SLIP ALL THESE MONTHS.
THANKS FOR YOUR HELP IN RUNNING HIM TO GROUND...
....AND OF COURSE YOU CAN BORROW SOME OF THE SUPPLY YOU HELPED RECLAIM. IT'S THE LEAST I CAN DO.
WE ARE GRATEFUL, KA-ZAR. AND WE WILL RETURN IT AT OUR EARLIEST OPPORTUNITY.
AT LAST WE RETURN TO THE MATTER AT HAND!
BUT TELL ME, PHASTOS: DO YOU THINK THE PRIESTLORD WILL BE AS GOOD AS HIS WORD?
WILL HE NOW RELEASE RANSAK AND KARKAS FROM HIS THRALL, THAT THEY MAY AID ME IN LOCATING ERESHKIGAL BEFORE SHE INADVERTENTLY PUTS AN END TO ALL REALITY?
MY FRIEND, I'M SORRY TO SAY IT...
...BUT THERE'S NO CHANCE.
GHAUR WON'T HONOR HIS WORD, BECAUSE WE'RE NOT HONORING OURS.
WHAT DO YOU MEAN?

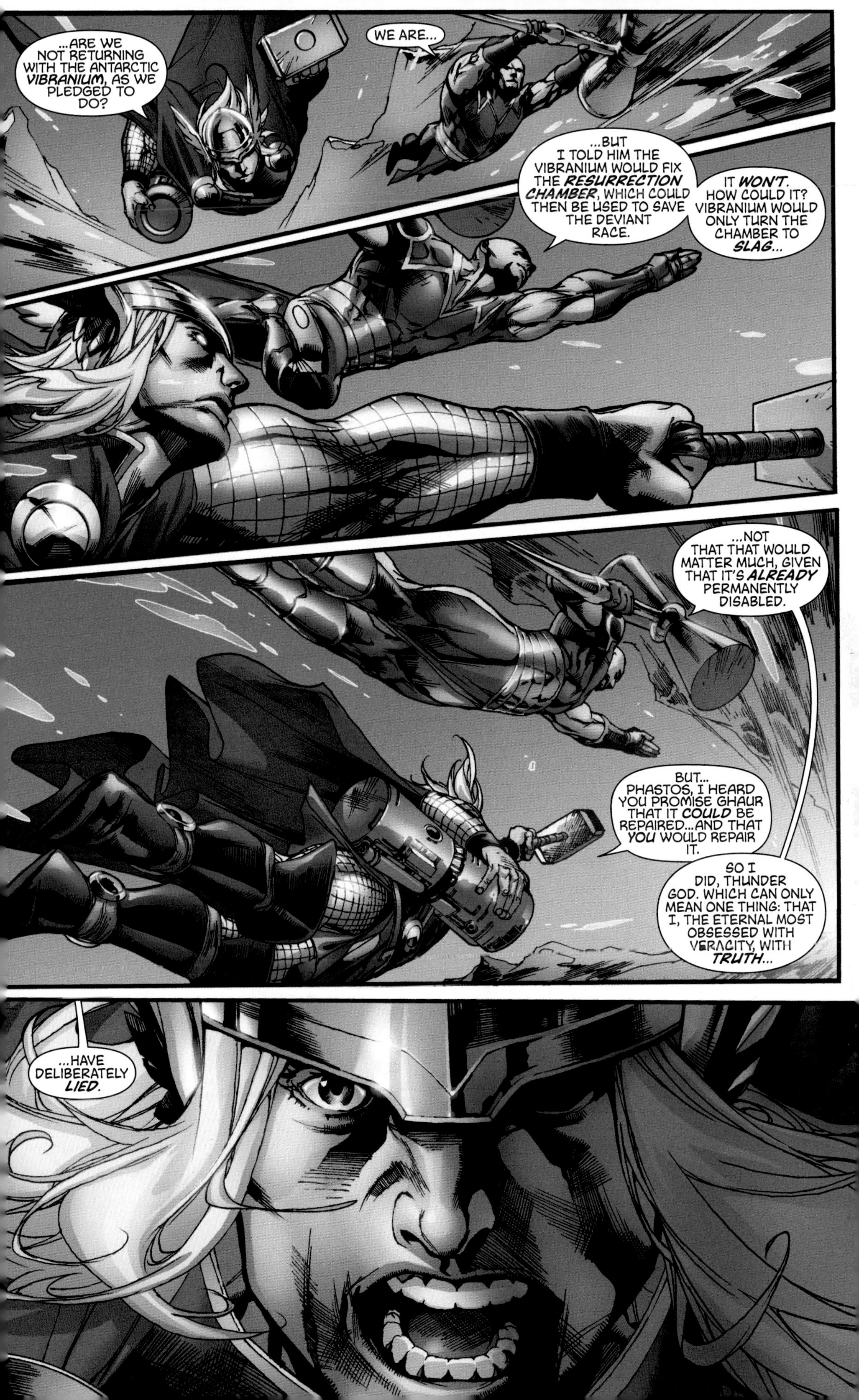
...ARE WE NOT RETURNING WITH THE ANTARCTIC VIBRANIUM, AS WE PLEDGED TO DO?
WE ARE...
...BUT I TOLD HIM THE VIBRANIUM WOULD FIX THE RESURRECTION CHAMBER, WHICH COULD THEN BE USED TO SAVE THE DEVIANT RACE.
IT WON'T. HOW COULD IT? VIBRANIUM WOULD ONLY TURN THE CHAMBER TO SLAG...
...NOT THAT THAT WOULD MATTER MUCH, GIVEN THAT IT'S ALREADY PERMANENTLY DISABLED.
BUT... PHASTOS, I HEARD YOU PROMISE GHAUR THAT IT COULD BE REPAIRED...AND THAT YOU WOULD REPAIR IT.
SO I DID, THUNDER GOD. WHICH CAN ONLY MEAN ONE THING: THAT I, THE ETERNAL MOST OBSESSED WITH VERACITY, WITH TRUTH...
...HAVE DELIBERATELY LIED.

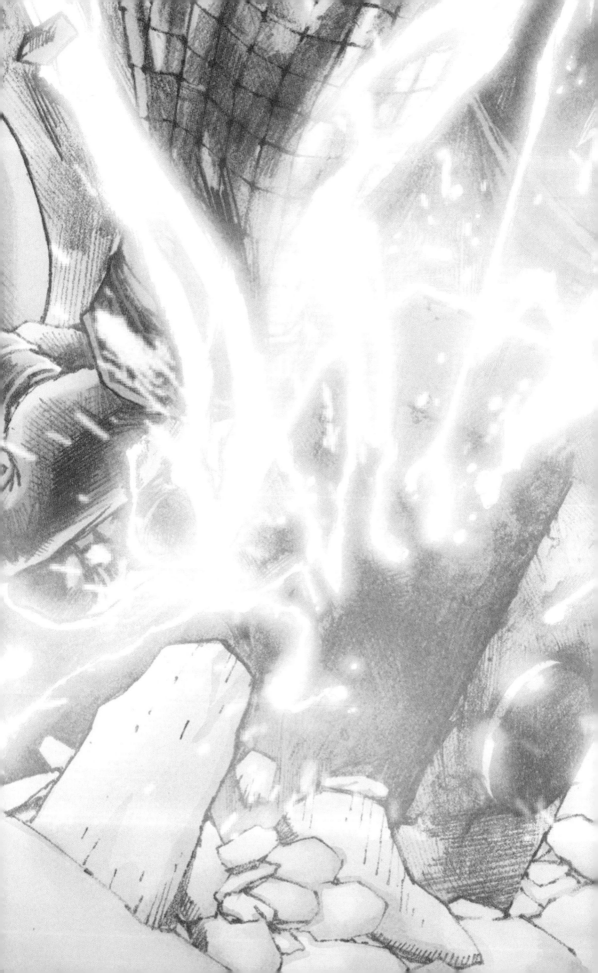

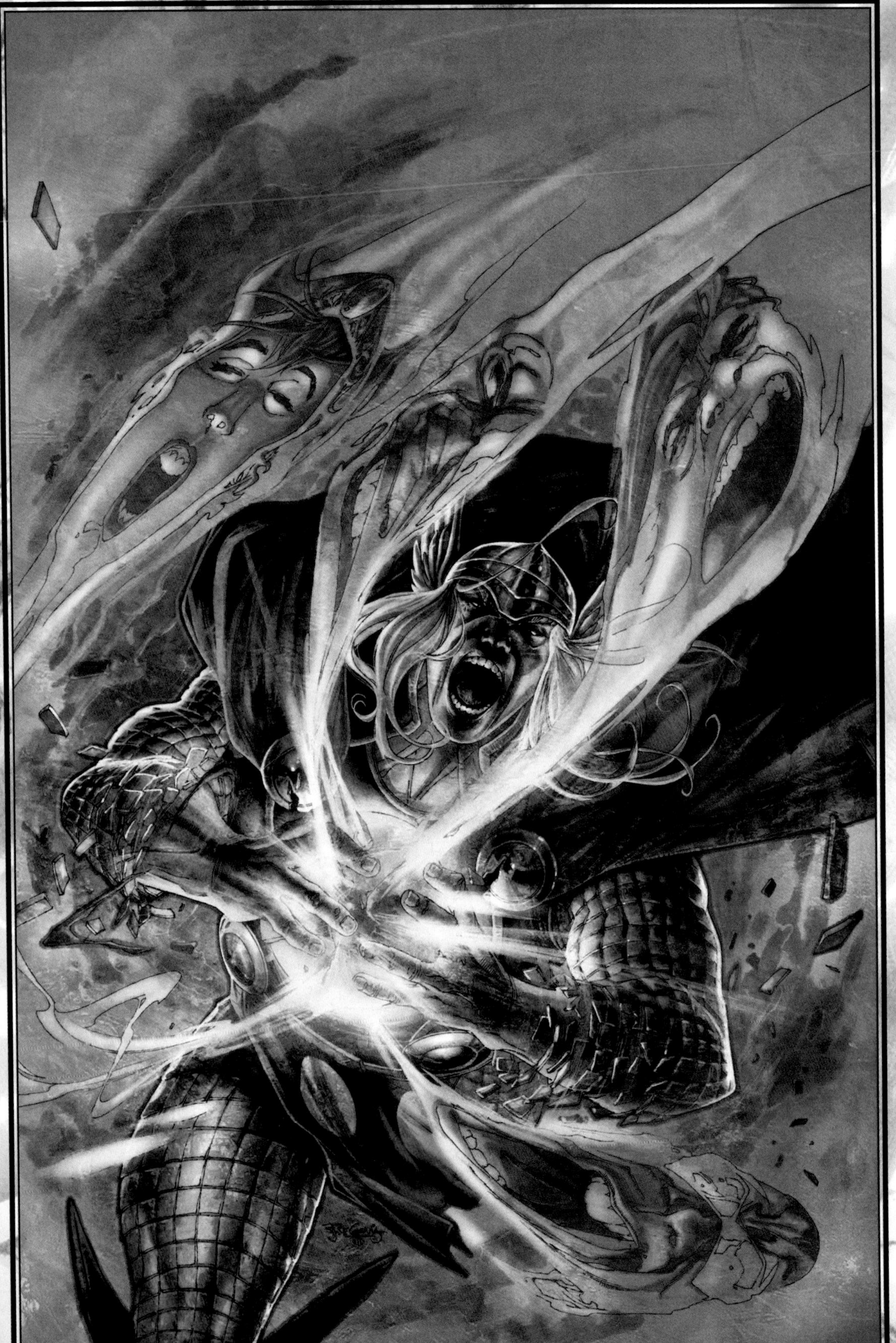

FIVE

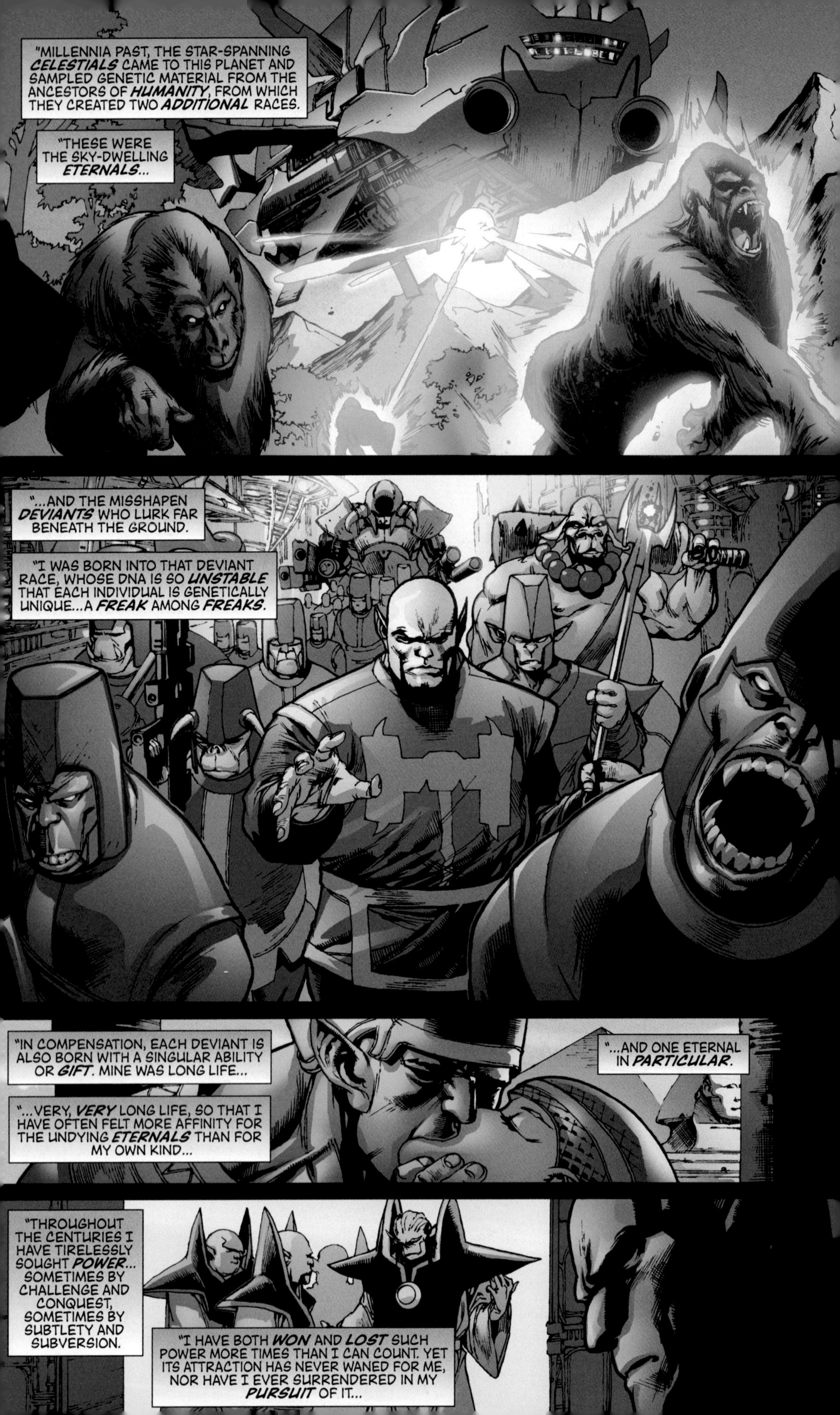
"MILLENNIA PAST, THE STAR-SPANNING CELESTIALS CAME TO THIS PLANET AND SAMPLED GENETIC MATERIAL FROM THE ANCESTORS OF HUMANITY, FROM WHICH THEY CREATED TWO ADDITIONAL RACES.
"THESE WERE THE SKY-DWELLING ETERNALS...
"...AND THE MISSHAPEN DEVIANTS WHO LURK FAR BENEATH THE GROUND.
"I WAS BORN INTO THAT DEVIANT RACE, WHOSE DNA IS SO UNSTABLE THAT EACH INDIVIDUAL IS GENETICALLY UNIQUE...A FREAK AMONG FREAKS.
"IN COMPENSATION, EACH DEVIANT IS ALSO BORN WITH A SINGULAR ABILITY OR GIFT. MINE WAS LONG LIFE...
"...VERY, VERY LONG LIFE, SO THAT I HAVE OFTEN FELT MORE AFFINITY FOR THE UNDYING ETERNALS THAN FOR MY OWN KIND...
"...AND ONE ETERNAL IN PARTICULAR.
"THROUGHOUT THE CENTURIES I HAVE TIRELESSLY SOUGHT POWER... SOMETIMES BY CHALLENGE AND CONQUEST, SOMETIMES BY SUBTLETY AND SUBVERSION.
"I HAVE BOTH WON AND LOST SUCH POWER MORE TIMES THAN I CAN COUNT. YET ITS ATTRACTION HAS NEVER WANED FOR ME, NOR HAVE I EVER SURRENDERED IN MY PURSUIT OF IT...

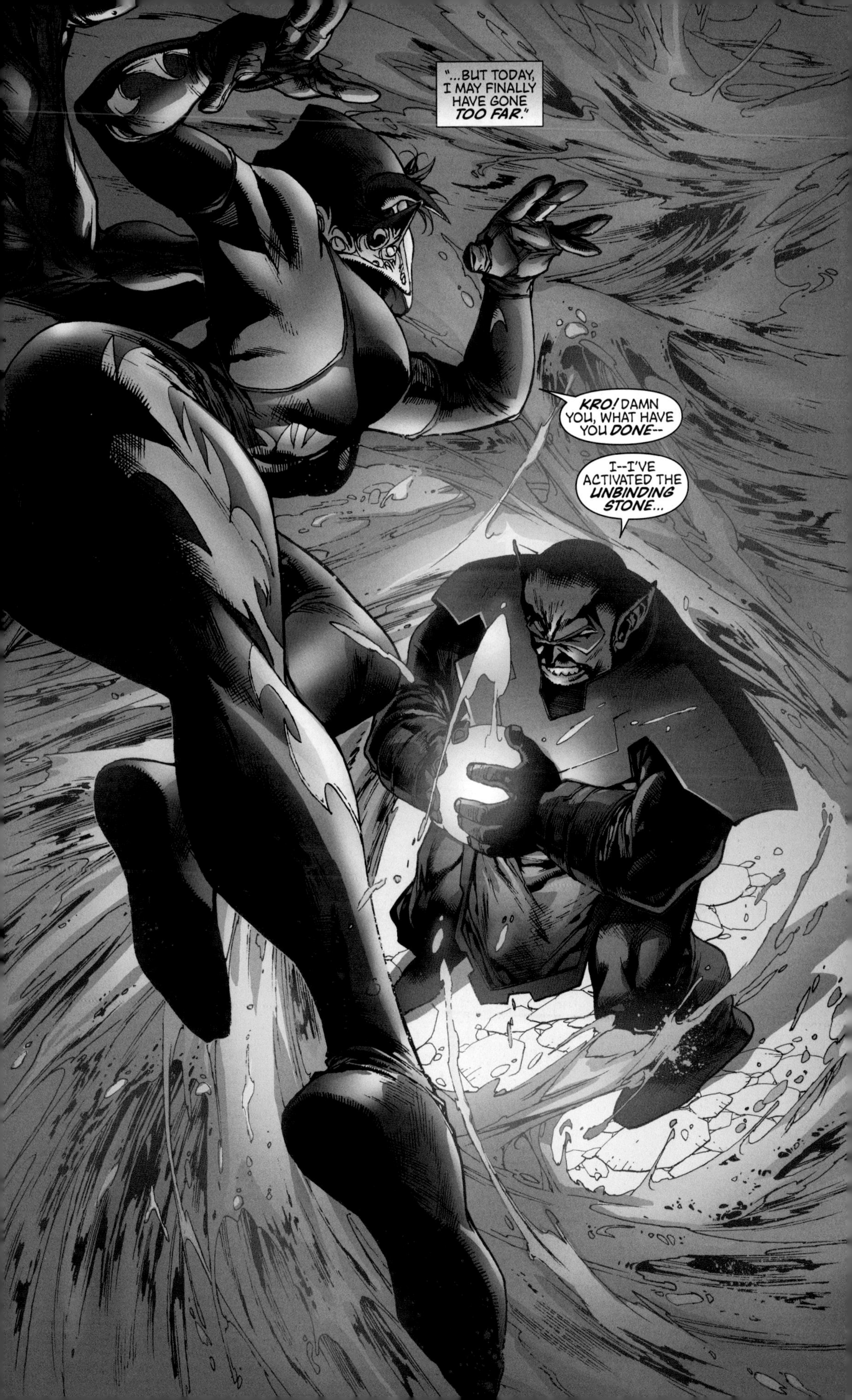
"...BUT TODAY, I MAY FINALLY HAVE GONE TOO FAR."
KRO! DAMN YOU, WHAT HAVE YOU DONE--
I--I'VE ACTIVATED THE UNBINDING STONE...

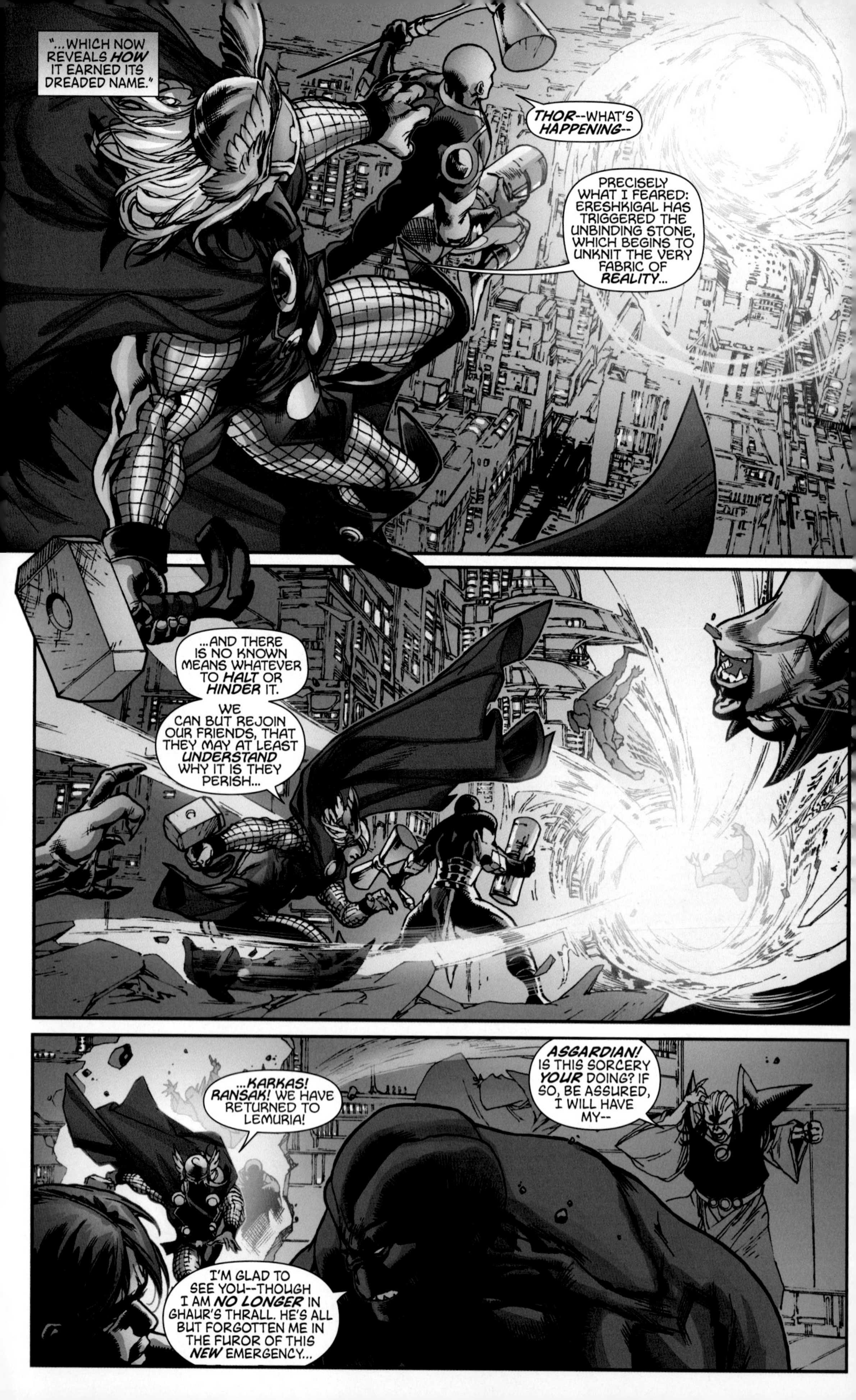
"...WHICH NOW REVEALS *HOW* IT EARNED ITS DREADED NAME."
THOR--WHAT'S *HAPPENING*--
PRECISELY WHAT I FEARED: ERESHKIGAL HAS TRIGGERED THE UNBINDING STONE, WHICH BEGINS TO UNKNIT THE VERY FABRIC OF *REALITY*...
...AND THERE IS NO KNOWN MEANS WHATEVER TO *HALT* OR *HINDER* IT.
WE CAN BUT REJOIN OUR FRIENDS, THAT THEY MAY AT LEAST *UNDERSTAND* WHY IT IS THEY PERISH...
...*KARKAS! RANSAK!* WE HAVE RETURNED TO LEMURIA!
ASGARDIAN! IS THIS SORCERY *YOUR* DOING? IF SO, BE ASSURED, I WILL HAVE MY--
I'M GLAD TO SEE YOU--THOUGH I AM *NO LONGER* IN GHAUR'S THRALL. HE'S ALL BUT FORGOTTEN ME IN THE FUROR OF THIS *NEW* EMERGENCY...

--REVENNNNNGE

STAY *CLOSE*-- OR WE'LL BE PULLED *APART*--

THAT WILL HAPPEN IN *ANY* CASE, PHASTOS...

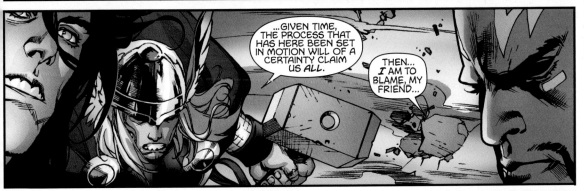

...GIVEN TIME, THE PROCESS THAT HAS HERE BEEN SET IN MOTION WILL OF A CERTAINTY CLAIM US *ALL.*

THEN... *I* AM TO BLAME, MY FRIEND...

...BECAUSE I HOLD IN MY HANDS THE MEANS BY WHICH WE MIGHT HAVE *PREVENTED* IT, IF I'D ONLY LISTENED TO YOU AND MADE *HASTE.*

WHAT ARE YOU SAYING, PHASTOS? OUR MISSION TO OBTAIN THE *VIBRANIUM*...THAT WAS *NOT* A FOOL'S ERRAND?

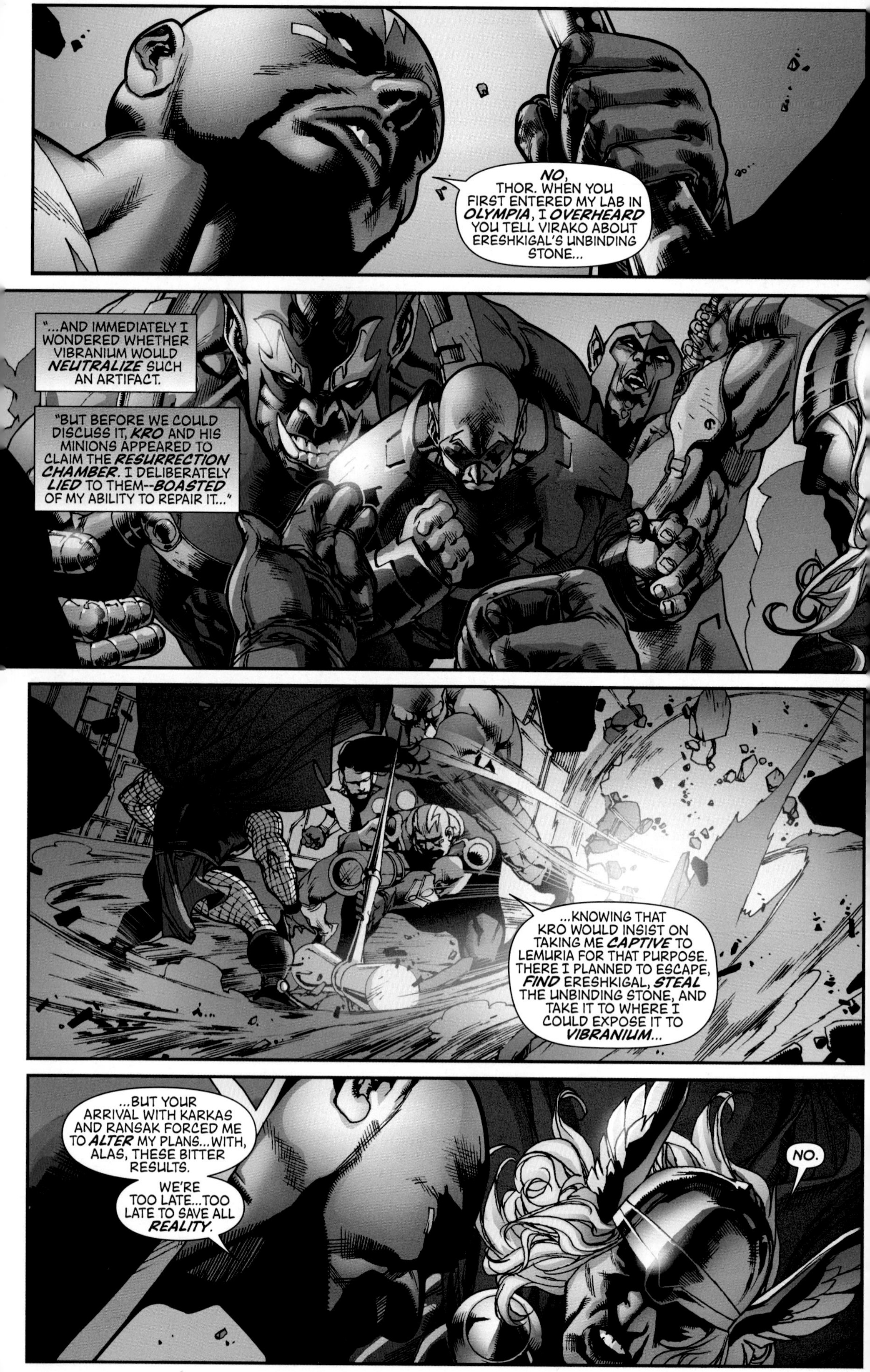
NO, THOR. WHEN YOU FIRST ENTERED MY LAB IN OLYMPIA, I OVERHEARD YOU TELL VIRAKO ABOUT ERESHKIGAL'S UNBINDING STONE...
"...AND IMMEDIATELY I WONDERED WHETHER VIBRANIUM WOULD NEUTRALIZE SUCH AN ARTIFACT.
"BUT BEFORE WE COULD DISCUSS IT, KRO AND HIS MINIONS APPEARED TO CLAIM THE RESURRECTION CHAMBER. I DELIBERATELY LIED TO THEM--BOASTED OF MY ABILITY TO REPAIR IT..."
...KNOWING THAT KRO WOULD INSIST ON TAKING ME CAPTIVE TO LEMURIA FOR THAT PURPOSE. THERE I PLANNED TO ESCAPE, FIND ERESHKIGAL, STEAL THE UNBINDING STONE, AND TAKE IT TO WHERE I COULD EXPOSE IT TO VIBRANIUM...
...BUT YOUR ARRIVAL WITH KARKAS AND RANSAK FORCED ME TO ALTER MY PLANS...WITH, ALAS, THESE BITTER RESULTS.
WE'RE TOO LATE...TOO LATE TO SAVE ALL REALITY.
NO.

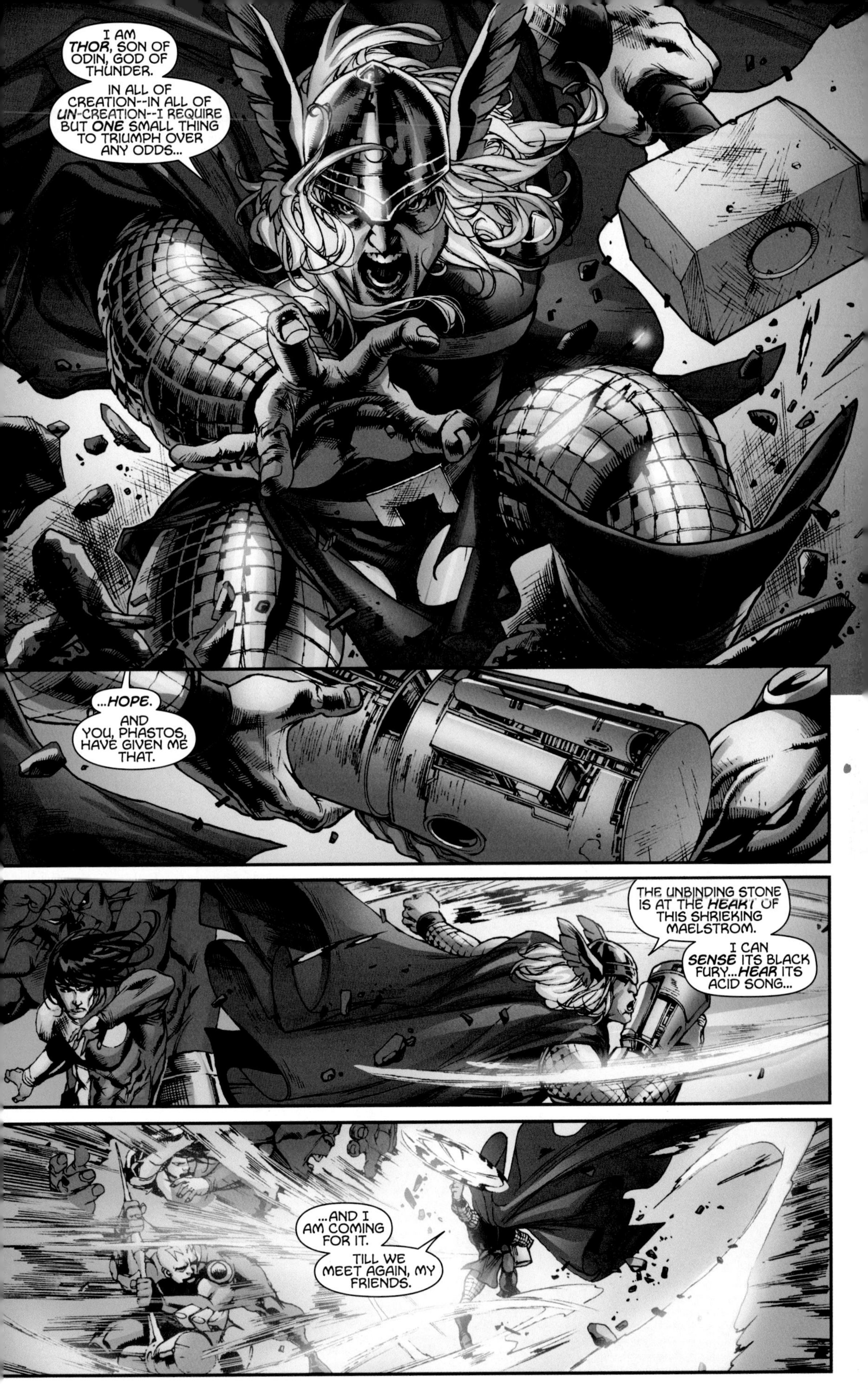
I AM THOR, SON OF ODIN, GOD OF THUNDER.
IN ALL OF CREATION--IN ALL OF UN-CREATION--I REQUIRE BUT ONE SMALL THING TO TRIUMPH OVER ANY ODDS...
...HOPE.
AND YOU, PHASTOS, HAVE GIVEN ME THAT.
THE UNBINDING STONE IS AT THE HEART OF THIS SHRIEKING MAELSTROM.
I CAN SENSE ITS BLACK FURY...HEAR ITS ACID SONG...
...AND I AM COMING FOR IT.
TILL WE MEET AGAIN, MY FRIENDS.

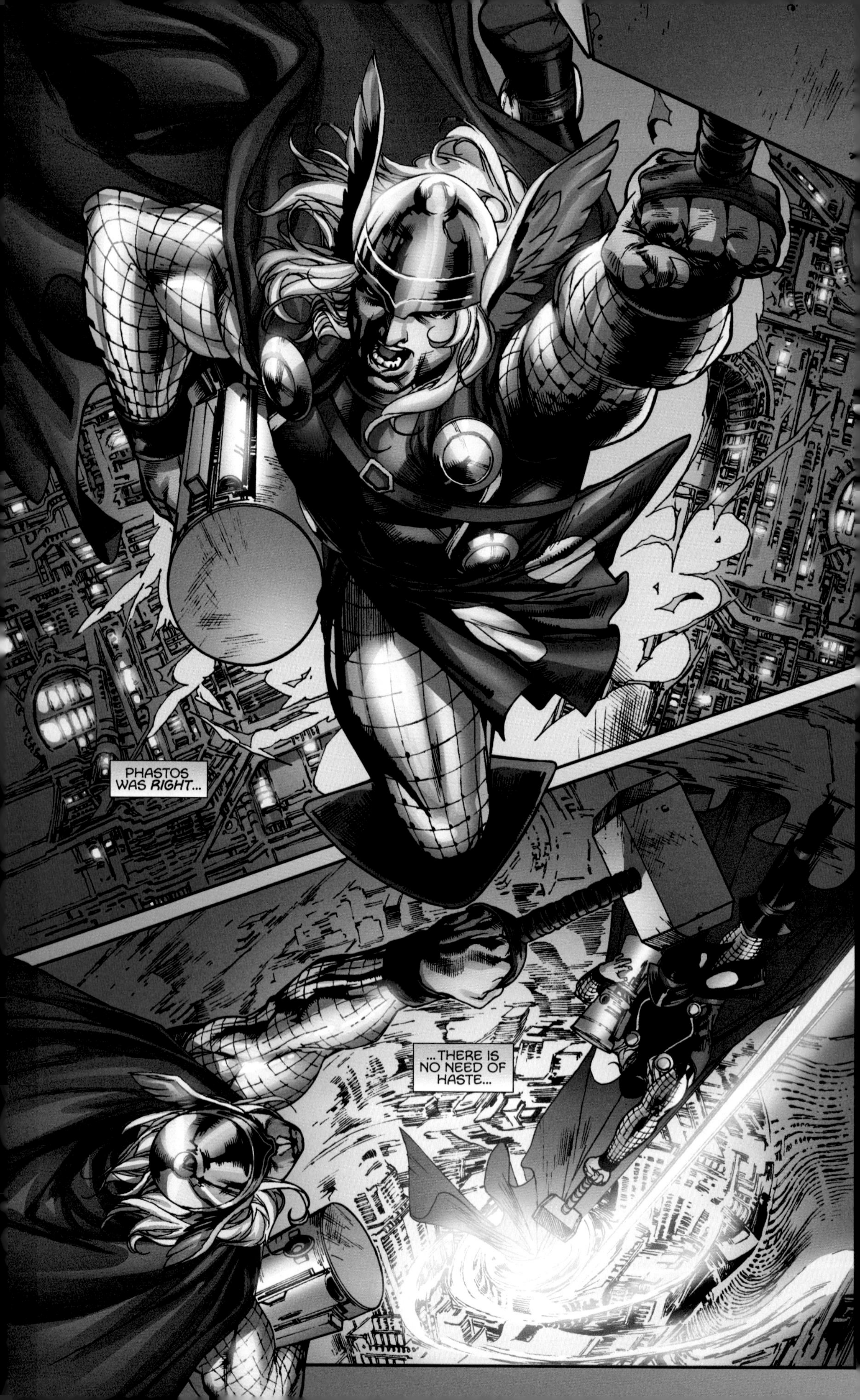
PHASTOS WAS RIGHT...
...THERE IS NO NEED OF HASTE...

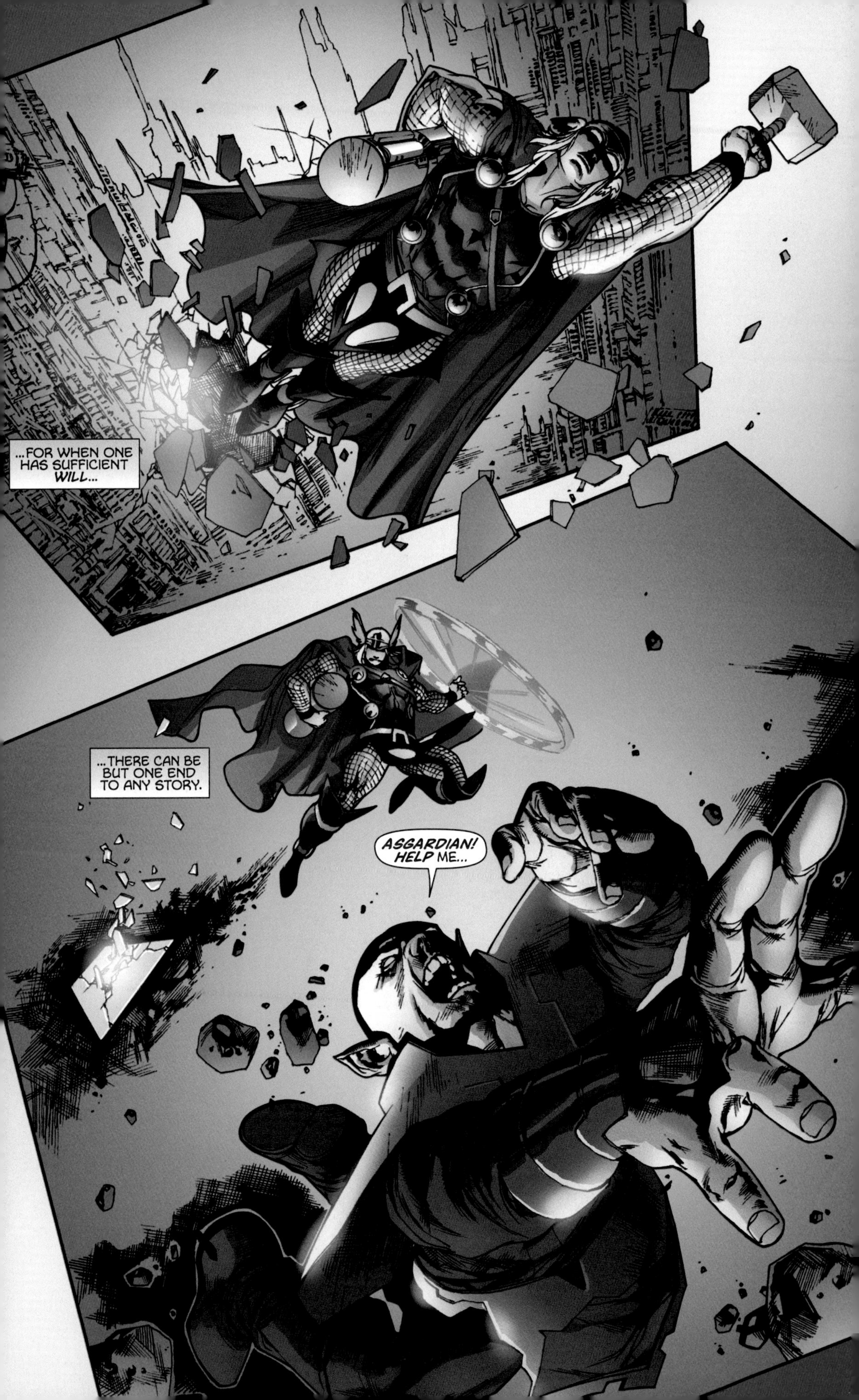
...FOR WHEN ONE HAS SUFFICIENT WILL...
...THERE CAN BE BUT ONE END TO ANY STORY.
ASGARDIAN! HELP ME...

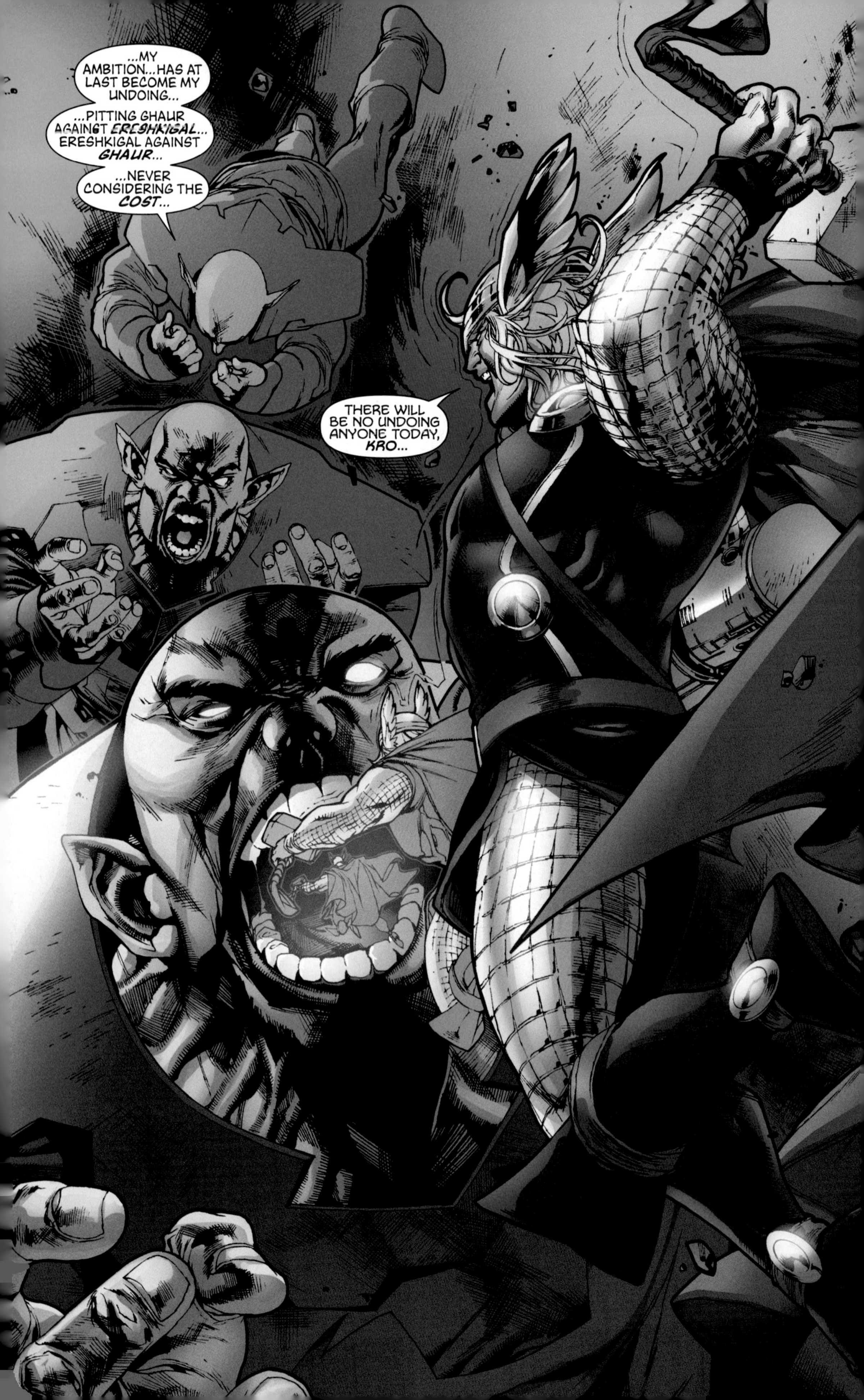
...MY AMBITION...HAS AT LAST BECOME MY UNDOING...
...PITTING GHAUR AGAINST EREȘHKIGAL... EREȘHKIGAL AGAINST GHAUR...
...NEVER CONSIDERING THE COST...
THERE WILL BE NO UNDOING ANYONE TODAY, KRO...

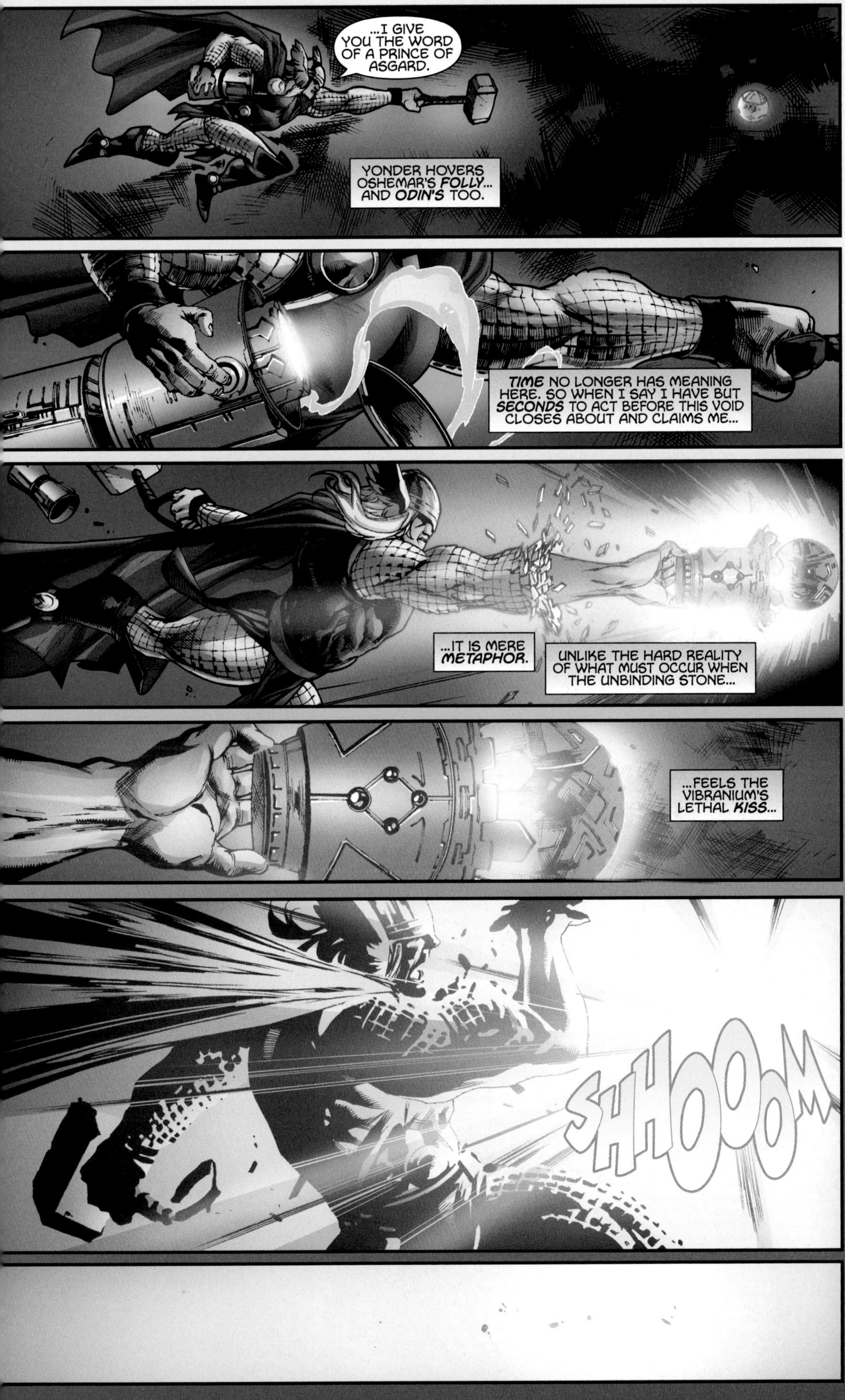
...I GIVE YOU THE WORD OF A PRINCE OF ASGARD.
YONDER HOVERS OSHEMAR'S FOLLY... AND ODIN'S TOO.
TIME NO LONGER HAS MEANING HERE. SO WHEN I SAY I HAVE BUT SECONDS TO ACT BEFORE THIS VOID CLOSES ABOUT AND CLAIMS ME...
...IT IS MERE METAPHOR.
UNLIKE THE HARD REALITY OF WHAT MUST OCCUR WHEN THE UNBINDING STONE...
...FEELS THE VIBRANIUM'S LETHAL KISS...
SHHOOOM

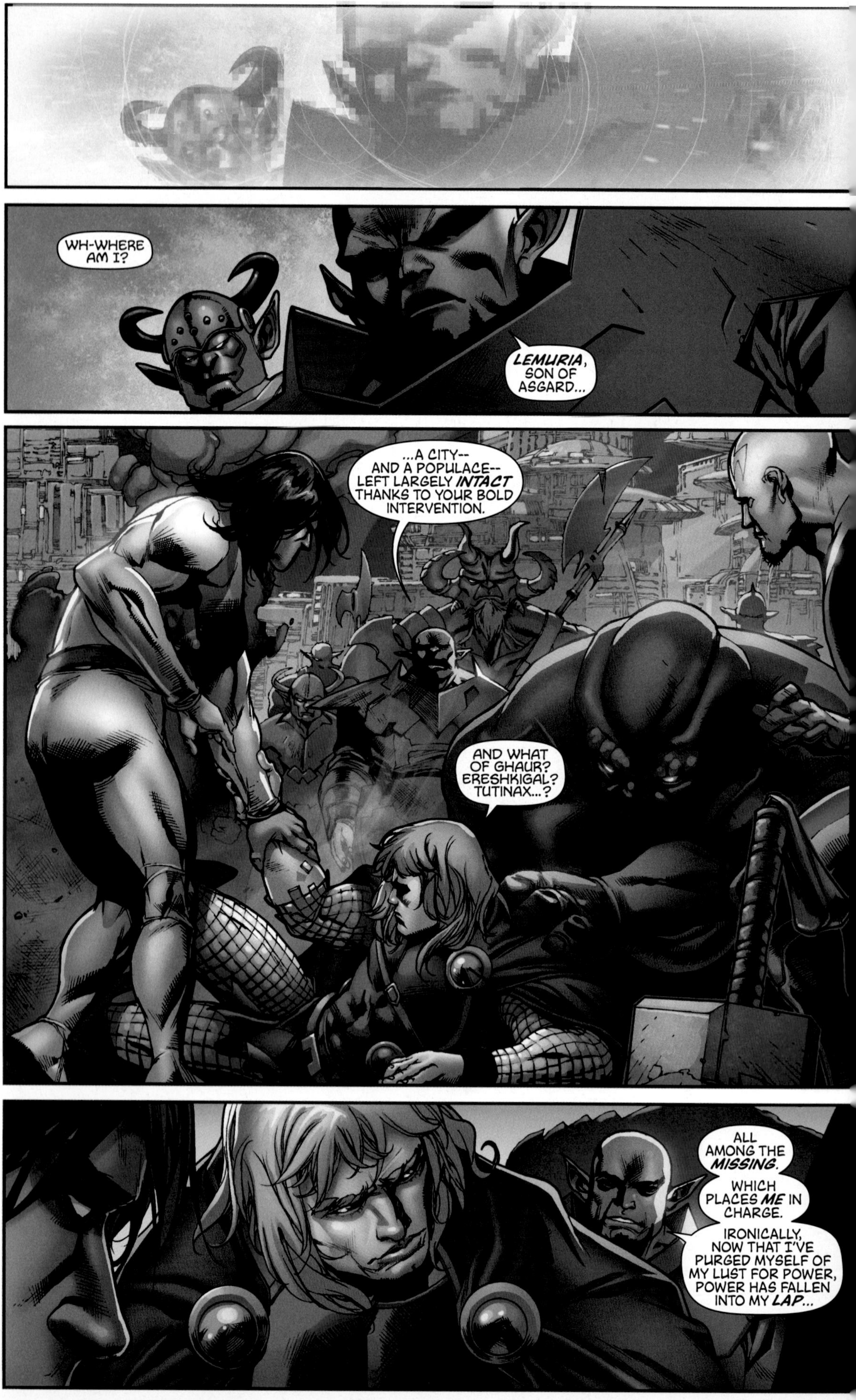
WH-WHERE AM I?
LEMURIA, SON OF ASGARD...
...A CITY-- AND A POPULACE-- LEFT LARGELY INTACT THANKS TO YOUR BOLD INTERVENTION.
AND WHAT OF GHAUR? ERESHKIGAL? TUTINAX...?
ALL AMONG THE MISSING.
WHICH PLACES ME IN CHARGE.
IRONICALLY, NOW THAT I'VE PURGED MYSELF OF MY LUST FOR POWER, POWER HAS FALLEN INTO MY LAP...

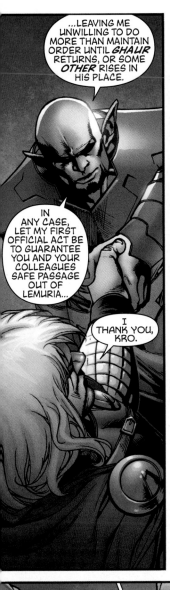

...LEAVING ME UNWILLING TO DO MORE THAN MAINTAIN ORDER UNTIL *GHAUR* RETURNS, OR SOME *OTHER* RISES IN HIS PLACE.

IN ANY CASE, LET MY FIRST OFFICIAL ACT BE TO GUARANTEE YOU AND YOUR COLLEAGUES SAFE PASSAGE OUT OF LEMURIA...

I THANK YOU, KRO.

...WITH THE EXCEPTION OF *RANSAK.*

WHAT?-- *ME?*--WHY AM I SINGLED OUT FOR DETENTION?

BECAUSE YOU'RE A DEVIANT...

...THE *ONLY* DEVIANT MALE STILL LIVING WHO HASN'T BEEN RENDERED *STERILE* BY THE PLAGUE.

IT IS YOUR DUTY TO STAY AND *REPOPULATE* THE DEVIANT RACE... SAVE US FROM *EXTINCTION*...

...AND SINCE YOUR DNA IS UNIQUELY *STABLE,* YOU WILL *GALVANIZE* OUR UNRULY GENETIC STOCK--CREATE A NEW GENERATION OF *SUPER-DEVIANTS.*

NO--I REFUSE. THE IDEA IS *DISGUSTING.*

I AM RANSAK THE *REJECT*--CREATED FOR THE *BATTLE-FIELD,* NOT THE *BOUDOIR.*

YOU DON'T UNDERSTAND. I'M NOT OFFERING YOU A *CHOICE.*

THAT IS UNFORTUNATE, KRO...FOR IT BRINGS YOU INTO OPPOSITION TO *ME.*

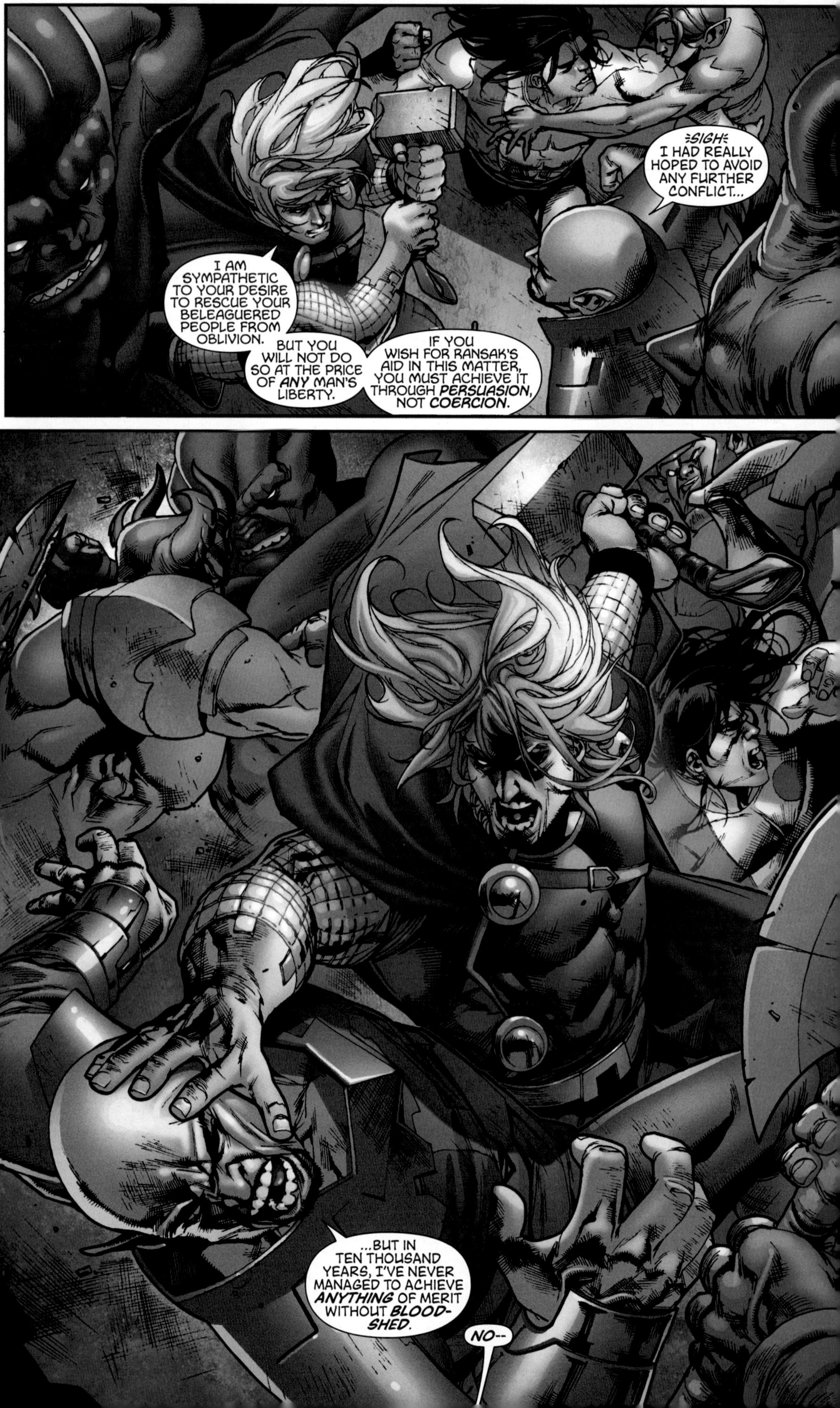
I AM SYMPATHETIC TO YOUR DESIRE TO RESCUE YOUR BELEAGUERED PEOPLE FROM OBLIVION.
BUT YOU WILL NOT DO SO AT THE PRICE OF ANY MAN'S LIBERTY.
IF YOU WISH FOR RANSAK'S AID IN THIS MATTER, YOU MUST ACHIEVE IT THROUGH PERSUASION, NOT COERCION.
≈SIGH≈ I HAD REALLY HOPED TO AVOID ANY FURTHER CONFLICT...
...BUT IN TEN THOUSAND YEARS, I'VE NEVER MANAGED TO ACHIEVE ANYTHING OF MERIT WITHOUT BLOOD-SHED.
NO--

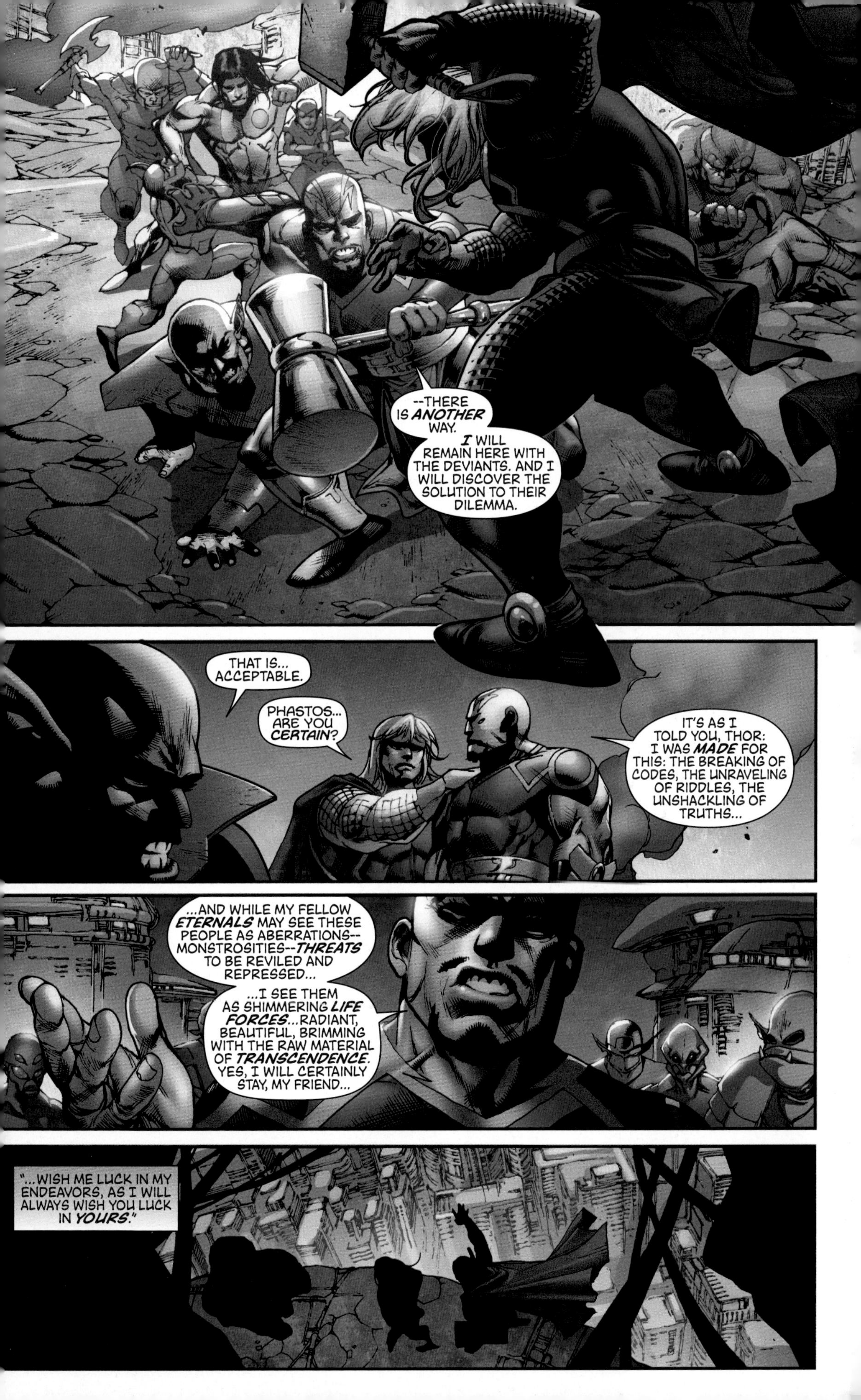
--THERE IS ANOTHER WAY.
I WILL REMAIN HERE WITH THE DEVIANTS. AND I WILL DISCOVER THE SOLUTION TO THEIR DILEMMA.
THAT IS... ACCEPTABLE.
PHASTOS... ARE YOU CERTAIN?
IT'S AS I TOLD YOU, THOR: I WAS MADE FOR THIS: THE BREAKING OF CODES, THE UNRAVELING OF RIDDLES, THE UNSHACKLING OF TRUTHS...
...AND WHILE MY FELLOW ETERNALS MAY SEE THESE PEOPLE AS ABERRATIONS--MONSTROSITIES--THREATS TO BE REVILED AND REPRESSED...
...I SEE THEM AS SHIMMERING LIFE FORCES...RADIANT, BEAUTIFUL, BRIMMING WITH THE RAW MATERIAL OF TRANSCENDENCE. YES, I WILL CERTAINLY STAY, MY FRIEND...
"...WISH ME LUCK IN MY ENDEAVORS, AS I WILL ALWAYS WISH YOU LUCK IN YOURS."

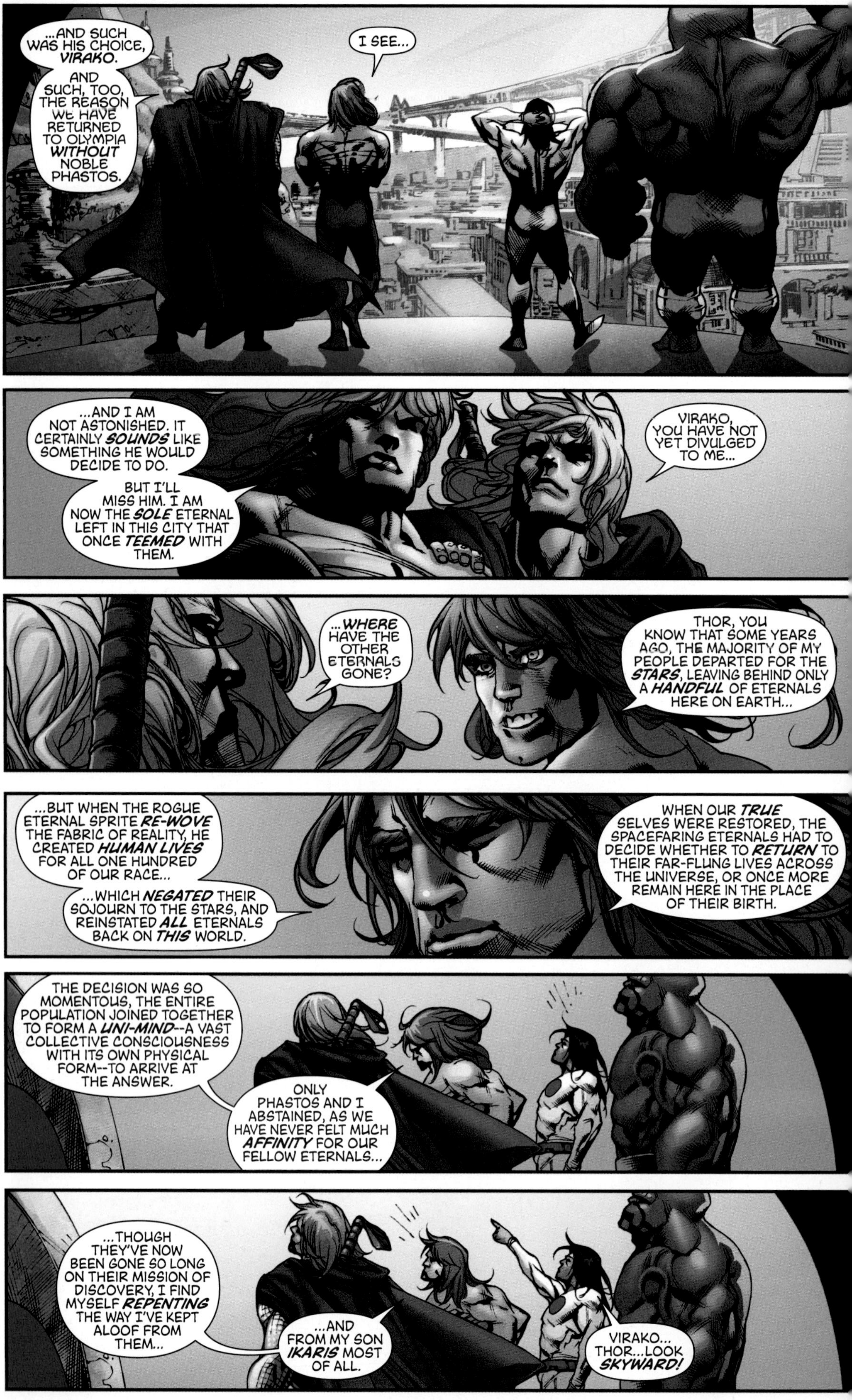
...AND SUCH WAS HIS CHOICE, VIRAKO.
AND SUCH, TOO, THE REASON WE HAVE RETURNED TO OLYMPIA WITHOUT NOBLE PHASTOS.
I SEE...
...AND I AM NOT ASTONISHED. IT CERTAINLY SOUNDS LIKE SOMETHING HE WOULD DECIDE TO DO.
BUT I'LL MISS HIM. I AM NOW THE SOLE ETERNAL LEFT IN THIS CITY THAT ONCE TEEMED WITH THEM.
VIRAKO, YOU HAVE NOT YET DIVULGED TO ME...
...WHERE HAVE THE OTHER ETERNALS GONE?
THOR, YOU KNOW THAT SOME YEARS AGO, THE MAJORITY OF MY PEOPLE DEPARTED FOR THE STARS, LEAVING BEHIND ONLY A HANDFUL OF ETERNALS HERE ON EARTH...
...BUT WHEN THE ROGUE ETERNAL SPRITE RE-WOVE THE FABRIC OF REALITY, HE CREATED HUMAN LIVES FOR ALL ONE HUNDRED OF OUR RACE...
...WHICH NEGATED THEIR SOJOURN TO THE STARS, AND REINSTATED ALL ETERNALS BACK ON THIS WORLD.
WHEN OUR TRUE SELVES WERE RESTORED, THE SPACEFARING ETERNALS HAD TO DECIDE WHETHER TO RETURN TO THEIR FAR-FLUNG LIVES ACROSS THE UNIVERSE, OR ONCE MORE REMAIN HERE IN THE PLACE OF THEIR BIRTH.
THE DECISION WAS SO MOMENTOUS, THE ENTIRE POPULATION JOINED TOGETHER TO FORM A UNI-MIND--A VAST COLLECTIVE CONSCIOUSNESS WITH ITS OWN PHYSICAL FORM--TO ARRIVE AT THE ANSWER.
ONLY PHASTOS AND I ABSTAINED, AS WE HAVE NEVER FELT MUCH AFFINITY FOR OUR FELLOW ETERNALS...
...THOUGH THEY'VE NOW BEEN GONE SO LONG ON THEIR MISSION OF DISCOVERY, I FIND MYSELF REPENTING THE WAY I'VE KEPT ALOOF FROM THEM...
...AND FROM MY SON IKARIS MOST OF ALL.
VIRAKO... THOR...LOOK SKYWARD!

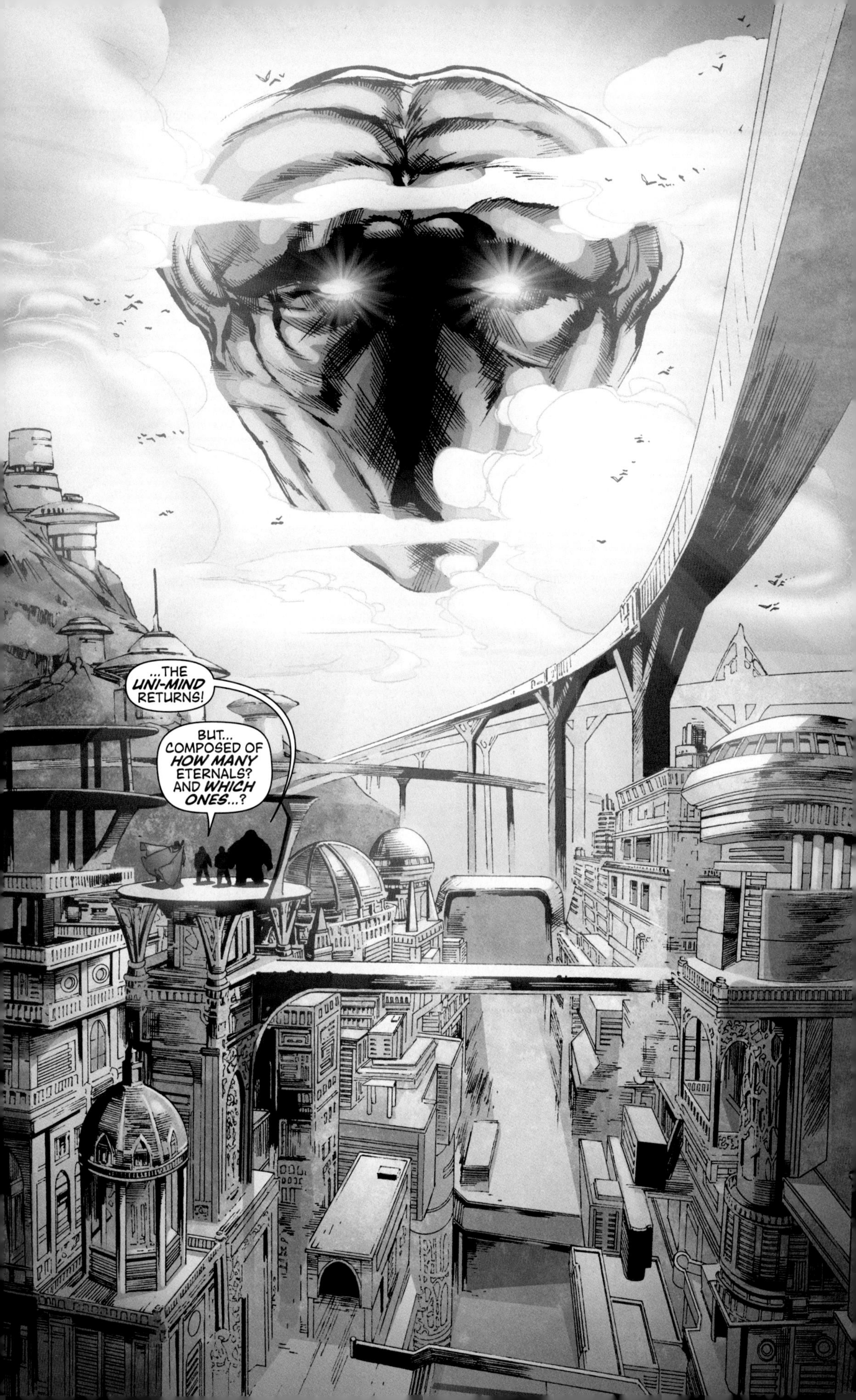
...THE UNI-MIND RETURNS!
BUT... COMPOSED OF HOW MANY ETERNALS? AND WHICH ONES...?

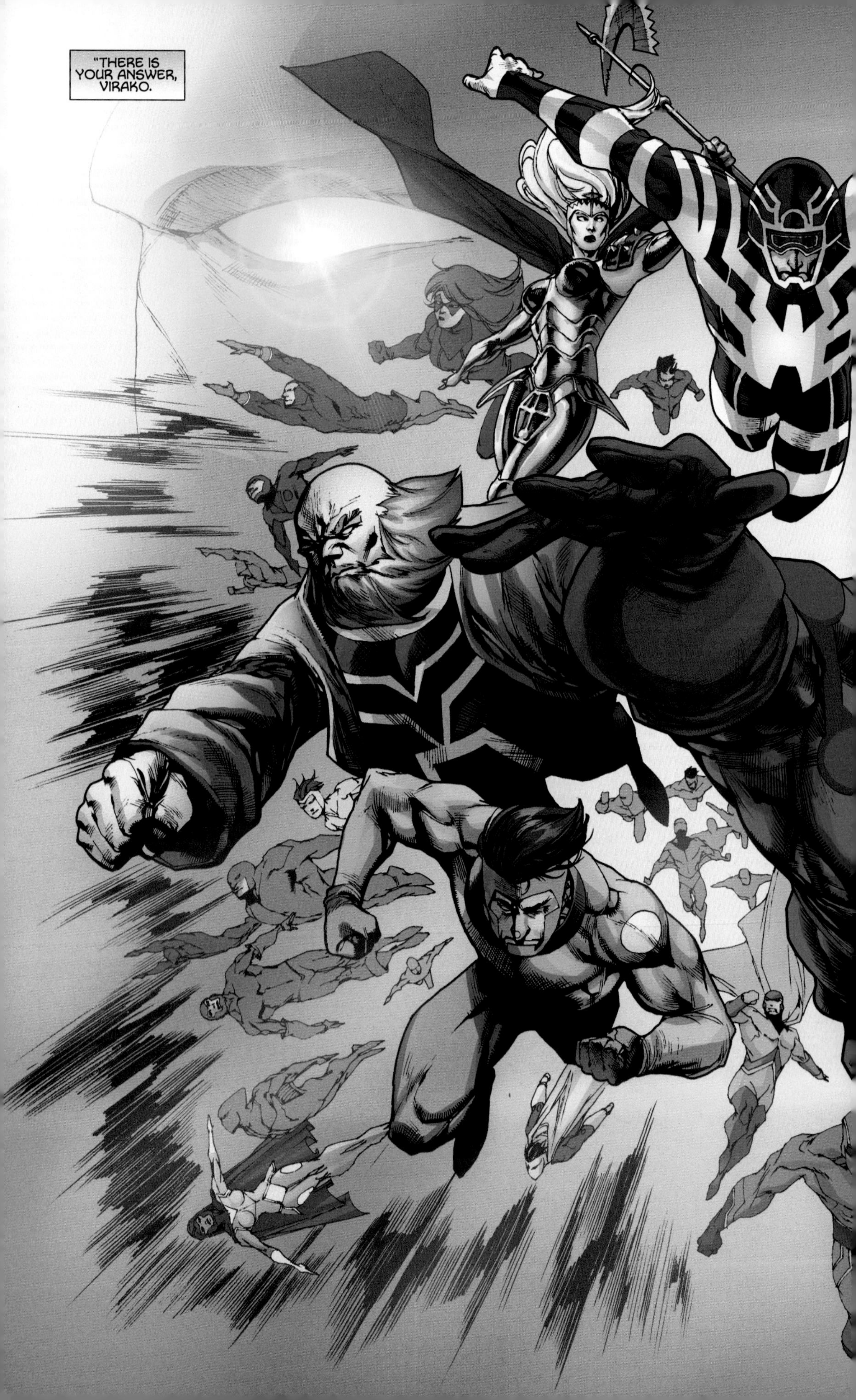
"THERE IS YOUR ANSWER, VIRAKO.

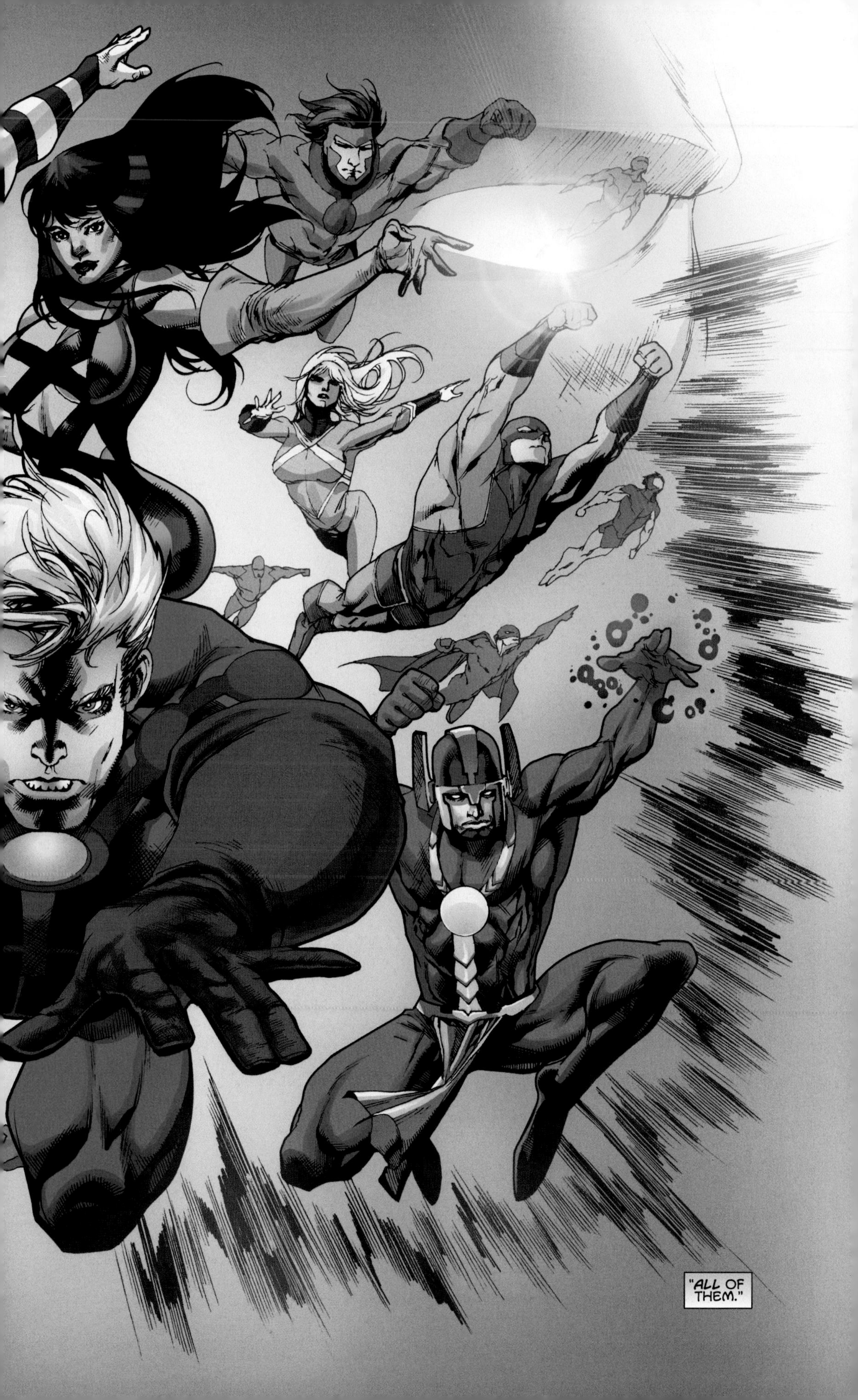
"ALL OF THEM."

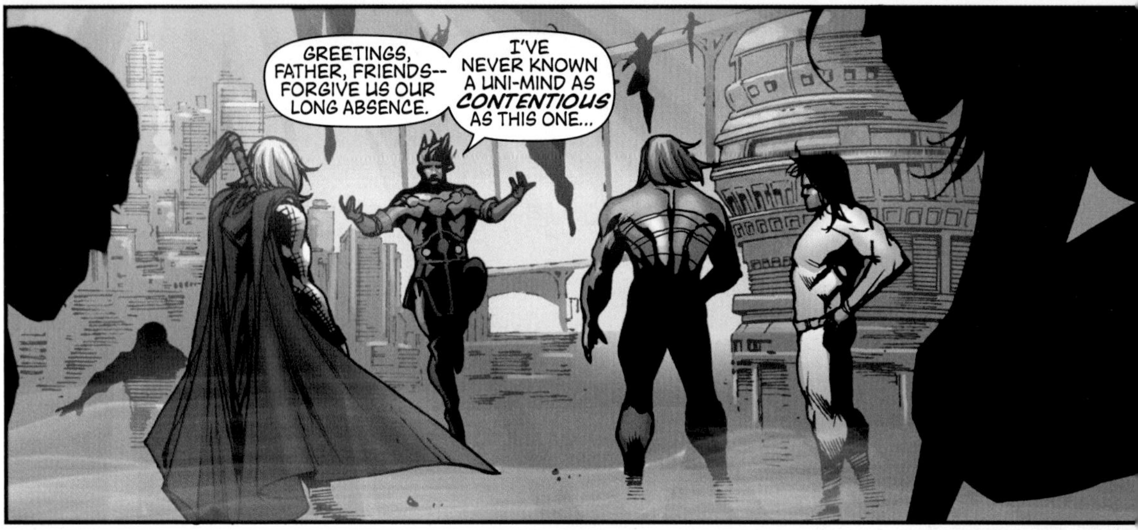
GREETINGS, FATHER, FRIENDS-- FORGIVE US OUR LONG ABSENCE.
I'VE NEVER KNOWN A UNI-MIND AS CONTENTIOUS AS THIS ONE...

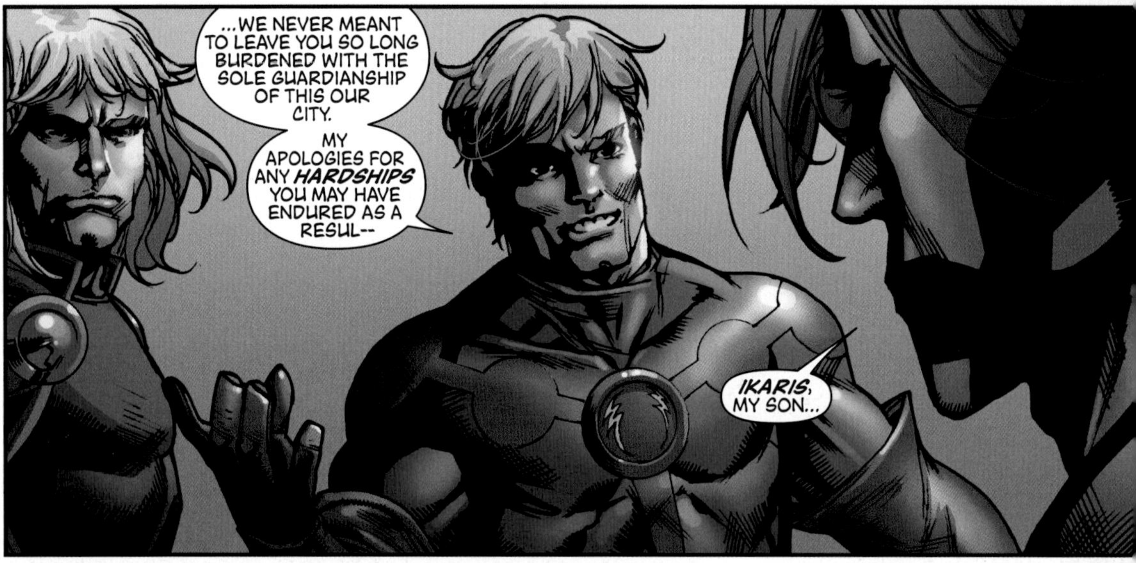
...WE NEVER MEANT TO LEAVE YOU SO LONG BURDENED WITH THE SOLE GUARDIANSHIP OF THIS OUR CITY.
MY APOLOGIES FOR ANY HARDSHIPS YOU MAY HAVE ENDURED AS A RESUL--
IKARIS, MY SON...

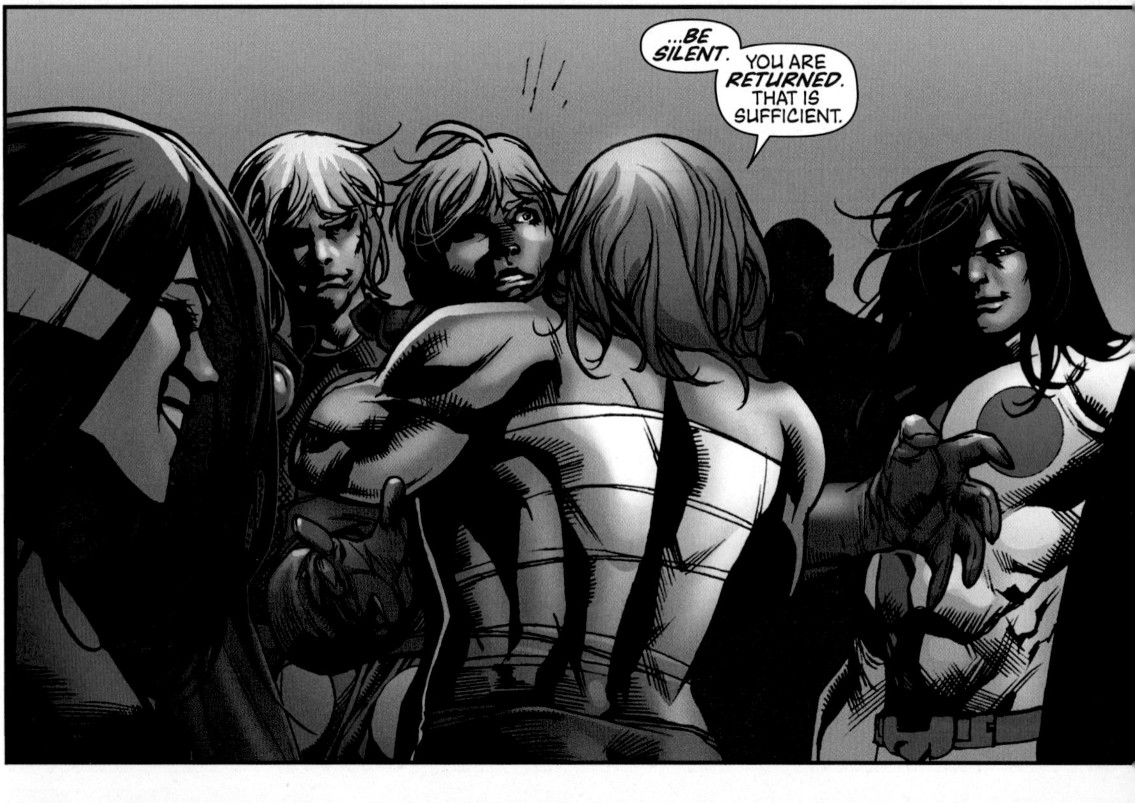
...BE SILENT.
YOU ARE RETURNED. THAT IS SUFFICIENT.

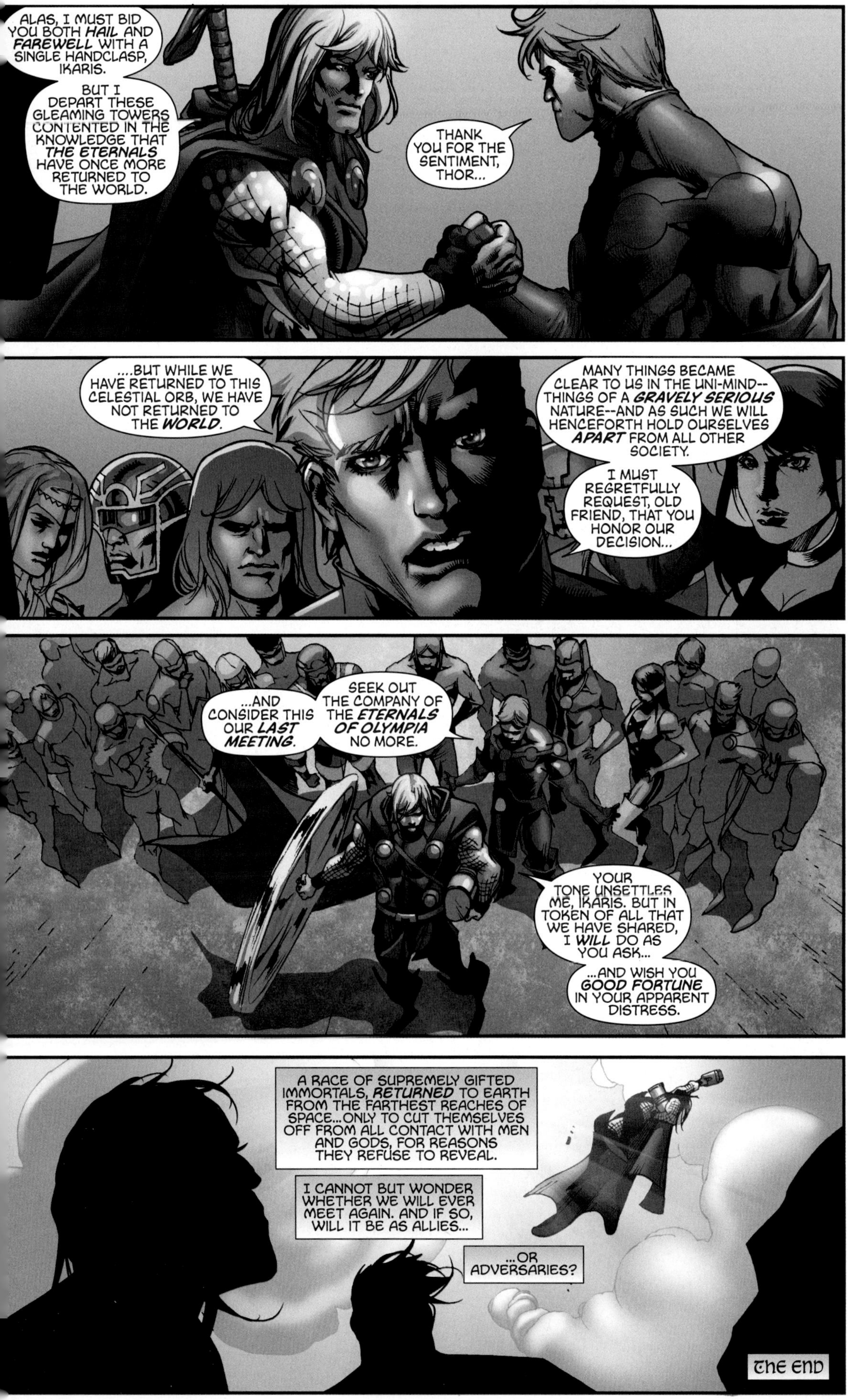
ALAS, I MUST BID YOU BOTH HAIL AND FAREWELL WITH A SINGLE HANDCLASP, IKARIS.
BUT I DEPART THESE GLEAMING TOWERS CONTENTED IN THE KNOWLEDGE THAT THE ETERNALS HAVE ONCE MORE RETURNED TO THE WORLD.
THANK YOU FOR THE SENTIMENT, THOR...
....BUT WHILE WE HAVE RETURNED TO THIS CELESTIAL ORB, WE HAVE NOT RETURNED TO THE WORLD.
MANY THINGS BECAME CLEAR TO US IN THE UNI-MIND--THINGS OF A GRAVELY SERIOUS NATURE--AND AS SUCH WE WILL HENCEFORTH HOLD OURSELVES APART FROM ALL OTHER SOCIETY.
I MUST REGRETFULLY REQUEST, OLD FRIEND, THAT YOU HONOR OUR DECISION...
SEEK OUT THE COMPANY OF THE ETERNALS OF OLYMPIA NO MORE.
...AND CONSIDER THIS OUR LAST MEETING.
YOUR TONE UNSETTLES ME, IKARIS. BUT IN TOKEN OF ALL THAT WE HAVE SHARED, I WILL DO AS YOU ASK...
...AND WISH YOU GOOD FORTUNE IN YOUR APPARENT DISTRESS.
A RACE OF SUPREMELY GIFTED IMMORTALS, RETURNED TO EARTH FROM THE FARTHEST REACHES OF SPACE...ONLY TO CUT THEMSELVES OFF FROM ALL CONTACT WITH MEN AND GODS, FOR REASONS THEY REFUSE TO REVEAL.
I CANNOT BUT WONDER WHETHER WE WILL EVER MEET AGAIN. AND IF SO, WILL IT BE AS ALLIES...
...OR ADVERSARIES?
THE END

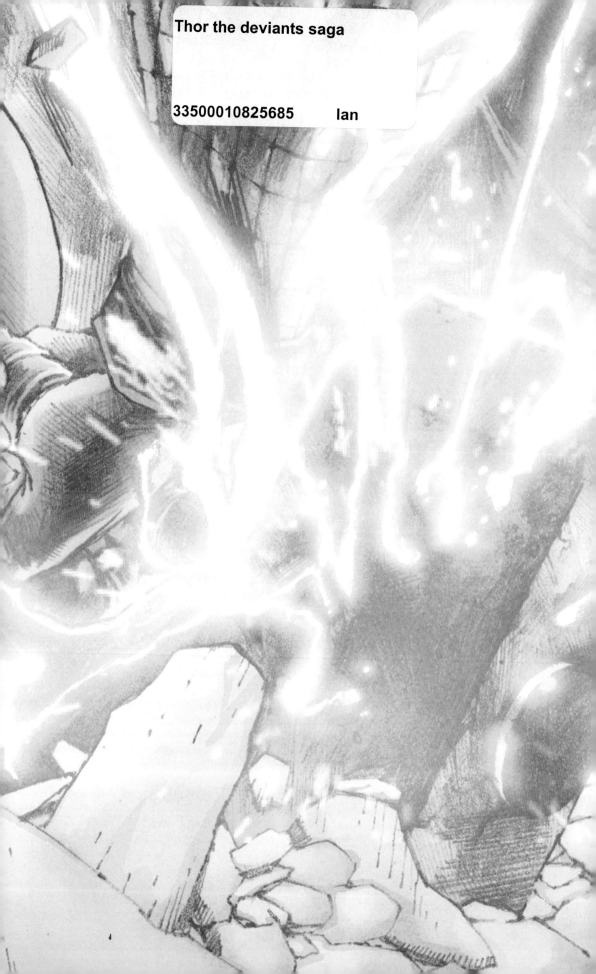

Thor the deviants saga

33500010825685   Ian